The Dye of God

Anthony H Johns

Scholars Collection

The volumes in this Collection aim to celebrate the quality of work by scholars whose reputation has been established through a substantial career. They bring together essays, articles from journals and chapters in publications around a particular theme or topic, often showing a development or progression in thinking over time. ATF Press is pleased to promote the series that highlights an author's significant contribution within theology, biblical studies, history, ethics or social issues. The purpose of the Collection is to provide a valuable resource for current and future generations by those who have contributed at an international level in their respective field.

1. *Opening the Bible*, 2014, Antony Campbell, SJ
2. *Amplifying that Still Small Voice*, 2015, Frank Brennan, SJ
3. *Gospel Interpretation and Christian Life*, 2017, Francis J Moloney, SDB
4. *The Natural World and God: Theological Explorations*, 2017, Denis Edwards
5. *Thinking Faith: Moods, Methods and Mystery*, 2017, Anthony J Kelly, CSsR
6. *Colonial Religion: Conflict and Change in Church and State*, 2020, Bruce Kaye
7. *Creation, Matter and the Image of God: Essays on John*, 2020, Dorothy Lee
8. *The Other Side of the Story: Essays of Jews, Christians, Cults, Women, Atheists & Artists*, 2021, Rachael Kohn
9. *Jesus Left Loose Ends: Collected Essays*, William RG Loader, 2021
10. *Now and Then: Australian Catholic Experiences*, Edmund Campion, 2021
11. *Early Christian Witnesses: Biblical and Theological Explorations*, Victor C Pfitzner, 2021

The Dye of God

Essays on Islam and the Qur'an

Anthony H Johns

ATF PRESS
Adelaide
2023

Cover design:	Gabriel Bueno Siquiera
Layout:	Extel Solutions, India
Font:	Minion Pro, size 11pts

ISBN:	978-1-922582-85-0	soft
	978-1-922582-86-7	hard
	978-1-922582-87-4	epub
	978-1-922582-88-1	pdf

SCAN ME

Published and edited by

Making a lasting impact
An imprint of the ATF Press Publishing Group
owned by ATF (Australia) Ltd.
PO Box 234
Brompton, SA 5007
Australia
ABN 90 116 359 963
www.atfpress.com

Table of Contents

Acknowledgments vii

Introduction ix

1. Discovering the Qur'an: A personal Odyssey 1
2. Joseph in the Qur'an: Dramatic Dialogue, Human Emotion and Prophetic Wisdom 19
3. Moses in the Qur'an: Finite and Infinite Dimensions of Prophecy 49
4. Shu'ayb, Orator of the Prophets: Reflections On Qur'anic Narrative 77
5. Narrative, Intertext and Allusion in the Quranic Presentation of Job 93
6. Jonah in the Qur'an: An Essay on Thematic Counter-point 125
7. Solomon and the Queen of Sheba 165
8. Sufism in Southeast Asia: Reflections and Reconsiderations 191
9. Perspectives of Islamic Spirituality in Southeast Asia: Reflections and Encounters 213
10. '. . . . Abraham, our father in faith . . . ?' 239

Acknowledgments

The following articles are taken from the respective journals with details given after the title of the article. Thank you to the respective publishers for giving approval for use of the articles which in most case have been updated from the original.

1. 'Discovering the Qur'an: A personal Odyssey', in *Hamdard Islamicus* (Bait al-Hikmah, Pakistan) Volume XXX (October-December 2007): 7–15.
2. 'Joseph in the Qur'an: Dramatic Dialogue, Human Emotion and Prophetic Wisdom', in *Islamochristiana* (Rome: Pontificio Istituto di Studi Arabi e Islamici, Centre of Studies for Muslim-Christian Dialogue, 1981), 29–55.
3. 'Moses in the Qur'an: Finite and Infinite Dimensions of Prophecy', in *The Charles Strong Lectures 1972–1984*, edited by Robert B Crotty, 1982, 123–138.
4. 'Shu'ayb, Orator of the Prophets: Reflections On Qur'anic Narrative', in *Journal of Qur'anic Studies*, Volume V Number XIII/2, Issue 2 (2011): 136–148.
5. 'Narrative, Intertext and Allusion in the Quranic Presentation of Job', in *Journal of Qur'anic Studies*, Volume I, Issue I, (1999): 1–25.
6. 'Jonah in the Qur'an: An Essay on Thematic Counterpoint', in *Journal of Qur'anic Studies* (London: Centre of Islamic Studies School of Oriental and African Studies, University of London) Volume V, Issue 2 (2003): 48–71.
7. Solomon and the Queen of Sheba ABR-NAHRAIN Volume XXIV 1986 Leiden E.J. Brill pp.58–81
8. 'Sufism in Southeast Asia: Reflections and Reconsiderations', in *Journal of Southeast Asian Studies* 26 (March 1995) National University of Singapore: 169–183.

9. Perspectives of Islamic Spirituality in Southeast Asia: reflections and encounters', in *Islam and Christian-Muslim Relations*, Volume 12 Number 1 (January 2001): 5–21.
10. '. . . Abraham, our father in faith . . .?', in *St Mark's Review*, 206, (November 2008)

Introduction

These essays, first published between 1981–2008, are the result of encounters with a tradition that for many 'westerners' is 'other'. These encounters are essentially a cognitive exercise, but one infused with a sense of the richness of the religious and humanist traditions of Islam, and beyond that, they are 'a religious quest'—a phrase difficult to explain—an effort bring to light something of the mystery of 'the other'. They were written, in the first instance, as a response to an engagement with the foundation texts of that tradition, and the ways they are lived and understood. They are a personal exploration, but one with appreciative wonder of what is in the life of that tradition. Though not arranged in chronological order, they are milestones along a continuing journey.

Seeds of an interest in Islam were planted in my grandfather's book room in southwest England in 1939, but did not germinate until circumstances beyond my control took me to what was then British Malaya in 1947. The circumstances were conscription into the British army and an overseas posting to Singapore and Johor Bahru. It was an experience that led me, after demobilisation to a degree in Malay and Arabic, and a PhD on Malay Sufism at the London School of Oriental and African Studies. Yet the foundation proper for what was to come did not begin until I arrived in Indonesia in 1954 as a teacher of English as a foreign language. It was there I realised how much of what I had learned of Islam at University (during the 1950's) was more words than meanings. And equally important, that Southeast Asia, no less than the Middle East was a gateway to the world of Islam; and further, that any study of Islam in Indonesia ineluctably drew one into the great traditions of learning that belong to and define the patrimony of the Islamic world as a whole.

From the late fourteenth century on, numbers of the city states around the littoral of the region were transformed into sultanates. As such, they became members of an exclusive club, and were recognised by other sultanates, great and small as centres of the Islamic community across the Islamic world, and with them participated in the trading systems of the Indian Ocean. They developed institutions for the study of the core traditions of Islamic learning—Qur'an exegesis, scholastic theology, the mystical tradition, and jurisprudence, yet at the same time reflecting some of the distinctive emphases and colourings of the cultures of the regions, sacred and profane, in which they were set. A wonderful and haunting Qur'anic metaphor for the religion of Islam is the 'dye of God' in the verse, 'And who, better than God, can spread the tincture of a dye: and Him we adore' (Qur'an 2:138) intimating the multiple textures and levels of intensity and shading in the living of the religion that serves as a title for the collection.

The journey has been as much one of unlearning as of learning; progress at times stirred by feelings of empathy, at others halted by issues of cognitive dissonance. For the Westerner, thanks to an overlap in the broad outlines of salvation history in Judaism and Christianity, and the shared names of the dramatis personae in this history, much in Islam appears familiar. Yet behind these common elements lie a number of stubborn incompatibilities.

Academically, the journey has followed a winding path. It began in Southeast Asia with a study of seventeenth century writings in Malay by Sufi authors in north Sumatra; it progressed to a study of their teachers, whether local or itinerant and the traditions of learning they followed, turning to the Arabic language texts of the disciplines they taught. It was only later that it arrived at the place any study of Islam should properly have begun: the Qur'an. It is the experience of the foundation text itself that illumines the responses to it of the diverse communities of the Muslim world, and enables an enhanced insight into the diffusion of *the dye of God*.

The first essay, 'Odyssey'—for convenience the titles are abridged)—is in part autobiographical. It gives an account of some of the difficulties that confronted me on a first encounter with the Qur'an in translation. The following six are on the prophetic figures, Joseph (2), Moses (3) Shu 'ayb (4), Job (5) Jonah (6) and Solomon (7). Apart from Shu'ayb, these figures and the defining events in their lives largely overlap with those in the biblical tradition. But when these events are presented in the Qur'an, for example when God addresses Moses from the burning bush, Jonah is spewed from the belly of the great fish, when Joseph in goal interprets the dreams of his fellow prisoners, and is appointed administrator of Egypt, one must be aware that whatever they have in common, they are *dramatis personae* on a different stage, playing their roles in a different drama.

At the heart of the First Testament is the Covenant between God and Abraham: God's promise to him of a son in his old age, of descendants as many as the stars of heaven and a land 'extending from the river of Egypt to the Great River and the Euphrates.' Abraham, his son Isaac and grandson Jacob are the patriarchs of the Jewish people, central to the salvation history of the First Testament. Joseph, son of Jacob, establishes them in Egypt, where they are to be enslaved. Moses, responding to God's call from the burning bush leads them out of Egypt. After the great theophany on Mount Sinai, where God speaks with Moses, Joshua leads them across the Jordan into the promised land, where David establishes the kingdom of Israel, and his son Solomon builds the first temple.

In the Islamic narrative of salvation history, Adam (as in Genesis) is the first man. Notwithstanding his disobedience, and banishment from the garden, Adam repents, and as the first prophet and first teacher of his progeny, establishes the primal shrine for the worship of God on earth, the Ka'ba at Mecca.

From the time of Adam up to that of Muhammad, God sent many prophets, each chosen from and preaching to his own people, some known, many unknown, twenty five of whom are named in the Qur'an. All preach the same message: that God is one, that he reveals a Law, and that at the end of time, all humankind will be resurrected for judgement. Muhammad is the final prophet and the Qur'an the final revelation. Earlier prophets had been sent to their own peoples, but the Qur'an, the Arabic book revealed to him, an Arab, is not for his people alone, but for all mankind, consecrating Arabic as the ultimate language of revelation.

In the Islamic narrative, the Jews have no special role. They are not a chosen people with a teleological vocation, but one of the many peoples to whom prophets had been sent. Abraham, Isaac and Jacob are not seen as the patriarchs of a uniquely chosen people, but as prophets, Jewish messengers sent to the Jews. Abraham has a central role. He resumes the monotheism of Noah, the great prophet who warned his people of the flood, rejects the idolatry of his father, and leaves home as a migrant for God. With his son Ismail, he restores the primal site of worship, established by Adam, the Ka'ba the house of God at Mecca, and according to tradition destroyed by Noah's flood. In this narrative, the prophets include Joseph, dreamer of dreams and victim of fraternal jealousy, and skilful administrator of Egypt, Moses who spoke with God on mount Sinai, and supreme role model to Muhammad; among them too are the prophet kings David and Solomon. The number of names, as the Qur'an puts it, testifies to the fact that the Jews had been sent more prophets than any other people, yet remained the most obstinate in their rejection of the final revelation made to Muhammad.

The Qur'an is not a narrative text, but an arrangement 'by wisdom' of the revelations made to Muhammad over twenty two years. It is divided into one hundred and fourteen units called suras (chapters), arranged roughly in order of decreasing length, the longest 286 verses and the shortest 3. A short sura may be dedicated to a single theme or event. The longest ones are complex literary structures, weaving together pericopes of prayer and praise, exhortation, homiletic narrative, debate, criminal, ritual and family law, and opening a space for moments of silent ecstasy.

It gives little in the way of biographical information about the prophets. Rather it presents sequences of scenes or episodes from their lives that are crucial to its message. It does so in various ways. Their names may appear in pericopes, individually or in choruses. Sometimes the mention of a name in a verse is sufficient to set sounding waves of resonances. A vignette may give a vivid picture of prophetic challenge and unbeliever response. A sequence of episodes of the same figure may extend over a hundred verses. Sometimes a narrative may be broken up, and its scenes strategically set in different suras. On the other hand, a single scene may be re-presented in a number of suras, the change in context serving to highlight different aspects and emphases in the role the prophet is playing. This iteration of episodes adds to the mood meanings and movement of the suras in which they are set. Events in their careers often parallel the experience of Muhammad himself as he preaches his message. Their stories are told to comfort and encourage him in face of rejection, give authority to his argument, establish the historical depth of the religion he is teaching, and enhance inner themes and intertext continuities: all combining to yield a moving texture of sound and sense.

These complexities easily pass unrecognized when the Qur'an is read in translation. and this lack of awareness was among the reasons for the cognitive dissonances I encountered when first I read an English rendering. 'Discovering the Qur'an' (1), is in part an account of my experience in confronting these dissonances.

'Joseph' (2) shows how an acceptance of the Genesis telling of the story as normative, hinders a positive response to the Qur'anic presentation. It was necessary to look at it hard and long to see it in its own terms and its place in the context of the Islamic narrative of salvation history, and then for it to look hard back at me to disclose its proper form and dynamic role in its own narrative framework.

'Moses' (3) explores the multiple levels of his role in the Islamic tradition. His presence in the Qur'an, greater than that of any other prophetic figure. He is the supreme predecessor and role model for Muhammad, celebrated as *kalīmu'llāh*, the one who spoke with God. The great 'show-stopping' scenes of his career, God speaking to him from the burning bush and the theophany on Mount Sinai when he asks to see God—are placed and reiterated and echoed across a number of suras in language of radiant intensity. And added to the scenes known in the Bible, is his encounter with the mysterious figure of *al-Khidr* (the Green Man), who puts him to the test.

'Shu'ayb' (4), is little known outside the Muslim world, perhaps because he has no obvious association any biblical figure, although some have identified him with Jethro. He is a model of the Islamic prophet in its simplest form. He is called to warn his people of the dreadful doom they face if they do not repent of their besetting sins of greed and dishonesty, crying to them, *Give full weight and measure, and do not deprive people of the things that are theirs*! They reject his warning, claiming the right to have unfettered possession of what is theirs! They are destroyed, and left lying dead, face down in their dwellings. It is a passionate call for social justice.

Job (5) when compared with Moses, may appear a minor prophet. Although his name resonates among the choruses of prophetic names in a number of *suras*, there are only six verses dedicated to him, occuring in two pericopes in different suras, one of four verses, the other of two. Although they complement each other, they are allusive, and at first sight bewildering. Nevertheless, the exegetic tradition provides a contextual background which by and large is parallel to that in the biblical book of Job. As Tabari presents it, it resolves every difficulty in the Qur'anic text, and ensures that the six verses have complete clarity and coherence. Job, as every prophet, is put to the test, and his sufferings raise the question that challenges every theodicy: why do the innocent suffer?

There are eighteen verses dedicated to Jonah (6). They communicate vividly the focal scenes of his prophetic career—his flight on the ship, his prayer in the great fish that spews him on the shore, and his frustration that the people of Nineveh who rejected him have not been destroyed—are distributed over six suras. Even so, the story line is maintained across them and distant verses by sub-text, verbal echoes and parallelisms, and ensures a continuing presence. In one verse, God warns the Prophet not to be like the 'man of the fish' (Jonah), resentful because the punishment threatened the Meccans for rejecting him is delayed. The people of Nineveh at first had rejected Jonah, but God accepted their repentance. The people of the Hijaz who reject Muhammad too may repent.

The focus of 'Solomon' (6) is the prophet king's meeting with Bilqīs the great queen of the south (the Yemen). This is presented as the second of four prophet narrations that follow the exordium of Sura 27 al-Naml. (vv 6–14 Moses; vv 15–44 David and Solomon; vv 45–53, Sālih, and vv 54–58 Lot.)

The story is related as an episodic narrative, largely carried by dramatic dialogue. Over the episodes are a number of speakers, the dramatis personae including an ant, the hoopoe bird (remember that Solomon had the gift of understanding the speech of animals), an envoy, the ministers of both Solomon and Bilqīs a daemon from among the jinn, and 'one with knowledge of the Book' (not named)

And finally, climacticly, the encounter between Solomon and Bilqīs. All have a part to play in the complexities of the story line, that concludes with Bilqīs acknowledging Solomon not only as king but prophet. The narrative is vividly presented, and the dialogues, especially that between Bilqīs and her ministers, and that between her and Solomon grip the reader's (or listener's) attention. Fakhr al-Dīn al-Rāzī (d1209) in some ways greatest of the 'classical' exegetes, offers a multi-layered exegesis of the pericope, deriving from a deeply felt experience of the words. He presents the basic information necessary for an understanding of the text, dealing with the lexical, grammatical, and textual issues. But with the skill and sensitivity of a proto-novelist, and a marvellous literary skill he gives a personal response to the dramatis personae of the narrative, their thoughts, insights, psychological motivations and their relation with each other. He engages with character and personality, and uncovers lessons to be drawn from their exchanges. From the words of the ant, warning its followers to clear the road for Solomon and his army, he derives a traffic regulation. From the dialogue between Bilqis and her ministers, he finds an example of how rulers should treat their officials. Further, in the events of the narrative, he finds grounds for rebutting the doctrines of the Mu'tazilites whose philosophical beliefs would subject God to the limitations of human reason. Yet above all this he reveals spiritual insights not far removed from mysticism.

The next two essays, 'Sufism' (7) and 'Spirituality' (8) mark a return to expressions of Islamic life and thought in the region that had led me which had led me to the study of the Qur'an in the first place, Southeast Asia. The first is a revisiting of the scene of the Malay language Sufi tracts in north Sumatra I had worked on for my PhD thesis. This study had prompted an article I published in 1961, proposing that the Islamisation of the Malay/Indonesian world might be attributed principally to Sufi ascetics preaching a mystical dimension of Islam. This essay is a radical recalibration if not abandonment of that hypothesis. When writing it, I was not aware of the contextual setting in which they were a miniscule, and in themselves unimportant part; how the Indian Ocean was the arena of a trading system linking Southeast Asia, the Indian subcontinent and the Middle East, or that across the region were networks of trading communities with business confidence sustained by Islamic commercial law and itinerant religious scholars of varying traditions, linking Muslim communities at the city states round the littoral of the region. 'Ulama' from these states, along with colleagues from the Indian sub-continent and diverse regions of the Middle East regularly spent years in Madina or Mecca, getting to know each other, and each other's students. They wrote treatises on the Islamic disciplines, compiled biographies of their own teachers, and wrote letters to colleagues and students, letters that were carried in trading vessels across the ocean and of which the texts I had studied for my thesis were only an infinitesimally minor part.

There were then vigorous and many stranded traditions of social, intellectual and spiritual life in diverse communities, the Jawi (Malay peoples) from Southeast Asia among them, learning from, teaching, and interacting with their peers, and that Islamisation was a 'whole community' process, not reducible to a single component. Among them were indeed Sufis, and exponents of mystical authors, but a part is not greater than the whole. This sequel to the 1961 essay is an attempt to take account of what I had missed before, but at the same time not neglecting 'the mystical dimension of Islam', which indeed had its role to play. 'Spirituality' (9) in the title of the second is not intended as a 'feel good' word, let alone a sleight of hand to avoid an Islamic terminology. Rather it looks for and at the redolences, resonances, echoes, vibrations even—direct and indirect, of an underlying stratum of religious belief, and its interactions with everyday life; suffusing it at multiple levels, some not immediately identifiable, yielding a universe of symbols and images, fecundating an Islamic humanism with a regional character.

The religious elements behind this humanism may be immediate or remote and allusive. They may be seen in architecture, the design of public buildings, monuments and houses; insinuate themselves into local forms of music, dance and drama; They may be embedded in works of literary imagination in variety of literary forms: lyric poetry, the essay, and the novel, all forms that give a writer scope to include doubt, to question faith, to pursue problems to the very edge of unbelief, and even search for space outside the law.

The concluding essay (10) '. . . Abraham, our father-in-faith . . . ?' in a way ends the collection with a question. More simply, the title might be 'Abraham, Patriarch or Prophet?' for now 'Abrahamic' includes Muslims as among the descendants, uncountable as the stars of heaven, promised Abraham. The word is sometimes used to give a patina of solemnity to political negotiations; at a deeper level however, it is aspirational, and asks how the communities of three faiths might share the umbrella of his name. Each has a scriptural authority by which to claim him as a 'father in faith'. In what sense can each of them say along with the other two, 'Our father in faith' as a statement, not a question? As a question, does it put us to the test? If so, what is the test? And what the answer?

*****

The opportunity to reprint these essays in this collection has awoken waves of nostalgia for days long past, memories of colleagues and friends, some no longer with us, and places where learning and the exchange of ideas has been fruitful. They were stimulated by encounters with remarkable personalities at places far apart: the University of London Centre for Islamic Studies, the *Cairo Institut Dominicain des Etudes Orientales*, the State Islamic University of Syarif Hidayatullah in Jakarta, and the Canberra campus of the Australian Catholic University. My appreciation and thanks goes to all of them. Thanks are also due to Cathie, a daughter-in-law who scanned the texts to be sent to ATF Press; to a son Michael, who deigned a program to insert diacritical points on Arabic words, and very especially my friend Abdelghani, a calligrapher who designed for the cover the Qur'anic verse that inspired the title. All have contributed to preparing for re-publication these encounters with 'the dye of God'—that haunting metaphor for the diffusion of a faith, and of its transforming tincture spread across broad swathes of our world, 'And who better than God can spread the tincture of a dye!'

Discovering the Qur'an
A Personal Odyssey

My first encounter with the Qur'an was in February 1948. It was through the translation made by George Sale in 1734. I acquired it in a bookshop in Singapore when on leave from an army camp in south Malaya. When I first read it, I had no idea as to what kind of book it was, or what to expect from it. Sale's rendering used the language of the King James Bible, but the rhetorical movement and internal organisation of the book was so different to what I was familiar with in biblical narrative, that reading it resulted in an experience of cognitive dissonance that was to remain long unresolved.

The Qur'an, indeed, is not easily accessible to non-Muslims. The layout of the received text in book form inevitably presents problems to an unprepared reader. There are a number of reasons for this. Among them is the sheer stylistic unattractiveness of most renderings of it in English, an unattractiveness that discourages many from the attempt even to read it. But there are more serious obstacles. One is cultural, due to the absence in the Western literary tradition of signposts as to its distinctive character, and by which it can be recognized as Muslims see it, as an event in human history.

The problem is one of approach. Essentially, it needs to be recognised as an extended utterance addressed by God to the prophet Muhammad. God, as master narrator, speaks in the first person as 'I' or 'We', but also of Himself in the third person, as He presents to the prophet what his vocation is, and the message he is to give to those to whom he is sent. In this address, He shows concern for His prophet, offers him comfort for the burden that this responsibility of prophethood causes him, pain at the insults he received, fear at the thought of failing in his mission, and the thought of his people, his kin, possibly doomed to hell.

God comforts him, encourages him, and urges him to be patient. He accompanies the Prophet through the many events of his career, reminds him of the help He has given him and his followers in crises in the past and the good things they have received. He provides proofs of His might and His creative power. He sets out the core theological statements of true religion: that He God is One; that He sends prophets telling of Himself and His laws for humankind, and that there will be a Day of resurrection, on which all will be judged as to how they have lived according to those laws.

Through the Prophet Muhammad, He addresses them directly, warning them, and sometimes individuals among them, of the punishments for disobedience and ingratitude, and of the rewards they will receive for obedience and gratitude. He gives examples of those He has punished and those rewarded. There are words to remind them of His constant care, to guide them, support them through the various vicissitudes of life, and to teach them prayers by which to address and adore Him. He tells them of the names by which he may be known: He is Allāh, the Merciful, the Compassionate, The Guide, The Carer, the Beneficent, The Reprover, and so on through what Muslim devotion knows as the 99 most beautiful names of God. Within this same 'extended utterance' God also reveals a line of salvation history from the creation of Adam, by presenting narrations of episodes from the lives of the prophets He has sent prior to Muhammad. In part to show Muhammad that all of those He had sent had suffered the pains of rejection as had he, but also to show how great is His care for humanity, shown by this sending of prophets together with the proofs He had given them of the truth of messages they bring.

This extended utterance is not directly recognisable as such in the received text of the Qur'an, which does not present the pericopes in chronological order, or individually identify the occasions of revelation as it was revealed to the prophet over a period of twenty-three years. Rather the content of Revelation is organised then divided into 114 suras (chapters) of varying lengths. This division into suras with different mixes of content and distributions of emphases and mixed chronology is nevertheless directed by divine wisdom and is part of the message of the Book, and every pericope within each sura needs to be understood within the context of the whole extended utterance of which it is a part.

These 114 suras range from two hundred and eighty-six to three verses in length. There is a variety of rhetorical forms within them, descriptions of the wonders of nature, of land, sea and sky, multi-directional dialogue, rapid shifts of speaker, exhortations to battle, promulgation of laws, dramatic changes of scene, allusions to events in the immediate and remote past, reference to beliefs, memories and practices, and events occurring outside the text, although encoded within it. A rendering of the Qur'an in English may then be accurate at the level of the word, but it cannot of itself on the printed page provide signals to decode the shifts and contrasts in style, the modulations of tone, the changes in speakers for which there are no explicit signals in the printed text, and which need to be heard.

Thus a non-Muslim might read in translation the first words of sura 96: *iqra' bi'smi rabbika* 'Read in the name of your Lord', widely accepted as the first revelation made to the Prophet. 'Read' is indeed a correct rendering of the word, *iqra'*, but it is an anaemic equivalent for *iqra'*, and communicates nothing of the suddenness and intensity of it as a word of command, with the acoustic support of the assonance in the following four verses; neither could he relate to, or take as a reference point what is a matter of profound faith, almost visual in its vividness to any Muslim: the scene of the angel of revelation taking hold of the prophet as he meditated alone in the cave on Jabal al-Nūr, about ten miles to the north of Mecca, directing him to recite these verses, with this dramatic word of command *iqra'*!

For similar reasons, the core Christian credal phrase, 'The Word was made flesh' has no resonance and little meaning for Muslims, though for English speaking Christians, it is charged with awe. It summates the doctrine of the incarnation, and resonates at a number of levels. It is a consecrated phrase at which when uttered in a liturgical setting, the congregation kneels. The words have this power because they are part of the acculturation over centuries of Christian theology, shaped in English by the Authorised Version of the Bible, widely shared, and subsumed into the language of everyday living.

The narrations, images and structures of the Qur'an are not acculturated in this way in the English-speaking patrimony. Thus there are few, or at best inadequate reference points to illumine or reflect back its words and images, to create meanings that take the reader beyond the words on the page. To date, there is no rendering of the Qur'an that has a commanding presence in English. And even where there is overlap between the stories told of the prophetic figures in the Qur'an and the Bible, the unfamiliar ordering and rhetoric of the Qur'anic presentation makes them appear askew in a way that engenders a feeling of irritation rather than a glow of appreciation resulting from recognition and a sense of a heritage shared.

In the non-Arab speaking countries of the Muslim World such as Indonesia, Pakistan and Iran, the reverse is the case. There, multiple extra-textual reference points exist because the patrimony of Islam has become vernacularised. The Muslim concept of time and sacred history are established. The year itself is structured by Islamic rites and festivals, daily greetings, expressions of condolence, of surprise, and thanksgiving are often in Arabic. The stories of the prophetic figures as presented in the Qur'an are shared at all levels of society, and the symbols and institutions of Islamic life are integrated even into secular forms of culture. In them, Arabic words have become part of the vocabulary of local vernaculars, and even their equivalents in these languages have often achieved a sacral status, due to the shared living of the ethico-legal values and precepts of Islam, implanted through formal and informal religious education. In such an environment, vernacular renderings of the Qur'an can resonate, move and inspire in public utterances and live as symbols in secular literary works, just as Christian motifs have a role in the symbolic structures in Christian cultures, East or West, Dostoyevsky or Dickens. There is a texture of shared symbolic materials, ranging from the call and life of the Prophet, the varying contexts and occasions of revelation of pericopes of the Qur'an, and ultimately the status of the completed Book as, for Muslims, the central and ultimate event in divine revelation, and so of human history.

Without such reference points, Westerners have little sense of what the Qur'an is, or the ways in which it serves as the bed-rock of Muslim identity and culture, and so are often dismissive of it. A common view in 'the West', is that the Qur'an (in translation) is uninspiring, even though it may be conceded that listening to it recitated is an aesthetic and even religious experience, an encounter with the numinous, the holy, even though the words may not be understood. For in this cantillation is encoded the spiritual essence of the Book. On the lips of an accomplished reciter it has an almost physical presence, as he or she (and some of the greatest reciters are women) caresses the words with spell-binding melodic felicities of phrasing that pass from heart to heart. This sound of qur'anic cantillation is part of the defining ambience of the Muslim world, constantly renewing and refreshing Muslims' awareness of what has been part of their life from childhood.

This I had to learn. And the first seed of understanding was sown when Malay friends in 1949 invited me to be present at the congregational prayer of the 'Īd al-Adhā in the Abu Bakr mosque in Johor Baru. For half an hour before the formal prayer began, I listened to the *takbīr*, the congregational chanting of the phrase and prayer, *Allāhu akbar* 'God is most great'. There was a rhythm, a movement, an exultation in their voices that rolled like the swell of the sea. It stayed in my mind, and haunted my memory. It was an introduction to the resonances of Arabic as a liturgical language.

Little help in the germination of that seed was gained by formal study at the School of Oriental and African Studies (University of London)—in the early 1950s, be it emphasised. The Qur'an was referred to simply as a source of Muslim theology: uncertain and self-contradictory in some of its propositions, repetitive, and often dull. There was no explanation that the verses cited to establish particular theological or moral doctrines were organic parts of something larger than themselves. There was no appreciation of the richness and complexities within the Qur'an, or that it was a book that was lived, and above all experienced.

Even lectures on *taṣawwuf*, the Sufi movement in Islam, were of little help. True, they drew attention to the ascetic and ecstatic themes in the spiritual and mystical dimensions of Islam, and the inner life of Muslims, and pointed out that the Sufis had distinctive understanding of particular verses. They did not, however, show how the power of Qur'anic utterances lay behind, infused and were the ultimate motivation for the spiritual effort and aspiration of the Sufis and their longing for God. Nor did they make it clear that the roots of inspiration of this heightened spirituality which inspired the development of a rich and poetic theosophy, particularly in the writings of the great mystic Ibn 'Arabī (d 1240) was Qur'anic), and resonated with Qur'anic rhetoric through and through.

Nevertheless, in my journey I encountered many verses and shorter suras that even in English renderings served as points of entry into the world of the Qur'an, as ways of establishing a foothold in, a way of exploring that world, to appreciate it, to respect it as a revealed book. And despite the obstacles I have mentioned, there were phrases and verses that could the heart and mind of the non-Muslim as directly as the psalms, and are an authentic extension of that spirituality. Among them is the sublime verse of the throne,[1]

God, there is no god but He, The Living, the Eternal;
Neither slumber nor sleep seize Him.
To Him belongs all that is in the heavens and on earth.
Who is there who could intercede with Him without His leave?
He knows what is before men and what is past
But they know nothing of His knowledge, except in so far as He wills
His throne embraces the heavens and the earth:
to sustain them is no burden to Him.
He is the Exalted, the Almighty (Q 2:255).

There is the divine generosity revealed in the gifts of nature

We pour down the rain in abundance
We break open the earth,
and make spring from it grain and grapes and clover,
olives and date palms,
gardens planted thick with trees
and all the gifts of the earth (Q 80:25-31).

There are the resonances of the first verse of the penultimate sura:

Declare: I take refuge with the Lord of the Dawn (Q 113:1)

The sublime diction of such verses captivated me in my early encounter with the Qur'an. But there were two events that were for me literally life-changing in the way in which they carried me into the world of the Qur'an. One was a chance meeting with a remarkable Egyptian scholar and reciter, Dr Muhammad Ali al-Erian. He agreed to recite a number of passages of the Qur'an for an English-speaking audience, and asked me to prepare English renderings to distribute for the event. Among them was the celebrated Light Verse (Sūrat al-Nūr 24:35). In it, the light of God is compared to a radiance set in a niche, lit from the oil of an olive tree of neither east nor west, this oil

1. This, and subsequent renderings of Qur'anic verses are not offered as formal translations. They are simply to illustrate my personal experience of the Book

which would itself radiate light without even fire having touched it, light upon light (Q 24:35):

> *God is the light of the heavens and the earth*
> *His light may be compared to a niche*
> *in which is set a radiance*
> *this radiance is within a glass,*
> *the glass gleaming like a brilliant star.*
> *The radiance is lit [from the oil] of a blessed olive tree*
> *of neither east nor west*
> *an oil that would radiate light*
> *even without fire having touched it,*
> *light upon light.*

As he recited it in a superb cantillation, he dwelt on, caressed on his lips with loving, lingering embrace phrases that had a special meaning for him. And when he came to the words 'light upon light', *nūrun ʿalā nūr*, he halted, then repeated them time and again—up to seven times—before continuing. The hearing of him caress this phrase brought a kind of illumination similar to that I had experienced many years before when I first heard the *takbīr*. For when I heard these words of the Qur'an taken from the confines of the printed page, it was as though they had taken wing from the letters with which they were written. On another occasion we cooperated to present a lecture on the Qur'anic story of Joseph. He urged me to study it, analyse, and explain it, and then prepare English renderings for the passages that he would recite in Arabic. At first I resisted. At that stage I could not relate to it. There was a barrier of habit and custom to break through before I could appreciate it in its own terms, and share that appreciation with others. I am forever grateful to his memory for the insight he gave me. He provided the jolt necessary for this breakthrough, to hear and experience afresh the story I already knew in its biblical form. I then realised that the story of Joseph in its Qur'anic form, reflects a different vision of spiritual history to that of the Bible, and communicates it through a different rhetorical dynamic.

The second was when I encountered in Cairo the work of one of the great minds of human history, the philosopher and Qur'an exegete Fakhr al-Dīn al-Rāzī (d 1210) *Mafātīh al-Ghayb* (Keys to the word beyond vision), a work of exegesis in sixteen volumes (fasicules). Rāzi became for me a guide, and as it were, took me by the hand to lead me through the universe of the Qur'an. Because Dr el-Erian had sensitised me to the sura of Joseph, Rāzī's exegesis of this chapter was the first part of his work that I read. It demonstrated how the Qur'anic presentation of the story was not simply a collage of episodes from different sources inexpertly put together, as the methodology of higher critics contributing to the *Encyclopaedia of Islam* assessed it, but had an organic unity, as indeed the Muslim community had recognised from the moment of its revelation.

At critical points in his analysis of the sura, Rāzī shows his knowledge of phonetics and the physiology of the articulation of speech sounds. This information is not gratuitous, but rather demonstrates that the exegetic tradition was fully aware that the Qur'an as a revelation was to be heard. It shows the high level of his oral literacy, and the sensitivity with which he listened to the dialogues that carry the story. Thus when Joseph tells his father of his dream (v 4)

> *My father, I saw eleven stars and the sun and the moon*

Rāzi hears an ellipted

> 'What did you see them doing?'

to which Joseph's continuing words are the answer

> *I saw them bowing down before me*

thus showing his awareness of the dynamic character of dialogue in the Qur'an, and a response to signals that can only be detected from hearing the intonation of its words.

When Joseph's brothers, consumed with jealousy meet to discuss what to do with Joseph, the words 'Kill Joseph' (v 9) are uttered. One exegete understands this as uttered by the brothers in chorus. Rāzī opines that they are uttered by one of Joseph's brothers, or by a passing stranger listening to their discussion, or someone of whom advice is sought. It is a question of how the words are heard. But all contribute aspects of meaning and add to the drama of the scene.

There are other examples of ellipted phrases in dialogues that Rāzī hears. When Joseph in prison interprets the Baker's dream, saying it means that (v 41)

> *He will be crucified and birds feed on his head*

he hears an ellipted protestation from the two of them

> 'We don't believe a word of what you are saying'

prompting Joseph's insistence

> *The outcome of what you asked me is decreed.*

He also hears the silence after these concluding words, when, as an after-thought Joseph says to the prisoner who is to be re-instated in the ruler's service,

> *Mention me to your lord.*

In the story of Joseph, of the eighteen dramatis personae who take part in the drama, only two are referred to or identified by name, Joseph and Jacob. Nevertheless, Rāzī, (along with the exegetic tradition) hears the differences in speech patterns that identify the individual speakers. He recognises the situations in which individuals speak together or confront each other, and by supplying words and phrases that are ellipted, heightens the hearers awareness of the drama of the situations in which they are uttered. They are thus the more ready to recognize the prophetic mode of Jacob's utterances, and the shift in Joseph's style of speech when he assumes that mode; to detect whether Joseph's brothers speak in chorus, in succession, or one to the other, how distinct they are from the voices of the other characters, and the different tones in their voices on the various occasions in which they speak, whether whinging: 'Why don't you trust us with Joseph' (v 11); defensive: 'Even when we speak the truth, [you don't believe us]' (v 17); pleading: 'Father, we are not to be given any more corn! so send our brother with us, we'll get corn then' (v 63); and in contrition: recognising the wrong they have done after Joseph has identified himself to them, 'By God, God has preferred you to us, for we have been sinners.' (v 91).

He highlights the drama in some of the crises, the critical turning points of the unfolding of the story. One of these is Zulaykha's (the source of the name is Talmudic, not biblical or Qur'anic) attempt to seduce Joseph with her words *hayta laka*! which Arberry renders, 'Take me'.

Rāzī notes five different hearings/recitations of the consonantal outline of the words, with meanings such as 'Yipee, you're mine now' or 'I'm ready to embrace you', or 'I've been made ready for you', and 'Yes indeed!' The sense of these different recitations of the consonantal outlines, though different in nuance are cumulative. Taken together they express the passion with which Zulaykha offers herself to Joseph. This passion is explained academically by Rāzī, but the vitality and power of the language is universally recognized, and expressed in more demotic style by popular story tellers who spice up the story by telling how Zulaykha created a seductive setting of rich curtains, subdued lighting and perfume, and then dramatically stripped herself naked, to ensure that her attempt to seduce him will be successful. Yet even at this popular level, the theological message is clear. That Joseph was truly tempted; that with God's help he resisted the temptation, that his rejection of it is an example to all. Joseph flees, with her in pursuit, and as he reaches the door, her husband enters. Zulaykha claims that Joseph has attempted to assault her. And Rāzī hears in the long, hurried, tangled syntax of her accusation, 'What should the requital be for one who intends harm to a member of your household, what other than imprisonment, or [subjected to] a painful punishment' the guilt that she is trying to conceal in her words to him.

When years later, Joseph's brothers come to Egypt in search of food, unaware that Joseph is still alive, let alone that he occupies a position of authority, Rāzī also hears more details beyond the ones alluded to in the Book. He draws attention to this matching of linguistic style with inner emotion in the scene in which Joseph reveals his identity to his brothers, pointing out the uncertain bewildered half-unbelieving words of the brothers, in the complex (v 90) *a innaka la anta Yūsuf* 'Can it be that you are Joseph?', and the sublime simplicity of Joseph's reply, *ana Yūsuf* 'I am Joseph'. The vitality of the language that is carried throughout the sura, the impact it makes, with its energy felt continuously in the rhythm, and at every point along the line of every verse, is difficult even to approximate in English. But the impact of the sura goes beyond the story told, and the lessons taught, for the presentation of individuals among the *dramatis personae* is so vivid that one is drawn to identify with them, and learn from their predicaments, and to see in the Qur'anic text a mirror of one's own predicaments and emotions.

One of the themes of the story is the grief of a father who has lost a son. Rāzī too had lost a son. And this identification with the grief of Jacob is shown in his treatment of the scene in which the sons, who have taken Benjamin to Egypt as a condition imposed on them for getting more grain, return without him, because he has been imprisoned on a charge of theft. On hearing this news, instead of crying out for Benjamin, he responds with the name of the son he had lost years before (v 84), 'How I grieve for Joseph'.

Rāzī points out the psychological reason for this response. He explains that a new grief may intensify an old deeply buried grief, and that a new wound that falls on the site of an old one, makes the older one all the more painful. And to make the point clearer, he cites a poet who 600 years earlier had written an elegy on his brother Malik, killed in battle in defence of Islam during the *ridda* wars after the death of the prophet. In the conventional imagery of poetry of the time, he is reproached for weeping tears of blood whenever he passes through a cemetery, and was asked, 'Do you weep at every grave you see?' And he replies, 'Sorrow simply adds to sorrow, so let me be, for every grave here is the grave of my brother Malik. When a new grief falls upon an old grief, it is as though the scar is torn off an old wound, which then bleeds afresh'

The significance of this excursus is revealed at the conclusion of Rāzī's commentary on the sura. He wrote this when his heart grieved for the loss of his own son, and asks whoever reads it, and gains something from it, to recite recite al-Fātiha (the first sura of the Qur'an, a prayer of seven verses, that has the same status among Muslims as the Lord's prayer for Christians) for the son, and for himself, and to pray for those who die away from home, far from brethren and mother and father as he himself will pray for them. A conclusion showing that for all his literary insight into the story, he lives the religious message implicit within it.

Parables and the telling of stories of the prophets are one of the Qur'anic modes of presenting the truths central to its message. The story of Joseph is the best known of them, and is unique in that an entire sura is devoted to it. In the case of other prophets, information about them, and episodes in their careers are distributed across a number of suras, sometimes retold from different perspectives and with different emphases. They include Noah, Abraham, Moses, David, Solomon, Job and Jonah.

Among them is an account of Solomon meeting Bilqīs, the Queen of Sheba (Sūrat al-Naml 27:15–44). Rāzī, is again an insightful guide to its interpretation. Solomon has a bird that attends him, the hoopoe. One day it vanishes [from Jerusalem] without explanation. Later it returns to inform him—for in the Talmudic and Qur'anc traditions alike, Solomon knew the language of birds and animals—that it had discovered a great queen in the Yemen, who worshipped the sun.

Solomon, in his role as prophet, is appalled at her unbelief. He sends a letter to her carried by the hoopoe, ordering her to come to Jerusalem in submission to him [and to the one God he worships].

The hoopoe duly delivers it. Bilqīs announced the content of the letter to her ministers, and asked their advice. Their reply was, 'We have awesome might and the power to wage war', though adding that the decision is hers to make. Cognizant of the pointlessness of war, she replies (v 34), 'Kings when they enter a town lay it waste, and reduce its most powerful citizens to the lowliest'. She sent Solomon a gift, but he rejected it. Therefore she went to Solomon in Jerusalem.

He decided to put her to the test. He had her throne miraculously brought from the Yemen to Jerusalem, and ordered his courtiers to alter it slightly. He then questioned her about it. After that, he had her approach him across a forecourt of glass that looked like water and she lifted her skirt to avoid it getting wet as she walked across it. However, her eyes had deceived her. She had made a mistake. And in the wake of the jolt she received from realizing her mistake, she recognised Solomon not just as a ruler, but as a prophet. Rāzī expands on this information, and responding to the power of her personality implicit in what the Qur'an tells of her, fills in details of the events it records. The Qur'an, for example, does not say how the hoopoe delivered the letter to her. But Rāzī, to contextualize the event, suggests that she was asleep, that the bird entered her room through the window, cast it on her breast, and pecked her gently so that she awoke with a start. When she announces to her ministers that she has received this letter, Rāzī once again offers a plausible reconstruction of the sequence of events. They ask her, 'Who is the letter from, what does it say?' She replies that it is from Solomon; and that he demands that she come to him in submission. Rāzī's contemporary, the great mystic Ibn 'Arabī, observes that these answers show her skill as a ruler. She does not divulge to her ministers how the letter was delivered to her, or who brought it. For if this became known, false information could be delivered to her, and her lines of communication be corrupted. Rāzī notes her skill in maintaining the loyalty of her ministers by consulting with them, while reserving for herself the prerogative of making the decision.

He also emphasises her astuteness. Her armies indeed have awesome might, but she knows the cost of war (v 34), 'Kings, when they enter a town lay it waste'. She plays for time by sending a gift to Solomon. But Solomon will be satisfied with nothing less than her acceptance of belief in one God. She is bold enough to confront him. He puts her to the test by the sight of her throne which he had slightly altered, and asks her a trick question: 'Is your throne like this one?' Instead of giving a yes or no answer, she neatly dodges the question and replies, 'Well, it could be'. In this, Rāzī sees her as the equal of the wisest man of her age, Solomon. But in the next scene, Solomon orders her to enter the palace, to walk across glass, which she confuses with a path through water. So she raises her skirt, she was mistaken, and confused. And in this momentary loss of self-assurance, she recognised the charisma of prophethood in Solomon, and, as had Solomon, makes her submission to God, *rabb al-ʿālamīn* 'Lord of the Worlds'. In his exegesis of this episode, Rāzī shows an appreciation of the qualities of Bilqīs as a ruler, and shows her as among the great women mentioned in the Qur'an.

Such story-telling is central in the Qur'an's presentation of its teaching. From the diverse personalities of the prophets, the situations they face, their role in enlarging Muhammad's understanding of what it is to be a prophet, the pain of rejection they too suffered, much of the economy of the human relationship with the divine can be understood.

But there are other ways in which the Qur'an teaches. The suras themselves are structured in various ways to give different emphases and insights of the revelation to those who live surrounded by the sound of them, and direct their lives according to them. The shorter ones often convey a lesson through a single idea with great power. The longer ones are often episodic, the various episodes relating to each other in different ways, without fracturing the unity of the sura. The study of the sura as a unity is a relatively recent emphasis in Qur'anic interpretation. It moves away from the traditional methodology of exegesis based on a sequential verse by verse commentary, and offers new perspectives of insight and meaning in the text. It contributes to a deeper appreciation of the Book as a literary as well as a religious event; it facilitates an understanding of the relationship of the suras to each other, demonstrating that, as a single extended utterance addressed to the prophet, every pericope within it needs to be understood as dominated by the concerns of the whole, and the over-riding values that it teaches, and so making clear a hierarchy of values and instructional priorities. It is simplistic to expect to find a common basic template as a result of such an investigation into the text, as simplistic as to accept the assertion of Richard Bell that the internal organization of the sura is largely arbitrary.

Form is a protean concept not easy, possible or even desirable to define with precision. Often it is a presence that has to be felt, before any attempt can be made to analyse it. The Qur'an offers various forms of sura structure. The sura of Joseph for example, is self-evidently a unity, both in its subject, the linear character of its narrative, and the circumstances of its revelation. Sūrat al-A'rāf (7) on the other hand is significantly longer, more various in its content, and without the authority of a single dominant narrative line. Its unity resides in its consisting of four parts, each structurally integrated with its neighbours, presented in an ascending order of rhetorical power. It opens in Mecca as God addresses the prophet. It presents narrations of five of the early prophets. It presents the story of Moses, and concludes with the climactic point of divine revelation at the place and in the time that it opened, with the call and preaching of Muhammad, the unlettered prophet, in Mecca.

Sura 25, al-Furqān, is in a different form again. Its structure is marked by challenges put to the prophet and divine responses, interposed with passages of doxology and divine allocutions. The challenges to the prophet, 'This (the Qur'an) is nothing but a lie! He has made it up' (v 4), are in a demotic style of language; the responses put on the prophet's lips have a solemnity and authority, and this mingling and contrasting of naturalistic and formal language is one of the striking features of the sura. It concludes with a triumphant vindication of Muhammad as a servant of The Merciful, al-Rahmān.

This sura also provides exquisite examples of how the verbal music and imagery of the Qur'an is carried within the sura and between suras. It opens with the celebratory formulaic ejaculation: 'Blessed be He who revealed the Qur'an to His servant [Muhammad]', *tabāraka'l-ladhī nazzala'l-furqāna 'alā 'abdihi*. The celebratory phrase 'Blessed be He who . . . *tabaraka'lladhi* . . . occurs four times at strategic points in the sura, binding it together, and establishing its pulse and movement. It occurs at crucial points in a number of other suras as if sung in chorus with this utterance of the phrase, celebrating God's wonderful deeds, with perhaps most strikingly at the opening of sura *al-Isrā' (17:1)*), celebrating Muhammad's night journey to Jerusalem and ascent to the throne of God, 'Blessed be He who took His servant by night from the Sacred Mosque [at Mecca] to the furthest Mosque [at Jerusalem]' *tabāraka'l-ladhī asrā bi-'abdihi laylan min al- masjidi'l-harām ilā'l-masjidi'l-aqsā*

It presents striking images of God's power. One is the movement of shadow (*zill*) over the earth (v 45)

> *Have you not reflected on how your Lord*
> *extended [over the earth]a shadow.*
> *Had He wished, He could have made [this shadow] stay at rest.*
> *But We directed the sun to make it move,*
> *and so drew it gently towards Us.*

The word for shadow, *zill*, is lexically simple, but rich in its connotations and associations, among them protection from the heat of the sun, and so comfort, and shelter in this and the world to come. In sura 28, after fleeing from Pharaoh, the young Moses, having reached safety and helping two young women water their sheep, moves into the shadow (v 24). Elsewhere, the movement of shadows over the earth is a symbol of obedience to God. Here, however, it is used in a broader sense, and the image is one of cosmic grandeur.

In the exegetic tradition, *zill* is glossed as *safar*, referring to the yellowish half-light of dawn when the eastern sky is brightening, but the sun has not yet risen. The shadow of night still lies over the earth. But in a little while, looking to the West, the first rays of the sun can be seen to strike the highest point of the horizon with light. From that moment on, as the sun further rises, the whole mass of shadow, of darkness in the west, gradually but inexorably rolls back eastwards. The image then shows the power of God on a vast scale over the processes of nature. Nevertheless, for its significance to be understood, the situation it depicts must be experienced, and the Qur'anic words of divine simplicity with which it begins, *a-lam tara* 'have you not reflected on' are an invitation to share this experience, paradoxically, at dawn they look to the West, not to the East.

But this verse is also an exquisite example of another feature of Qur'anic rhetoric. It opens with God questioning the prophet

> *Have you not reflected on how your Lord extended*
> *[over the earth] a shadow.*

God then speaks of Himself in the third person.

> *Had He wished, He could have made it stay at rest.*

For whether day dawns or not is a matter of God's will. All creation is totally dependent on Him. Then He switches to speak in the first person

> *But We directed the sun to make it move,*
> *and so drew it gently towards Us.*

The effect is electrifying. The words are no longer an account of God's power, but of God himself telling how He exercises his power, and how all creation is in His charge.

There are other images of the dawn in the Qur'an. Taken together they have a cumulative effect which contributes to the power of the whole. It is as though it is a symbol which functioning as a pressure point in one context, replicates the pressure it exerts everywhere else it occurs. I have already referred to the evocative power of God's command to Muhammad: Declare, I take refuge with the Lord of the Dawn (113:1). In sura 100, the suddenness of a dawn attack on an enemy encampment at an oasis, the hooves of the horses of the attackers striking fire as they raise the dust, is an image of the suddenness of the coming of the day of judgment (100:1–3). And in sura 81, Muhammad is called on to swear by the first breath of morning as it stirs across the desert, at the closing of night (vv18–20) that the words of the Qur'an are brought to him by a mighty messenger, the angel Gabriel, stationed at the divine throne.

In this account of a personal odyssey, I have attempted to give an outline of what the Qur'an is. It is based primarily on a literal understanding of the Book, as the inescapable first stage of any literary appreciation of it. From this one can move to its metaphorical, moral and mystical significances, for the Qur'an can be and has to be understood at all these levels.

I have been able only to hint at these. But perhaps this is sufficient to give some idea of what unites Muslims with the Qur'an, and what gives them the assurance of finding in it the wisdom needed in face of modernity. For the Qur'an presents a vision, a spirituality and ideals that transcends, even though it has inspired, the best efforts of the jurisconsults of all the schools of Law. Fakhr al-Dīn al-Rāzī, my guide, my friend, great intellect that he was, saw this clearly, and in his last years devoted himself entirely to the study of the Qur'an.

It is indeed a guide to faith and works. It speaks with authority. It is this authority that has demanded and created the marvellous tradition of *tafsīr* as one of the great disciplines in Islamic learning. Over one and a half millennia, it ranges from the lucidity and charm of Muqātil b Sulaymān to the searching, probative questionings of Nasr Hamid Abū Zayd and others, who in the wake of post-modernist theories, explore the relation between the text and the context in which it was revealed, the relation between text and receptor over all these years, and the implication of these theories for the understanding and application of the positive laws stipulated in the Qur'an. The emphases of *tafsīr* during this long history have been rich and diverse: historical and meta-historical, philological, grammatical and literary, mystical, theosophical, philosophical and theological—and even political. Some of the greatest minds in human history, such as my beloved Fakhr al-Dīn al-Rāzī have devoted all their energies to it.

Yet alongside all the calls for modernisation in approach to this discipline, and to reduce meanings of the Qur'an to what the contempoprary mind deems 'modern' or 'rational', an approach that Muhammad Asad in his rendering, *The Message of the Qur'an*, takes to extremes, the rhetorical and moral core of the Qur'an needs no more apology or modernisation than do the Psalms. Its essential message is timeless. It is not only for reading, but meditation and reflection. Moses, at one point, reflecting on the many blessings God has given him, withdraws to the shadow of palm-trees next to a watering place for flocks of sheep, and murmurs, Lord God, how deep indeed has been my need for the blessings You have given me. ((*rabbī/innī limā anzalta ilayya min khayrin faqīr)*) [al-Qaṣaṣ (28:24)]. When Muhammad has endured the turmoil of argument and rejection in the Meccan marketplace, weary and perhaps disheartened, God counsels him, 'Think on your Lord, morning and evening, humbly and filled with awe, speechless with adoration' (al-A'rāf 7:205).

Joseph in The Qur'an: Dramatic Dialogue, Human Emotion and Prophetic Wisdom[1]

In Memoriam Dom Gregory Burke OSB
Monk of Buckfast

The story of Joseph is world class. Like that of Alexander it has generated numerous retellings, elaborating or emphasising one or another of its episodes, and provided a frame-work into which various sub-plots and episodes might be inserted.

Knowledge of the story in the Christian and Judaic traditions, and through these traditions, in western literature generally, has been from the version presented in Genesis, chapters 37–50. Its diffusion and numerous retellings from the Rabbinic period down to the great novel created out of it by Thomas Mann have been extraordinary.[2]

Yet the presentation of the story in sura 12 of the Qur'an has fecundated an equally remarkable diffusion of the Joseph story in the various languages of the Muslim world, whether in Spanish (a heritage of Muslim rule in Spain), Arabic, Persian or Turkish, or the numerous vernaculars of the Indian subcontinent or the island archipelago of Southeast Asia. There are versions for all social and educational levels of society, from the great literary version of Jāmī *Yūsuf u Zulaikha* to those of the popular story-tellers of Baghdad. One of these story-tellers claimed to tell a version of the tale that would reveal the name of the wolf that ate Joseph. When reproved by ibn Ḥanbal on the grounds that the wolf had not eaten Joseph, the

1. This essay took shape at the Dominican Institut of Oriental Studies in Cairo, July–August 1980. My deepest appreciation is due to the Dominican Friars for their hospitality and friendship and especially to Fr Jacques Jomier who first introduced me to that spiritual and intellectual colossus, Fakhr al-Dīn al-Rāzī.
2. Thomas Mann, *Joseph and His Brothers* (London: Sphere Books, 1968), i–iv.

story-teller promptly re-phrased his claim, and promised the name of the wolf that had not eaten Joseph.[3]

For any one brought up in the ambience of the Judaic or Christian tradition, the Genesis version of the story inevitably is regarded as a norm. Von Rad remarks that it is novel through and through,[4] and indeed the emotional climaxes, the distribution of tensions, aspects of the dialogue, and some of the techniques of story-telling—the description of a character from various reference points, for example—are not only effective in their own right, but are among the features recognized as characteristic of the novel.

One whose literary imagination, sense of style and expectations of the story have since childhood been formed in this tradition may well be disappointed in the Qur'anic version, and regard it as unworthy of serious attention. Thus a scholar of the stature of Torrey treats it almost frivolously. Of the vision which warns Joseph against adultery when Zulaikha tempts him, he remarks, 'This is characteristic of the angel Gabriel's manner of spoiling a good story', and of the scene in which Joseph reveals his identity: 'This is simple routine; no one in the party appears to be excited.'[5]

Yet the individuality, force and beauty that the Muslim tradition has found in it is amply attested in the writings of exegetes, poets and mystics.

Even so, on a first encounter, the Qur'anic presentation of the material may to the Westerner appear disjointed and incomplete, requiring its readers to supply out of their imaginations or prior knowledge, both the links between the events occurring in the narrative and the framework in which they are set, without which the story could not exist.

The reason for this reaction, I suggest, is the way in which the material is presented. In order to see the sura in its own terms, and without the interference of expectations brought about by the unconscious conditioning of other versions, it is necessary to be aware of the rhetorical idiom in which the story is told. The character of this

3. See Ignaz Goldzier in Muslim studies, edited by SM Stern (Sydney: Allen and Unwin, 1967), II, 157.
4. Gerhardt von Rad, *The Problems of the Hexateuch and Other Essays* (Edinburgh: T&T Clark, 1966), 292.
5. Charles Cutler Torrey, *The Jewish Foundations of Islam* (New York: Ktav Publishing House, 1967), 112–123.

idiom is obscured by the assumption that its wealth of meaning is accessible from a silent reading. Essentially, the Qur'anic presentation of the story is to be heard, and just as the asseverative, argumentative and hortatory episodes of the Qur'an can only make their full impact when heard, so too, the stories, narrative episodes and dialogues in the Qur'an, can only be grasped to best effect when heard, and their phrasing and emphases are informed by the intonation of the speaking or reciting voice. The Genesis version on the other hand, is accessible to a silent reader—von Rad's remark that it is 'novel through and through' being particularly apposite.

Therefore, the art of the reciter is crucial to the western reader's perception of the difference between the rhetorical idioms of Joseph in Genesis and in the Qur'an. For it is the declamatory projection of the voices of Joseph, of Jacob, of Joseph's brothers, of the Governor, al-'Azīz (aka Potiphar), of Zulaikha, of the women, of Joseph's fellow prisoners, and of the king (Pharaoh)—even the exclamation of the drawer of water who finds Joseph in the well 'What luck! Here's a young man!' *yā bushrā, hādhā ghulām*! (v 19)—all reveal the vibrant life and excitement of the sura. Only then is the setting of the story clear: Muhammad's response to the challenge made him by the Meccans, that if he is indeed a prophet he will be able to tell them the story of Joseph and why Jacob's family moved from Canaan to Egypt. Once this has been grasped, the structure of the chapter and its episodic character are set into relief; it can then be seen how the sura is constructed out of a rapidly moving sequence of scenes, something like a morality play, and the events of the story are for the most part communicated through the dialogue. The scenes are not watertight and at times merge into another.

The scenes may be set out as follows:

(I) 1–7 God's words addressed to Muhammad, announcing the story to be revealed to him which will provide evidence.

(II) 8–15 The brothers' envy; their plot to get rid of him; they throw him deep into the well.

(III) 16–18 They return to Jacob with Joseph's garment daubed with blood; Jacob's patience.

(IV) 19–20 Joseph's rescue from the well; he is sold.

(V)	21–29 Joseph in Egypt; he is tempted by Zulaikha; she calumniates him; his innocence is proved.
(VI)	30–34 Women gossip about Zulaikha' infatuation with her servant; they see him for themselves how handsome he is, and cut their fingers—instead of the fruit—in amazement.
(VII)	35–42 Joseph is in prison; he interprets the dreams of the baker and the cup-bearer.
(VIII)	43–45 The King (Pharaoh) dreams of the fat and lean cattle, the green and the withered corn; The cup-bearer is sent to Joseph
(IX)	46–49 Joseph interprets Pharaoh's dreams to the cup-bearer.
(X)	50–57 Pharaoh summons Joseph. He demurs until Zulaika admits her guilt. He comes, and his position at court is established.
	54–57 The King has Joseph brought to him, and establishes his position at the court.
(XI)	58–62 Joseph's brothers come before him to ask for corn; they do not recognise him. He asks them to bring to him their younger brother as a condition for them to receive more corn
(XII)	63–67 The brothers return to their father; they ask to take Benjamin back to Egypt with them. Despite misgivings he allows him to go.
(XIII)	68–69 The brothers return to Egypt with Benjamin. Joseph reveals his identity to Benjamin.
(XIV)	70–76 Joseph has his cup put in Benjamin's bag, and he is accused of theft.
(XV)	77–81 The brothers plead for Joseph to release Benjamin for their father's sake. They offer one of themselves in his place. [episode of brothers return to their father understood].
(XVI)	82–87 Jacob is told that Benjamin has been held in Egypt; his grief yet steadfastness: only unbelievers despair of the kindness of God.
(XVII)	88–93 The brothers return to Joseph and plead with him. He reveals his identity, forgives them, and orders his garment be sent to Jacob.
(XVIII)	94–98 Jacob's eyesight is restored by Joseph's garment. [The re-union and journey to Egypt understood].

(XIX) 99–101 Joseph welcomes his father and brothers to Egypt; his final prayer.
(XX) 102–111 Conclusion to the sura: God's words addressed to Muhammad.

Description is sparse, and link passages between the scenes are minimal. Indeed, on several occasions one scene blends into another, but since the presentation is oral, the resonances and associations of the words, particularly for a non-literate audience, establish continuities not immediately evident to a silent reader. And because the primary exposition of events is more dramatic than descriptive or narrative, the effect of one scene following swiftly on another is cumulative, and becomes a strength not a weakness. The series of scenes is held together by the voice of God transmitted by Gabriel (Jibril) both at the opening of the sura, and in the magnificent peroration with which it ends.

Thus if the modern analogue for the Genesis version of the story is the novel, that for the Qur'anic, is drama: one might well describe it as 'a play for voices'.

Of course the sura *Yūsuf* is not unique in this. There are striking dialogues in Maryam (19:18–32) between Mary and the angel, between Abraham and his father in the same sura vv 41–48 and in many other suras. One might say that the Qur'an is a mosaic of voices, and in sura *Yūsuf*, this feature is especially clear.

There are the voices of the characters to each other throughout the story; there is the voice of Gabriel (Jibrīl), bearing the words of God, which, something in the manner of a chorus, comments on and draws the lesson from the episode just concluded. In scene X for example (vv 56–57), after Joseph has been set over the storehouses in the land, the Voice declares, 'This is how we established Joseph in the land, to live in it wherever he pleased' (v 56), and then presents to the listening crowd of Meccans the lesson to be drawn from God's providence: 'We give our mercy to those whom we will, and do not stint the reward of those who do good. Indeed, the reward of the world to come is better (than this) for those who believe and are devout' (v 57).

There are other examples of the voices turning outwards from the internal drama of the story to the audience listening to it. A notable one occurs in scene VII (v 39–40) when Joseph, in prison, addresses first his fellow prisoners, using the dual, 'My two fellow prisoners (*yā ṣāḥibayi'l-sijn*) which is better, to have many lords, or God, the One, the Almighty?' Then using the plural, he turns to the world outside the story, 'All that you worshp other than He are but names, names you yourselves and your fathers have made up.. God has not given them any dominion, such authority is God's alone, He has commanded that you worship none other than He—'this is the true religion' (v 40). Then, reverting to the dual, he turns back to the two prisoners, and interprets their dreams.

The style of utterance of the various *dramatis personae* likewise is consistent with the need to distinguish one individual from another in a dramatic presentation: it ranges from the emphatic and ornate to the simplest and most direct forms of address. I have already referred to the exclamation (v 19) 'What luck! Here's a young man!' (*yā bushrā hādhā ghulām*). Syntactically it could hardly be simpler. But consider the scene (V v 25) in which Zulaikha is pursuing Joseph; they come to the locked door, and unexpectedly Zulaikha's husband is standing there. Zulaikha hardly drawing a breath says, 'What is the penalty for one intending evil to your household, other than he be imprisoned or endure a painful punishment?' (*mā jazā'u man arāda bi ahlika sū'an illā an yusjana aw adhābun alīm*?) The complicated syntax and the manner in which she suggests these penalties reflects her confusion and sense of guilt. Rāzī notes this, and asks why does she *demand first imprisonment*, and as an afterthought only, severe punishment, when the crime of which she is accusing him is punishable by death? Rāzī's explanation is that she does not want to put her hope of seducing him permanently out of reach.[6]

Joseph's answer (v 26) by contrast is simple and brief, 'She tried to seduce me' (*hiya rawādatnī 'an nafsi*), Indeed, Joseph's words which are at times grandiloquent, on occasion have a moving simplicity, as when in scene XVII (vv 88–93) he reveals his identity to his brothers, saying 'I am Joseph, and this is my brother' (*ana Yūsuf wa hādhā akhī* v 90). This aspect of dialogue in the Qur'an deserves careful study.

This vitality deriving from the role of the spoken word in the sura gives some idea of how it might effectively have been presented to the Meccans, against a background of noise, bustle and scepticism, at length to win and hold attention. And indeed, there is a suggestion that

6. Fakhr al-DIn al-Rāzī, *al-Tafsīr al-Kabīr*, also known as *Mafātīh al-Ghayb*, Tehran, Dār al-Kutub al-'ilmiyya (2nd impression, no date). The work is in 16 volumes. Reference is to *TK* volume and page. Here, *TK* 18:122.

Muhammad himself did present it in this way. Kisā'ī quotes a tradition from Ibn 'Abbās telling how 'Abdullāh b Salām challenged Muhammad to tell the story of Joseph and his brethren, and then described how the Prophet recited it, raising his voice sometimes and lowering it at others (*wa yarfa'u ṣawtahu marratan wa yakhfiduhu ukhrā*).[7]

In the last resort however, the effectiveness of the sura derives from its inner coherence and thematic unity.[8] This can be shown in various ways. The first and most obvious is that of chronological sequence despite the transitions between scenes, which at times have to be understood. Chronology however is only one element, and indeed the simplest element that contributes to the structure, and thus to the impact of the sura as a unity. There is a variety of techniques that can be distinguished by which the scenes are interlocked, and the sura held tightly together.

One is a series of replays: incidents which occur a first time to result in evil, then a second time to result in good, the effect of which is heightened by juxtapositions and inversions.

Joseph's first encounter with Zulaikha in scenes V and VI (vv 23 and 35 respectively) for example, results in evil: when he resists her attempts at seduction, she calumniates him, and has him imprisoned. At a second encounter, on his release from prison, (scene X v 51) she admits her guilt and he forgives her. Indeed, on the tongues of the story tellers and in Kisā'ī too, the couple are wedded, her former marriage to 'Azīz (Potiphar) being invalid due to his impotence[9]—which explains a great deal.

Another example of such a replay is the brothers' request to Jacob to allow Joseph to accompany them (scene II v 12), assuring Jacob, 'We will watch over him well' (*wa innā lahu la ḥāfiẓun*). In this case the promise is false, and the harm that befalls Joseph is real: he is thrown into the well and sold into bondage. When in scene XII v 63 they ask Jacob to allow Benjamin to accompany them back to Egypt, otherwise they will not be given any more corn, they again assure him in identical words, 'We will take good care of him' (*wa innā lahu la ḥāfiẓun*), giving Jacob the opportunity to reproach them in v 64, 'Can I trust him to you any more than I trusted his brother to you years ago?

7. al-Kisā'ī, *Qiṣaṣ anbiyā'*, edited by Isaac Eisenberg (Leiden: Brill, 1922), I, 179.
8. Professor H Bajouda, Head of the Department of Arabic, King Abdul Aziz University at Mecca, has devoted a full length study to this topic: *al-Waḥda al-Mawdū'iyya fi sūra Yūsuf 'alayhi'l-salām* (Cairo: 1974).
9. Kisā'ī, Qisas, 179.

In his reply there is a double irony. The first is that in scene II v 12 the brothers were lying, but here they are telling the truth. Jacob was prepared, albeit reluctantly, to believe the first assurance that they would care for their brother, but not the second one. The second irony is that in scene III v 17, when they are lying to Jacob, insisting to him that Joseph has been taken by a wolf, they hypocritically complain 'Yet you never believe us, even if we are speaking the truth' (*wa ma anta bi mu'minin lanā, wa law kunnā ṣadiqīn*). Having had to accept the lie they told then, now Jacob cannot accept the truth or sincerity of their words. Yet in the first instance the harm that has befallen Joseph is real, in the second, the harm that Jacob is led to think has befallen Benjamin has not occurred.

This repetition of key words or phrases within such replays is another of the key devices by which the sura makes its impact. Another example occurs in scene II v 8 in which the brothers, jealous of Joseph and contemptuous of their father say of him, 'Our father is clearly deluded' *(inna abānā la-fī ḍalālin mubīn).* In face of such words and attitudes, Jacob has no redress. It is to be understood that throughout the years of Joseph's absence, Jacob has had to endure these insults. But eventually, when (scene XVIII v 90) Joseph reveals his identity, he tells his brothers to take a garment of his to cast on the old man's face in order to restore his sight. No sooner has the caravan set out from Egypt bearing Joseph's garment, than Jacob (v 94) declares, 'I sense the fragrance of Joseph. Did you not think I was senile, you would believe me'. The household (not the brothers, who are in Egypt), who have learnt how to treat the old man from his sons, in v 95 retort: 'By God, you are still in your old delusion' *(fī ḍalālika'l-qadīm).* But on this occasion, Jacob's patience *(ṣabr)* is proved to be justified. The messenger arrives (v 96), casts the garment on his face and he regains his sight. With confidence he can (v 96) at last reply: 'Did I not tell you, I know from God what you do not know' (*a lam aqul lakum innī a'lamu mina 'Allāhi mā lā ta'lamūn).* The root *'ilm* in fact occurs at many points in the sura, showing various facets of meaning in order to highlight the knowledge of God, the ignorance of so many of mankind, and the knowledge that God may give to a prophet—here Jacob—that is hidden to others.

There are many other instances of such repetitions, which sometimes serve to call attention to, or heighten the perception of replays of events, at others to keep particular themes or ideas in the listeners' mind. They have a function analogous to that of a repetition or suggestion of a theme in a piece of music.

For example in scene II v 18, when Jacob believes he has lost Joseph, he exclaims 'So gracious patience [is my sole recourse] *(fa ṣabrun jamīl)*.[10] In v 83, when he is told that Benjamin has been held in Egypt and Judah has remained there with him, despite these new sorrows after so many years of grief, he can still respond with the same words 'So gracious patience [is my sole recourse]'.

Another theme woven in to the texture of the sura is the ineffectiveness of human trickery and deceit.

In scene I (v 5), Jacob warns Joseph, 'Do not tell your brothers of your dreams, for they will scheme against you' (*fa yakīdu laka kaydan*); in scene V v 28, al-'Azīz reproves Zulaikha, after it has been proved that her accusations against Joseph are false, saying, 'This comes of your scheming, your guile is overwhelming' (*innahu min kaydikunna, inna kaydakunna 'aẓīm*).

In scene X v 50, Joseph, having interpreted the King's dreams, and being summoned from prison to the king's presence, instead of obeying, sends the messenger back to enquire: 'How is it with the women who cut their fingers? My Lord knows all their scheming' (*inna rabbī bi kaydihinna 'aẓīm*), and in v 52 he declares: 'God does not guide the guile of those who deceive.'

God however is able to surpass all human machinations. Thus when Joseph has his cup put into Benjamin's bag, the trick which brings about the triumphant has his cup put into Benjamin's bag, the trick which brings about the triumphant replay in which, as we shall see, it is proved that the brothers' dispositions have changed, and leads to the final reconciliation, God says, (*kadhālika kidnā li Yūsuf*) (v 76).

There are many other examples of words repeated at different points, sometimes far apart in the story, to highlight lessons which the sura has to teach. In scene XV v 80, after Benjamin has been arrested on a charge of theft, the brothers are desperate, and do their

10. *Fa ṣabrun jamīlun*. The commentators (for example al-Zamakhsharī, Rāzī, Nasafī) point out that two undefined nouns can, grammatically, only constitute a phrase, and that therefore these words must either be a *mubtada'* with a *khabar* understood, or vice-versa, *ṣabrun jamīlun* being defined as' a patience in which there is no complaint, for he who complains does not endure with patience.' (A tradition from al-Ḥasan cited by Rāzī, *TK* 18:103).

best to persuade Joseph to release him. And when they despair of this (*fa lammā'stay'asū minhu*) they are forced to face the truth about themselves, and the implications of the pledge they made before God to their father not to return without Benjamin. They had despaired of a man. But Jacob, in scene XVI v 87, assures them, 'Only unbelievers despair of the kindness of God' (*wā lā tay'asū min rawḥi'llāhi illā' l-qawmu' l-kāfirūn*), and then in v 110, the same word is used in a reminder that sometimes circumstances become so hard that even the messengers were on the point of despair (*ḥattā idhā'stay' asa' l-rusul*), but at that very moment 'Our help came to them' (*jā'ahum naṣrunā*)!

Most of these examples have been located in replays. There is one replay however which has a special role and a sublime grandeur. It is set in motion by Joseph's ploy of placing his cup in Benjamin's saddle-pack so that he will be accused of theft. How will the brothers react?

It will be recalled that at the beginning of the story the brothers are envious and materialistic. In scene II, v 8, they say: 'Joseph and his brother are dearer to our father than are we, although we are many' (*'usba*).

They see their father's affection as a commodity, as merchandise to be shared out, and calculate that ten should receive more than two. It is this envy which leads them to plot against Joseph, and to jeer at their father's continuing grief for his lost son.

The arrest of Benjamin has a dramatic effect upon them. Placed once again between their father and a younger brother that he loves dearly in their charge, on this occasion they put their father before their own interests. They plead with Joseph to let Benjamin go. They appeal to his compassion in scene XV v 78, saying, 'He has a father advanced in years, so take one of us in his place'. Joseph (v 79) refuses, 'God forbid that we should take anyone other than the man on whom we found our property, for then we would be acting unjustly.'

Having failed to move Joseph, they draw aside, and whisper among themselves, trying to find a way of saving their brother for their father's sake, just as they had drawn aside, long before, to devise a way of getting rid of Joseph without any regard for their father's pain. And instead of giving up Benjamin for lost, the senior of them (Judah or Reuben—the commentators are divided) refuses to leave Egypt without him, ordering the remaining nine to return to Canaan and tell the bad news to their father.

This then was the outcome of Joseph's stratagem, the plot that God made for Joseph (v 76) brought to a climax by his refusal to accept anyone in place of Benjamin.

Von Rad's commentary on this episode in Genesis is apposite for a deeper understanding of its counterpart in the Qur'an:

> But what is behind Joseph's strict refusal in 44,17? Here is the most important part of the test which Joseph made his brothers endure: he wants to isolate them from Benjamin; he wants to prove them, to learn whether they will seize the opportunity to go free without Benjamin. Now they could again return to their father and announce to him the loss of a son; they could even justify themselves, for so far as they knew Benjamin was actually guilty. (In the Qur'an in fact scene XV v 77—some of the brothers say: If he has stolen, a brother of his also stole in former times) and the balance of power was completely unfavourable to them. Joseph's test, therefore, was that he constructed a situation in which it had to become evident whether they would act as they once had done, or whether they had changed in the meantime.[11]

In the great speech of Judah in Genesis (44:18–34), and in the brothers' drawing aside to whisper together in the Qur'an, (v 80) it is shown how they 'have changed in their relationship to each other and above all in their relationship to their father. Judah now sees the situation completely from his father's view-point, and is ready even to surrender his own life in order to protect that of Benjamin. It is now clear that the brothers have passed the great test which Joseph set them.'[12]

The sura has yet other aspects of a direct human concern; some of which were of special significance to Muhammad, others to certain of the great exegetes, and still others to the Muslim community as a whole. They may derive directly from the structure of the story or the way the tale is told. Take for example the role of Joseph's garment. It is a garment daubed with false blood (v 18) which is the beginning of Jacob's troubles, and a garment which cast on his face and restoring his sight, signals the end of them. This is brought out by Rāzī, who

11. Gerhard von Rad, *Genesis A Commentary*, Old Testament Library, text revised on the basis of the ninth German edition (London: SCM Press, 1972), 393.
12. Gerhard von Rad, *Genesis*, 395.

quotes Sha'bī as saying 'the story of Joseph is all in his garment. This is because when they threw him in the well, they took: his garment, daubed it with blood, and showed it to his father (scene III v 18); and the witness testified 'If his garment is torn from the back she has lied' (scene V v 26) and when the garment was cast on Jacob's face, his sight was restored' (scene XVIII v 96).[13] He refers also to other commentators who, suggesting that it was Yahuda (Judah) who brought to Jacob the news that his son was alive, attribute to him the words, 'I went to him with the garment stained with blood, and I said that a wolf had taken Joseph. And I came today with the same garment, and I gladdened him just as I had grieved him.'[14]

Because the sura of Joseph is episodic, it is possible to regard one theme or another as dominant, according to the way one or another of the episodes is weighted in relation to the whole. For many, the love between Joseph and Zulaikha has been central to it and stories have been woven to show this love brought to a happy conclusion. For others, a particular scene has had a special attraction, such as scene VI v 31–32 in which the women cut their fingers instead of their fruit at the sight of Joseph's beauty.

One effective way to discern the relative emphasis that may be accorded the various episodes, or the resonances that inevitably suggest echoes from other parts of the Qur'an, is to listen carefully to the presentation of the sura by different reciters. This is a mode of study that has only really become practical with the availability of cassette recordings. In a version made by the Pakistani reciter Khushi Muhammad, there is a distinct heightening of tension in the reciter's voice in scene XII at v 99 when Joseph says to his father and brothers, 'Come into Egypt, God willing, safe from any harm' (*udkhulū miṣra in shā'allāhu āminīn),* with a remarkable ornamentation on the phrase *in shā'allāh.* The quickening of the pulse of the recitation here, as though at this point were located the climax of the sura—if I have perceived the dynamics of the reciter's voice correctly—may be because he was aware of a parallel phrase in *Sūra*t *al-Fatḥ* (48:27) when Muhammad is assured 'You will indeed enter the sacred mosque, if God so wills, secure from all harm' (*la tadkhulunna' l-masjida' l-ḥarāma in sha'allāhu āminīn*) and thus understood the command to enter Egypt

13. Rāzī, *TK* 18:101.
14. Rāzī, *TK* 18:101.

as a prefiguring of the assurance that Muhammad would return to Mecca triumphant. It is Rāzī, in his discussion of the sura, who draws attention to the parallelism between these two phrases.[15]

In addition, audience response to a reciter's 'realisation' of the text provides an invaluable guide to the ways in which the story is appreciated and understood among the Muslim community. A friend[16] informed me that once, at a village mosque in Egypt at which he was present, he observed an extraordinarily long interruption for expressions of admiration and delight after the verse 28 in scene V in which Joseph's innocence of Zulaikha's accusation was proved, it being demonstrated that his garment had been torn from the back, not from the front. In other cases, this scene had passed without any special response.

This still begs the question as to the ways in which its unifying theme might be expressed. Von Rad provides a clue in his remark that 'the Joseph story is really conceived as a Jacob story'.[17] This is not to underestimate the role of Joseph.

Yet surely one way to summate the story is to describe it as that of a father whose son is lost and then found. In which case, the theme that dominates the story is Jacob's grief at losing Joseph, a grief compounded by the fear that he has lost also Benjamin, and with him the brother who refused to return from Egypt without him, variously identified as Reuben, Simeon or Judah.

Indeed, among the most moving verses of the sura are those presenting Jacob's words uttered in scene XVI v 83 on hearing that Benjamin was held in Egypt 'So gracious patience [is my sole recourse]'. It may be that God will bring them all back to me, he is the all knowing, the all wise. 84 Then he turned from them and said, 'how I grieve for Joseph'. His eyes had whitened with sorrow, and he was blind with grief.

85 They said, 'By God, you will not cease speaking of Joseph until you have wasted away and died'.

86 He replied, 'My unbearable grief and pain I share with God alone, for I know from Him what you do not know.

---

15. Rāzī, *TK* 18:211.
16. Fr J Jomier of the Dominican Institute of Oriental Studies, Cairo, in a private communication.
17. Gerhard von Rad, *Genesis*, 350.

87 My sons, go and enquire of Joseph and his brother, and do not despair of the kindness of God; only unbelievers despair of the kindness of God '.

These verses show in Jacob two contrasting moods. Alongside his grief, expressed in much weeping, is his total trust in God, a trust expressed in the words "So gracious patience [is my sole recourse]'and in v 86: 'I know from Him what you do not know' (*wa a'lamu mina'llāhi mā lā ta'lamūna).* In Genesis (45:26) Jacob cannot believe that his son is alive. 'He was as one stunned, for he did not believe them',[18] whereas in the Qur'an, Jacob cannot really accept that his son is dead, and is continually abused for his 'old delusion"

This grief of Jacob has a bearing on a broader question much discussed among early Muslims: is it permitted to weep at a bereavement?

The best known example of the Prophet's view is his answer to the question put to him when he wept at the death—perhaps in 632—of his infant son Ibrāhīm, born to him by Mariya the Copt, at a time when he could have had little expectation of fathering another child, 'The heart grieves and the eye weeps without offending God—yet at being parted from you, Ibrāhīm, we are overwhelmed with sorrow.'[19]

There are in fact many examples of Muhammad's tears. Zamakasharī remarks that the prophet wept at many bereavements, including the death of a grandson.[20] This was probably 'Abdullāh, the son of Ruqayya and 'Uthmān b 'Affān, later to be the third Caliph. Ibn Sa'd says that Ruqayya migrated to Abyssinia with 'Uthmān, and while there, first had a miscarriage, and then gave birth to a son 'Abdullāh - perhaps named after another son of Muhammad who had died in childhood, around 612, or even after his grandfather. Muhammad, after all, was Muhammad ibn 'Abdullāh. The child reached the age. of one or two, when a cock pecked him in the face. The wound became infected and the child died. Ruqayya had no further children.[21]

In the same narrative, Ibn Sa'd gives a telling example of Muhammad's attitude to the expression of grief. Ruqayya died during the battle of Badr, seventeenth months after the Migration,

18. The rendering is from *The New Jerusalem Bible* (London, Darton, Longman & Todd, 1985).
19. As cited by Zamakhsharī, *al-Kashshāf 'an haqā'iq al-tanzīl wa 'uyūn al-aqāwīl fī wujūh al ta'wīl* (Beirut, No date), 498.
20. Zamakhsharī *Kashshāf*, II, 498.
21. Ibn Sa'd, *Kitāb al-Tabaqāt al-Kabīr* (Leiden: Brill), 1321 AH, Vlll, 24.

and Zayd b Ḥāritha entered Medina with news of the victory as they were smoothing the soil of her grave. The women were weeping for Ruqayya when 'Umar came up, and began beating them with his whip. Muhammad took him by the hand, and said, 'Let them weep, 'Umar'. Then he said, 'Weep, and we drive away the devil. For whatever comes from the heart and the eye is from God and mercy, and whatever comes from the head and the tongue is from the devil'.

Fāṭima sat at the edge of the grave next to the prophet and began to weep, and the Messenger of God wiped the tears from her eyes with the edge of his garment.[22]

Jacob's grief in this sura was also used to prove that it was not forbidden to weep with grief. Zamakhsharī, commenting on the words in scene XVI verse 84 'and his eyes had whitened' *(wa-byaḍḍat a'ynāhu)* notes, 'It is said that Jacob's eyes were never dry from the time he was separated from Joseph until he was reunited with him after eighty years—yet there was no one on the face of the earth more honoured of God than Jacob. And from the Messenger of God (thus showing, as we shall see, a close feeling of kinship with Jacob) that he asked Gabriel (Jibrīl) how great was Jacob's grief for Joseph? Gabriel replied, 'The grief of seventy bereaved mothers'. He asked, and what was his reward? He replied, 'The reward of a hundred martyrs'; he never thought ill of God, even for a moment. Nor is this the only reference by Muhammad to the grief and tears of Jacob. Zamakhsharī reports from al-Ḥasan that whenever Muhammad wept at the death of a child or at some other bereavement and was asked about it, he replied, 'I do not think that God made Jacob grieve in order to disgrace him'.[23]

There are many examples in *ḥadith* and *sīra* material of the use of phrases or motifs from sura *Yūsuf* both by Muhammad and other members of the community, in addition to the echoes from this sura in other parts of the Qur'an. In fact the role and standing of Joseph among the prophets of Islam is illustrated by Muhammad's meeting with him in the account of the *mi'rāj* given by Ibn Ishāq.[24]

22. Ibn Sa'd, *Tabaqāt*, VIH, 25.
23. Zamakhsharī, *Kashshāf*, II, 498.
24. A Guillaume, *The Life of Muhammad* (London: Oxford University Press, 1955), 186. It may be noted that during the ascent to the Divine Presence through the seven heavens, Muhammad sees at the first and lowest Adam, then, respectively in order of ascent, Jesus and together with him, John his maternal cousin, Joseph (whose face is like the moon when it is full), Idris, Aaron, Moses, and finally, in the seventh heaven, Abraham.

Reference has already been made to the verse in *al-Fatḥ* 48:7 assuring Muhammad that he will enter the sacred mosque at Mecca, in virtually the same words as Jacob and his sons are told to enter Egypt. The phrase 'So gracious patience [is my sole recourse]', occurring in sura *Yūsuf* (verses 18 and 83) it seems, developed the currency of a proverb, and Muhammad's wife 'Ā'isha used it to console herself when accused of misconduct until a revelation established her innocence.[25]

There is however a report of Muhammad's association of himself with Yūsuf which gives the sura a special place in the development of the ethos of the Muslim community.

Zamakhsharī, in commenting on the words in scene XVII v 92, 'No reproach is held against you today. God forgives you, for He is the most merciful of all who show mercy' (*lā tathrība 'alaykum al-yawm, yaghfiru' llāhu lakum, wa huwa arḥamu' l-rāḥimīn*) says, 'It is related that the messenger of God put his hands on two pillars of the door of the Ka'ba on the Day of Victory, and said to the Quraysh, 'What do you think I will do to you?' They replied, 'Something good, noble brother, and son of a noble brother, and you have the power'. He said, 'I say to you what my brother Joseph said, "No reproach is held against you today"'. And it is related that when Abū Sufyān came to accept Islam, 'Abbās said to him, 'When you go to the messenger of God recite to him, "He said no reproach is held against you today"' (*qāla lā tathrība 'alaykum al-yawm*) and he did that. The messenger of God then said, 'May God be merciful to you and to him who taught you.'[26]

Such instances of Muhammad's perception of an image of himself and his own role now in Jacob, now in Joseph, are striking. But there are further reasons for considering that *Sūrat Yūsuf*, so far from being simply a story to present the divine message, was of particular significance to Muhammad personally, and has parallels to his own experience; and in addition, that it presents in microcosm a review of his past, prepares the ground for a new stage in his development, and provides an indication of what his future is to be.

It is not possible to establish with certainty the date of revelation of the Sura. If Bell's periodisation of the Meccan suras is correct, placing sura *Yūsuf* as late Meccan,[27] it could be 619/620. By this time

25. Rāzī, *TK* 18:103. See also the Qur'an Sura 24 (al-Nūr):11 sura 24.
26. Zamakhsharī, *Kashshāf*, II, 503.
27. Bell and Watt, *Introduction to the Qur'an* (Edinburgh: Edinburgh paperbacks, 1970), 110.

Khadīja, who died in 619, had born him four daughters and two sons, al-Qāsim and 'Abdullāh both of whom died in infancy. 'Abdullāh was Khadīja's last child. Ibn Sa'd says that he was born after the Call (*fī l-Islām*), and died in Mecca.[28] This could hardly have been later than 612. Reference has already been made to the death of 'Abdullāh, the grandson born in Abyssinia around 618. Thus Muhammad knew what grief for the loss of a son was; he also knew the biting pain of the contemptuous soubriquet *abtar*—without a male heir—that his enemies gave him, an insult referred to in sura 108 (*al-Kawthar*), 3: 'It is he who insults you who shall be childless.' Thus he could identify with Jacob—share his grief and imitate his patience, saying with him the words, 'So gracious patience [is my sole recourse].'

But this apart, the most striking feature of the sura is the completeness of the resolution of conflict, the restoration of peace and harmony after the disruption caused by envy. Many of the early prophets of the Qur'an bring dire punishments upon those who rejected them. For example, sura 54 *al-Qamar* warns of various peoples destroyed because they rejected the messengers sent to them. The people of Noah said their prophet was a madman. He called upon his Lord to avenge him, and they were drowned (54: 9–17).

The people of 'Ād rejected their prophet, and they were carried away by a roaring wind (54:18–22).

The people of Thamūd called their prophet Ṣāliḥ an imposter, and at one cry of the angel Gabriel they were reduced to dry sticks, with which one hardly build a cattle pen (54:23–32).

The people of Lūṭ (Lot) were destroyed by a wind driving a shower of stones (54:33–40).

Moses punished the people of Pharaoh, and destroyed Pharaoh's army, and then led the faithful Israelites through the desert (54:41–48).

By contrast neither Jacob nor Joseph make threats or need to exact vengeance. Jacob accepts his trials, he forgives his penitent sons for the pain they caused him. His patience and endurance never waver. Joseph likewise forgives Zulaikha for her lies, and his brothers for their envy, declaring, 'No reproach is held against you today'.

It is interesting to note the words that Jacob utters to express acceptance of his pain, 'So gracious patience [is my sole recourse]' *(fa ṣabr jamīl . . .)* occur in slightly different forms in two earlier suras,

28. Ibn Sa'd, *Tabaqāt*, I, 8.

in 70 *(al-Ma'ārij),* 5, 'Endure with a gracious patience' *(fa'ṣbir sabran jamīlan)*,and in 73 *(al-Muzzammil),* 10, 'Bear patiently what they say, and leave them with dignity *(wa'ṣbir 'alā mā yaqūlūna wa'hjurhum hajran jamīlan.* These are counsels to Muhammad early in his career to be patient when his teaching of the world to come is rejected, yet is followed by the assurance that those who spurn him will be overtaken by the hell they deny.

In the peroration to this sura too (scene XX:107) there is a warning to those who disbelieve, 'Do they not realise that the punishment of God will come upon them, or that suddenly, when they least expect it, the Hour will overwhelm them?'

Yet sura *Yūsuf* communicates above all the grand design of reconciliation that marked Muhammad's return to Mecca. In which case it is no coincidence that Muhammad addresses the Quraysh at the Ka'ba, 'I say to you the words of my brother Joseph, no reproach is held against you today', or that 'Abbās tells Abū Sufyān to recite these words from the sura *Yūsuf* when making his approach to Muhammad to accept Islam.

The conclusion of the sura consoles Muhammad for the rejection of the Qur'an by many, even though it is a message for all creatures, and urges him to endure it patiently (scene XX, v 103, 105, 110), 'Yet most men—though you yearn for it, will not believe' '. . . no matter how many signs there are in the heavens and on earth, they pass them by, and look the other way . . .' This rejection of the earlier prophets continued until even the prophets began to despair and fear that they had been deceived—'But then our help came to them' (110). In doing so it re-echoes the phrase recurring in the various preceding verses of the story, 'Most of mankind do not know' (*aktharu' l-nāsi lā ya'lamūn*), and the words of Jacob (scene XVI v 87), 'Only unbelievers despair of the kindness of God.'

It is possible then to see both Jacob and Joseph as role models for Muhammad. Jacob endures with patience the loss of his son, and the mockery of 'You are still in your old delusion', because he lives in hope of finding Joseph alive. His hope is anchored in his conviction that he knows from God something that the others do not know. Muhammad endures a similar mockery, and perseveres in the same conviction. Joseph provides a role model of prophet as ruler. He endures rejection by his kin, is exiled from his homeland and is calumniated. But what his enemies intended as ill, God turns to good. He is vindicated and takes his place as a wise and just ruler. Perhaps it is not too far-fetched to see Joseph's rejection as a parallel to Muhammad's rejection, his imprisonment a parallel to the restriction of Muslim activities to the house of Arqam, and his establishment as a ruler in exile as a parallel to Muhammad's leadership in Medina, as a model for the Migration. In fact this is suggested in scene VII: 37 when Joseph says to his two fellow prisoners when they asked him to interpret their dreams, 'Truly I left a company of people who did not. believe in God and who denied the world to come', as did Abraham, and as Muhammad himself was to do at the Migration. If the sura were revealed in 619/20, the date would fit very well. Further it is probably not a coincidence that those suras and verses telling of prophet rulers, such as David and Solomon, were revealed around the same time.

The great commentators analyse and explain sura Yūsuf in great detail, revealing its many aspects. Rāzī's exegesis, cited several times, is of special importance. In his long treatment of it, with his apparatus of *mas'ala, sū'al, baḥth* and *qawl*, he raises numerous issues of morality, psychology and human emotions in the story which are important for an understanding of the prophets, whether as men or as Messengers. In discussing them he reveals a remarkable sensitivity to the complexities and tensions in human motivation. In particular he communicates the intensity of Jacob's grief at the loss of Joseph, and discusses at length the moral problem as to whether it is right to express grief publicly. This issue is more important to him than Zulaikha's love for Joseph, or the incident in scene VI v 31 where the women are so overcome. at the sight of his beauty that they cut their fingers instead of the fruit they held in their hands.

He was after all, something of a mysogynist, and frequently refers to the guile and treachery of women. In fact in commenting on scene IV v 28 in which 'Azīz (Potiphar), having discovered that his wife is lying, condemns the guile of all women, he cannot restrain himself from saying, 'The guile of women compared to that of men is enormous . . . in this chapter women have a guile and deviousness that men do not have.'[29] But there is another reason. He wrote this part of his commentary, as he says, when his heart was grieved for the loss of his son Ṣāliḥ Muḥammad, and in concluding it, asks whoever reads his book, and gains something from it, to recite

29. Rāzī, *TK* 18:124.

al-Fātiḥa for his son. and himself and to pray for those who die away from home, far from brethren and mother and father[30] 'I for my part', he says 'offer many prayers for one who does this, showing how he too, intellectual giant that he was, shared the grief, the tears and the faith of Jacob.

The chapter of joseph

A Rendering[31]

In the name of God, the Merciful, The Compassionate

Scene I

The story to be revealed

1. Alif Lām Rā'—these are verses of the lucid book,
2. We revealed it to be recited in Arabic, so that you all might understand it.
3. We are telling to you the best of stories in what We reveal in this recitation, though before this you had given it no thought.
4. It is of when Joseph said to his father, 'My father I saw eleven stars, and the sun and the moon, I saw them bow down before me'.
5. He replied, My dear son, do not tell your brothers of your dream for they will scheme against you. The devil is a self-declared enemy to man.
6. This is how your Lord is choosing you, teaching you the interpretation of dreams, and making perfect his favour upon you and the family of Jacob, as in former times he perfected on your two ancestors Abraham and Isaac. Truly your Lord is knowing and wise'.
7. In Joseph and his brothers there are wonders for those who ask questions.

---

30. Rāzī, *TK* 18:229.
31. This is an attempt to communicate the sense of the sura as I have understood it, and in the light of which the essay was written. It has no pretensions to be definitive, either from the standpoint of style or interpretation.
   - The meaning of these three letters of the Arabic alphabet are 'Known unto God'.

Scene II

The envy of Joseph's brothers

8. **[It is of] when they said, 'Joseph and his brother are dearer to our father than are we, even though we are many. Our father is clearly deluded'.**
9. [One of them said] 'Kill Joseph or get rid him to another land', then the face of your father will be unclouded towards you. After that, live as a righteous people'.
10. Another of them said, 'Do not kill Joseph, but throw him deep into the bottom of a well: a passing caravan will find him if you do this'.
11. They said, 'Beloved father, why do you not trust Joseph with us? We will take good care of him.
12. Send him with us tomorrow to play and amuse himself; we will watch over him well'.
13. He replied, 'It grieves me that you should go off with him. I fear the wolf may devour him while you neglect him.
14. They said, 'If the wolf devour him—despite us being many—we would be weaklings.'
15. So when they went off with him, and decided to throw him deep into the well. We then revealed to him, 'Assuredly you will tell them what they have done when they least expect it'.

Scene III

Joseph's blood stained garment

16. They came to their father at nightfall, weeping.
17. They said, 'Beloved father, we went racing one with another, and left Joseph with our belongings. Then the wolf devoured him - yet you never believe us, even when we speak the truth'.
18. And they brought his garment with false blood on it. He replied, 'No, your desires have deceived you, so gracious patience [is my sole recourse], and God is to be asked for help in face of what you tell me'.

Scene IV

He is rescued from the well

19. A caravan of travellers passed by, and sent their drawer of water [to the well]. He let down his bucket and exclaimed, 'What luck! Here's a young man!'. And they hid him in their merchandise—yet God knew what they were doing.
20. Then they sold him for a cheap price, a few dirham they counted out, for they had little use for him.

Scene V

Zulaikha attempts to seduce him

21. The man from Egypt who had bought him [al-'Azīz][32] said to his wife, 'Give him good quarters—perhaps he may be of use to us—or let us adopt him as a son.'
   This was how We established Joseph in the land, to teach him the interpretation of dreams. God is invincible in what He decrees, but this most of mankind do not know.
22. When he came of age, We gave him wisdom and knowledge—this is how We reward those who do good.
23. She in whose house he was tried to seduce him. She locked the doors, and said to him, 'Here now, come to me'. He replied, 'I take refuge with God! Surely my master has given me a good place in which to dwell; surely those who do evil come to no good.'
24. Yet she longed for him, and he longed for her. Had he not seen a sign from his Lord [he might have lain with her], a sign by which We turned from him wickedness and disgrace. Truly he was one of our chosen servants.
25. They chased each other to the door, and she tore his garment from the back. At the door the two came upon master. She said: 'What is the penalty for one intending evil to your household, other than he be imprisoned, or suffer a painful punishment?'
26. He replied, 'She tried to seduce me'. Then one of her house-hold testified, 'If his garment is torn from the front, she speaks the truth, and he is a liar,

32. In Genesis: Potiphar

27. but if it is torn from the back, she has lied, and what he says is true.'
28. When he (her master) saw the garment was torn from the back, he said to her 'This comes of your scheming, your guile is great.
29. Joseph, say nothing of this; you [woman] ask forgiveness for your sin, you are a sinner.'

Scene VI

His beauty confounds the women

30. The Women in the city said: 'The wife of the Governor [al-'Azīz] tried to seduce her servant. Her heart is pierced with love for him; we see she is clearly deluded.
31. So when she heard their backbiting, she sent an invitation to them, prepared for them fruit,[33] gave to each one of them a knife, and called him, 'Come out before them'. When they saw him, they marvelled at him, and cut their fingers [instead of the fruit], and said, 'God Almighty: this is no human being, he can be only be a gracious angel'.
32. She said, 'This is the one for whom you condemned me. I tried to seduce him but he kept himself from sin. If he will not do what I command him, let him be put into prison, let him be held in contempt'.
33. He replied, 'My Lord, prison is dearer to me than that to which they tempt me to, but unless you turn aside their cunning from me, I will give in to them, I will be as one ignorant of right and wrong'.
34. His Lord heard his prayer, and turned aside their cunning from him. Truly He is the Hearing, the Knowing.

Scene VII

Joseph in prison.

He interprets the dreams of the baker and the cup bearer.

35. Then it seemed to them, even after seeing these signs, that they should imprison him for a while.

33. Reading *muikaan* in place of the usual *muuttaka'an*.

36. There came into prison with him two servants. One of them said, I saw myself [in a dream] pressing wine. The other said, 'I saw myself [in a dream] carrying on my head bread, and birds ate it. Tell us the meaning of these dreams, for we see you are a righteous man.'
37. He replied, 'No food to nourish you both shall come to you before I have told you what they mean before it happens. This is of what my Lord has taught me. Truly, I left the company of a people who did not believe in God and who denied the world to come.
38. I followed the company of my forefathers, Abraham, Isaac and Jacob. It is not for us to attribute a partner to God. This [teaching] is of God's bounty to us and to mankind, yet most of them are unbelievers.
39. My two fellow prisoners, which is better, to have many lords, or God the One, the Almighty!
40. All that you worship other than He are but names, names you yourselves and your fathers have made up. God has given them no dominion. The right to worship is His alone. He has commanded that you worship none other than He—this is the true religion, but most of mankind do not know.
41. My two fellow prisoners, as for one of you, he will again serve his master wine; as for the other, he will be crucified, and birds feed on his head. The outcome of what you asked me is decreed.
42. Then he said to the one he thought would be spared, 'Mention me to your master.' But the devil made him forget to mention [Joseph] to his master, so he stayed in prison for several years.

Scene VIII

The King's dreams.[34]

43. The king said, 'I saw [in a dream] seven fat cattle: seven thin cattle devoured them; and seven green [ears of corn], and another [seven] withered ones. My nobles, if you are interpreters of dreams, interpret my dreams for me.'
44. They replied, 'Confused dreams! We are not of those who know the interpretation of dreams.'
45. The one of the two [prisoners] who had been spared—for after a while he had remembered—said, 'I will tell you what they mean, just send me [to Joseph].'

---

34. In Genesis: Pharaoh

Scene IX

Joseph interprets the King's dreams

46. 'Joseph, man of truth, tell us the [meaning of the] seven fat cattle devouring the seven lean ones and the seven green ears and the other withered ones so I can go back to the people and they too may understand'.
47. He replied, 'You are to sow for seven years as usual, but what you harvest, apart from the little you eat, leave in the ear.
48. After this seven grievous years will come and consume what you have saved up for those years, except for the little that you have kept [as seed corn].
49. But after that will come a year in which men will be saved [from famine], and in which they will use again the *presses [for wine and oil.*

Scene X

The King summons Joseph

50. The king said, 'Bring him to me', but when the messenger came to him, Joseph replied, 'Go back to your master, and ask him how is it with the women who cut their fingers. My Lord knows all their scheming.
51. [The king] said [to the women], 'What do you to say of when you tempted Joseph?. They replied, 'God Almighty, we know no evil of him'. The wife of the Governor said: 'Now the truth has been made clear. I did tempt him, and he is the one who was speaking the truth'.
52. [Joseph said], This is that [her husband] may know I did not betray him during his absence, and that God does not guide the guile of those who deceive.
53. I make no excuses for myself: everyone is inclined to evil, except those on whom my Lord is merciful. My Lord is pardoning, merciful'.
54. The king replied, 'Bring him to me. I will keep him solely for myself'. And when he had spoken to him, he said, 'Today, you are firmly established with us, you deserve our trust.
55. Joseph said: 'Set me over the store houses of the land', I am a trustworthy guardian with full understanding'.

56. This was how We established Joseph in the land, to live in it wherever he pleased. We give our mercy to those whom We will, and do not stint the reward of those who do good.
57. Indeed, the reward of the world to come is better [than this] for those who believe and are devout.

Scene XI

Joseph's brothers seek corn in Egypt

58. Then Joseph's brothers arrived and came into his presence. He recognised them, but they did not know him.
59. When he had supplied their needs, he said 'Bring me a brother of yours by your father. Do you not see that I give full measure, and that I am the best of hosts?
60. But if you do not come to me with him, I have no corn for you. Do not approach me [again].'
61. They replied: 'We will ask for him from his father. Certainly we will do as you ask.
62. And he said to his servants, "Put the goods '[they have bartered] back into their saddle packs so they will recognise them on their return to their family—and so come back to us again.'"

Scene XII

They return to their father

63. When they had returned to their father, they said, 'Our father, we have been refused more corn [unless we bring our brother]. So send our brother with us so we will be given more corn; we will care for him well.'
64. He replied, 'Can I trust him to you any more than I trusted his brother to you years ago? Yet God is best as a protector and He is most merciful of all who grant mercy'.
65. When they opened their saddle packs, they discovered their goods had been returned to them. They said, 'Beloved father, what more do we want? These our goods have been returned to us; [with them] we can provide for our family. We will take good care of our brother, and we will gain [an extra] camel's load of grain; what we brought then was only a light load.'

66. He replied, 'I will not send him with you unless you make a pledge before God that you will bring him back to me, unless something overwhelms you all'. When they had made their pledge, he said, 'God holds in trust what we say'.
67. Then he said, 'My sons, do not enter [the city] through a single gate, but by separate gates. Yet I cannot protect you against what God [may will]. Authority belongs to God alone, in Him do I trust. So let those who seek one to trust in, trust in Him'.

Scene XIII

Joseph reveals his identity to Benjamin

68. They entered the city as their father had ordered them, but this did not shield them from God's will. This order was from a yearning in Jacob's soul, for he had knowledge that We had taught him, yet this most men do not understand.
69. When they came before him, Joseph took his brother [Benjamin] apart, and said to him, 'Truly, I am your brother so do not be troubled at what they have been doing.'

Scene XIV

Joseph's ploy

70. When he had met their needs, he put his cup in his brother's bag [and the caravan set out.] But suddenly a crier called out to them, 'Men of the caravan, you are thieves'.
71. The brothers replied, turning to those following them, 'What do you miss?'
72. They said 'We miss a cup belonging to the king. For whoever brings it me is a camel-load of grain, I vouch for this',
73. The brothers replied: 'By God, you know that we did not come to do evil in the land, and that we are not thieves'.
74. They said'. 'What should be the punishment be if you lie?'
75. The brothers replied, 'The punishment for him in whose pack it is found is himself [to be a slave]. This is how we punish evil-doers.'
76. He began (to search) all their packs, then coming to that of his brother, then took it from the pack. In this way we schemed for Joseph, for he could not have taken his brother captive according to the law of the king unless God willed it. We raise in rank whomever We will; above anyone endowed with knowledge is one who knows more.

Scene XV

Joseph's brothers plead for Benjamin.

77. [They said: 'If he has stolen anything, a brother of his also stole in former times. But Joseph kept this to himself, he did not disclose it to them, and said [to himself]: you are in a worse state. God knows the truth of] what you are saying.'
78. They said, 'Your Excellency, he has a father advanced in years, so take one of us in his place—we see that you are a righteous man'.
79. He replied, 'God forbid that we should take anyone other than the man on whom we found our property, for then we would be acting unjustly',
80. So when they had despaired of [changing Joseph's mind], they drew aside and whispered together, and the eldest of them said, 'Do you not know that your father had you make a pledge before God, and how before that you had sinned against Joseph? Therefore I will not leave this land until my father permits me, or until God makes a judgement for me—and He is the best of judges.
81. You return to your father, and say, 'Beloved father, your son has been accused of theft. We tell only what we saw; we have no way of understanding what is hidden'.

Scene XVI

They plead their innocence to Jacob

82. Ask the people of the city in which we were, and the camel drivers we me there: We are speaking the truth.
83. He replied, 'Rather, your desires have deceived you. So gracious patience [is my sole recourse]. It may be that God will bring them all back to me. He is the Knowing, the Wise'.
84. Then he turned from them and said, 'How I grieve for Joseph.' His eyes had whitened with sorrow, and: he was blind with grief.
85. They said, 'By God, you will not cease speaking of Joseph until you have wasted away and died'.
86. He replied, My unbearable grief and pain I share with God alone, for I know from Him what you do not know.
87. My sons, go and enquire oft Joseph and his brother, and do not despair of the kindness of God; only unbelievers despair of the kindness of God'.

Scene XVII

They return to Joseph

88. When they came into his presence, they said, 'Your Excellency, famine has afflicted us and our family, and we come with few goods [to barter]; yet give us a full measure of grain, give it to us as alms, for God rewards those who give alms.'
89. He replied, 'Do you know what you did to Joseph and his brother in your time of ignorance'.
90. They said, 'Can it be that you are Joseph?' He replied, 'I am Joseph and this is my brother. God has been generous to us. He loves] those who are devout and steadfast, and does not stint the reward of those who do good'.
91. They said, 'By God, God has preferred you to us, for we have been sinners'.
92. He replied, 'No reproach is held against you today. God forgives you, He most merciful of all who show mercy,
93. Go, take this garment of mine, cast it on my father's face: his sight will be restored. Then come to me with all your family.'

Scene XVIII

Jacob's eyesight is restored

94. As the caravan set out [from Egypt] their father said, 'I sense the fragrance of Joseph. Did you not think I was senile [you would believe me].'
95. They said, 'By God, you are still in your old delusion.'
96. But when the messenger arrived, and cast the garment on his face, his sight was restored, and said, 'Did I not tell you I know from God things that you do not know'.
97. They said, 'Beloved father, forgive us our sins. Truly, we have been sinners'
98. He. said: 'I will ask pardon for you from my Lord, for He is the Pardoner, the Merciful'.

Scene XIX

Joseph receives Jacob and his brothers into Egypt

99. Then, when they entered Joseph's presence, he embraced his parents and said, Come into Egypt, God willing safe from any harm'.

100. Then he invited his parents to the dias, but they [and his brothers] bowed before him, and he said, 'My father, this is what my boyhood dream foretold. My Lord has made it come true. He has treated me with loving kindness since He freed me from prison, and brought you out of the desert after Satan had put enmity between me and my brothers. Truly my Lord is kind to whomever He wishes, He is the Knowing, the Wise.
101. My Lord, you have given me a share in kingship, and taught me the interpretation of dreams. Creator of heaven and earth, you are my protector here, and in the world to come. Let me die faithful to you, and place me among the righteous.'

Scene XX

The Peroration

102. This story is from chronicles that are concealed. We have revealed it to you. You were not with them when they decided what they would do and made their plot against him,
103. Yet most men—although you yearn for it—do not believe.
104. Though you do not ask them any reward for telling it. It is a message from God to all creatures,
105. yet no matter how many signs there are in the heavens and on earth, they pass them by, and look the other way,
106. and most of them do not believe in God. They are idolators.
107. Do they not realise that the punishment of God will come upon them, or that suddenly, when they least expect it, the Hour will overwhelm them!
108. Proclaim: 'This is my way! I call on God in sure knowledge, I and those who follow me. May God be exalted! I am not of the idolators',
109. And before you too, was it not only men We inspired, and sent out from the cities. Did [the unbelievers] not walk through the earth, and see the fate of those who had gone before them? Truly, the world to come is better [than this] for those who are devout. Do they not understand?
110. Time after time We sent them until even they almost despaired, and feared they had been deceived. But then our help came to them, and those whom We willed were saved. Our anger cannot be turned aside from those who do evil.
111. In the stories of them are lessons for those of understanding. This is not something invented, but a confirmation of everything [revealed]l before it, an account of everything [about which they asked], a guide and a mercy to those who believe.

Moses In The Qur'an
Finite and Infinite Dimensions of Prophecy

The prophetess Miriam, Aaron's sister, took up a timbourine in her hand, and all the women followed her with tambourines and dancing. Miriam took up from them the refrain:

> Sing to the Lord, for he has triumphed in glory.
> Horse and rider he has thrown into the sea.'[1]

This song of Moses celebrates one of the great scenes in world religious literature: the escape of the Israelites from Egypt, and the drowning in the sea of Pharaoh and the Egyptians pursuing them. It marks a central point in the career of Moses, flanked on the one hand by his encounter with the burning bush, and on the other, by the giving of the Law on Mt Sinai. It is a scene that has a crucial role in salvation history as perceived in the traditions of Judaism, Christianity and Islam.

For Judaism, the commemoration of the Passover, the prelude to the escape of the chosen people from Egypt marks the first month of the year, an event to be celebrated annually until the Messiah comes; for Christians the crossing of the Red Sea represents the passage from death to life, signifying dying to sin and rising to grace, and an image of the resurrection. For Muslims it is one of the proofs of God's power to overwhelm those who reject his messengers. He chose Moses to be the great law-giver and ruler of his people, and spoke to him, establishing a covenant that was to endure until the time of the final revelation to be made to Muhammad.

1. Ex 15:21–22 (Translation the **Revised New** *Jerusalem Bible* (New York: Image, 2019).

Each of these traditions has developed and elaborated its vision of Moses in line with its own understanding of salvation history. In the Muslim tradition he became a model of sanctity, privileged above all others, apart from Muhammad, by God's speaking to him; an example of heroic holiness that reached the threshold of God himself.

It is prudent to be sceptical of the significance of word or verse frequency counts, but the fact that in the Qur'an there are 93 verses relating to Jesus, 131 to Noah, 235 to Abraham, and by comparison an overwhelming 502 to Moses,[2] gives us an approximate idea of how central the role of Moses is in the tradition that for Muslims was to find its apogee in the vocation of Muhammad, and how Moses was the figure that the Qur'an presented to Muhammad above all others as the supreme model of deliverer and ruler of a community, the man chosen to present both knowledge of the one God. and a divinely revealed system of law, known in the Judaic and Christian traditions as the 10 commandments.

David Daiches remarks that 'the religious experience . . . Moses first underwent alone with his flock of sheep in the wilderness of Midian was a genuine experience undergone by the man who remoulded the religious consciousness of his people, and in doing so made possible the history of both Judaism and Christianity.'[3] The words are thrilling, sublime to both Jew and Christian alike. But how could Daiches have overlooked the role of Moses in Islam, as the first Muslim of his time in the Islamic design of salvation history, and as the greatest role model that the Qur'an presents to Muhammad, or the significance that Moses has in the Muslim tradition? A significance that Muhammad and the Qur'an attest time and again.

A superficial reader of the Qur'an, particularly one who has to rely on a translation, may not realise how important Moses is in the message of the Book. This is, in part, because of the character and internal organisation of the Qur'an, in part because non-Muslims often find it difficult to appreciate how seriously Muhammad took his predecessors, and their importance in his message. To grasp this it is necessary to perceive how he shared in their consciousness of their vocation, and how he re-lived the challenges they faced as challenges

2. Youakim, Moubarac, *Moise dans le Coran* in *Moise l'homme de l'alliance* (Paris: Sioniens Cahiers, 1954), 375.
3. David Daitches, Moses, *The Man and his Vision* (New York: Praeger Publishers, 1975), 9–IO.

that he had to face. It was as such they were known in the Muslim community; and members of this community in different degrees and at different levels responded to the Qur'anic accounts of them. They saw and see them as the architects of a universalistic salvation history.

Indeed, in the Qur'an, they are presented with such immediacy that that they create in the imagination of the faithful a desire to set them in a broader framework, elaborating details which even if they go beyond the information given by the Qur'an, or beyond the facts that can be given a date and place by historians, present a human dimension to these culture heroes, generating an important literary genre of story-telling. Of these, the best known is Joseph. His relations with Zulaikha have been interpreted in stories in moral, romantic and mystical senses. His magnanimity to his brothers is a model for Muhammad; and the comfort that comes to his grieving father Jacob for the loss of his son is a solace for all who grieve.

Never let it be forgotten that the figures of his predecessors presented in the Qur'an were real people to Muhammad, and that in sayings attributed to him, he spoke of them as his brothers, whose actions and whose judgments he revered and imitated.

The heart of the Qur'an is not easily accessible to the non-Muslim. It is full of echoes and resonances which react upon, reflect and reinforce one another. Thus to see the Book as it presents itself, a study of verses, words, and names selected from a concordance without a grasp of the whole in which these individual references are set is not sufficient. It is only on the basis of a response to the book as a whole that the repetitions, rewordings, re-phrasings of its central themes can be understood as integral parts of the whole hook and are not simply failures of inspiration—or as has been said of van Karajan's successive recordings of Beethoven's symphonies, another attempt to get it right!

The Qur'an has to be taken on its own terms: whether accepted, as by the Muslim, rejected, or seen simply as a mysterious refraction of the light of the jewel that is Abraham. Torrey, who seems to have had a kind of love-hate relationship with the Qur'an sometimes comes up with phrases that are magically ambivalent: he speaks of 'the kaleidoscope constantly turning, the thought leaping from one subject to another', and of the 'ever turning wheel of the Qur'an'.[4] If on the one hand these appear to be mechanistic images, yet on the other, they suggest an infinity of aspects.

References to Moses occur throughout the Qur'an. And if one regards the chronology of revelation as proposed by such scholars as Noeldeke, Bell and Blachere[5] as a rough guide, one can see references to Moses and his authority from the very earliest of suras to be revealed, increasing in frequency and detail towards the end of the Meccan period, culminating in splendidly dramatic accounts of two great encounters with God: in the burning bush where Moses receives his commission to warn Pharaoh, and on Mt Sinai, when he is given the Law. In the Medinan period, we see more fully developed, Moses' experience with his recalcitrant followers as a model for Muhammad's own debates with the Jews who refused to accept his message, his role, or his authority. These perspectives are not mutually exclusive; all reveal aspects of the role of Moses. It does not matter whether one takes them in sequence or simply as aspects of a single event—and commentators, philosophers and mystics have done both.

The accounts of Moses in the Qur'an, then, focus on the two occasions on which Moses speaks to God: at the burning bush, and on Mt Sinai.

A vivid presentation of the first is given in Sūrat Tā Hā (20:9-34):

9. Have you heard the story of Moses,?
10. Of when he saw a fire
And said to his family
'Stay here!
Indeed, I see a fire.
Perhaps I can bring you a brand
from it, or by the light
of the Fire find guidance.'
11. When he approached it,
A voice called: 'Moses!
12. I, indeed I am your Lord

4. Charles Cutler Torrey, *The Jewish Foundation of Islam* (New York: Ktav Publishing House Inc, 1967), 93 and 105 respectively.
5. See Bell & Watt, *Introduction to the Qur'an* (Edinburgh: Edinburgh Paperbacks, 1977), 109–113.

So, take off both your sandals.
You are in the holy valley of Tuwa

13. I have chosen you, so listen to what is to be he revealed to you:
14. I, truly, I am God
    There is no God, but I
    So worship me, and perform
    the prayer, so that you remember me.
15. The Hour is coming; it is
    soon to be revealed, then every soul will be recompensed for what it has done.
16. Do not do let not yourself be hindered from [believing in] it by those
    who do not believe in it, and follow their passions and do evil.
17. Moses! what is that in your right hand?
18. He replied: 'It is my staff. I support myself on it, I use it to pull down branches for my sheep. There are other uses too I have for it'.
19. God said: 'Moses, cast it down.'
20. So he threw it down, and behold, it was a writhing snake.
21. God said: 'Take hold of it, do not fear, we will return it to its former form.
22. Now, place your hand into your armpit, then draw it out, a brilliant white, without it suffering any harm as another sign,
23. so that we may show you the greatest of our signs.
24. Go to Pharaoh: He is acting arrogantly.'
25. Moses replied: 'My Lord, ease my breast.
26. make my task lighter for me;
27. loosen the knot on my tongue
28. that they may understand my words.
29. Give me from my family one to support me.
30. Aaron my brother.
31. Through him, strengthen my loins
32. and make him my partner in this task.
33. that we may praise you much,
34. and remember you often.'

...

God grants Moses his requests, and re-assures him, reminding him how on three earlier occasions he had shown his love for him, and formed him for himself. The sura continues:

35. 'When we told your mother what we told her:

36. 'Place him in a wooden box,
and place the box in the Nile;
and then let the Nile cast it on the shore; and
37. our enemy and his enemy take it',
and I gave you love from myself, so that you might be formed under my care.
38. Then, when your sister was walking, she said:
'Shall I take you to one who will take charge of him'?
So we returned you to your mother to sooth her eye, and put an end to her grief.
Then you killed a man, and we saved you from affliction, and set you trials to endure.
Then you passed some years among the people of Midian.
Then, Moses, you came to the appointed time
39. and I fashioned you for myself.
40. Go, you and your brother, with my signs, and do not slacken in remembering me.
Go to Pharaoh, for he is arrogant, and speak to him gently.
Perhaps he will reflect, and fear me.'

Further details of the narrative are elaborated in Sūrat al-Qasas(28:7–28), in verses which emphasise the love and concern of Moses' mother for him; assuring her that she will indeed suckle him (for in suckling him her role as a mother is fully realised); if she fears for him (for Pharaoh is having slain all the male children of the Israelites, and letting the female ones live) then she should place him in a box in the Nile, and neither fear nor grieve on his account, for as God promises her:

7. 'We will restore him to you, and make him one of our messengers.'

In verse 9, Pharaoh's wife urges her husband not to slay him, assuring him that the child will be a 'soothing of the eye' both to herself and to him, persuading him to adopt him as a son.

Then the scene shifts to the grieving mother of Moses who almost reveals the assurance that God has given her about her son, and would have done so had God not strengthened her heart so that she should be a true believer. She tells her daughter, Moses' older sister:

11. 'Follow him.' So she watched him from a distance, (the Egyptians) were not aware of this.

There is a shift of scene again, and it is told how Moses refused to accept any wet nurse offered to him. It was then that his sister. unrecognised as such by any of Pharaoh's court officers, offered to take him to someone who would look after him, and thus returns him to his mother to take her breast. Thus she learns that the promise of God is true (v 13).

This sura also gives an account of the third occasion on which God had shown his kindness to Moses.

The scenes shift rapidly. Moses is a young adult. He comes into the city when it is deserted, and finds two men fighting: one of his own people, an Israelite, and the other an Egyptian. The Israelite asks for help. Moses, traditionally a strong, swarthy man responds, by striking the Egyptian, and kills him (v 15).

He is overwhelmed by shock and grief at what he has done (v 17), and prays for pardon, for he knows that God is the Pardoner, the Merciful. The following day he is still in the city, fearful for what may befall him, looking anxiously around him. The same Israelite as the day before is engaged in a fight, and again asks for help. Moses is prepared to help. but the man who is the enemy of them both brings him to his senses:

19. Are you going to kill me as you killed a man yesterday?
Are you bent on being a tyrant, and not one of the righteous?

At that moment a man comes running from the farthest part of the city to warn him to flee (v 20). Moses flees, and prays for God to guide him. He finds his way to Midian and comes to a spring where men are watering their flocks. Standing at one side are two women, who are reticently waiting till the men have finished (v 21–22).

24. He watered their flocks for them, then withdrew to the shade, and said (in prayer): 'My Lord, how deeply in need am I of the good that you have given me.'

25. One of the two women approached him modestly, and said: 'My father invites you (to his home) to reward you for watering our sheep for us.'

Moses returns to the house. One of the daughters suggests to her father Shu'ayb, sometimes identified with the Jethro of Exodus, that he employ him. He does so, and marries him to one of them, with as a bride price, a pledge to work for him for eight or ten years {v 26).

When the term is complete, Moses leaves with his wife to return to his homeland (Egypt). It is on this journey that he encounters the burning bush, and the account in this sura (al-Qaṣaṣ) in part mirrors, in part creates new dimensions or perspectives to that given in in Sūrat Tā Hā.

For our purposes there is no need to go into the details of Moses' confrontation with Pharaoh, the manifestation of the two signs of his staff becoming a serpent, and his dark swarthy hand turning a brilliant white. Nor is there a need to tell of the defeat of Pharaoh's magicians, their acceptance of the faith of Moses, and their crucifixion.

After enduring the plagues of flood, locusts, lice, frogs and blood, Pharaoh allows the Israelites to leave Egypt. In Sūrat al-A'rāf (7:134 –137), the sequence of events is swiftly told: 'When the plague fell upon them, the Egyptians said: pray for us to your Lord to fulfil the promise he made to you. If he removes this plague from us, we will believe in you, and send the Israelites with you. But when We removed the plague from them, for after a determined time they went back on their word. So We took vengeance upon them, and drowned them in the sea, for they had said our signs were lies, and had ignored them. And We made those who had been down-trodden to inherit the land we had blessed to the East and the West.'

A dramatic and moving detail of the episode is given in Sūrat Yūnus (10:90): 'We parted the sea for the Israelites, then Pharaoh and his army followed them, filled with greed and enmity. Yet when drowning overwhelmed them, Pharaoh said: 'I believe that there is no God but the God in whom the Israelites believe; I am of those who submit myself to Him.'

This account of the conversion of Pharaoh has provided an issue for theologians and mystics who have debated for centuries whether Pharaoh's profession of faith was accepted or not.

The crossing of the sea leads inexorably to Mt Sinai, where Moses is summoned away from his people, to be addressed by God on the mountain, and for the Divine Law to be entrusted to him.

This awesome event occurs after the Israelites have begun to grumble at Moses. They pass by a people who worship idols, and say to him, in in Sūrat al-A'rāf (7:13), 'Make for us gods such as the gods of these people.' Moses addresses them:

138. You are an ignorant people.
139. What these people have is vain, and what they do is empty.
140. Do you really seek any god other than The God, He who has given you more favours than any other people on earth, and saved you from the people of Pharaoh!

The sura (v 141) continues: We commanded Moses to fast for thirty nights, to which We added another ten. Then, after these forty nights, the time his Lord had appointed came, and Moses said to his brother Aaron: Take charge of the people in my place. Act well, and do not follow the way of those who do evil upon the earth.

The next and central episode, with Moses on the mountain, follows swiftly:

143. Thus when Moses came to the moment we had decreed, and His Lord spoke to him, he said: 'My Lord, let me look upon you'. He replied: 'You shall not see me, but look at the mountain. If it stands firm in its place, then you shall see me'. But when his Lord revealed himself to the mountain, it shattered to dust.

Moses collapsed as one struck by lightning. When he recovered he said: 'Praise be to you. I turn to you. I am the first among those who believe in you.'

144. God said to him: 'Moses, I have chosen you out of all mankind for my Message and words. So take what I have given you, and be thankful.'

These scenes are communicated in the Qur'an with great power through the extraordinary rhetorical instrument that is Arabic. There are many further facets of meaning and internal relationships that could be explored: the style of the speakers—the initial gentleness of Moses in first addressing Pharaoh, and the bragging arrogance of Pharaoh, something akin to that attributed to Herod in the miracle plays. There is Moses' courage in speaking to God, setting as it were his terms if he is to accept his vocation, and at the same time his fear to go before Pharaoh in case Pharaoh mocks at his message, or recognises him as the murderer who had fled years before, and finally his rashness in asking to see God. Then there is the loving kindness, the compassion of God for Moses' mother, who sets him adrift in the Nile, but with the consolation that he will be returned to her—and the human touch of her almost revealing the assurance she has been given, a revelation that would imperil the divine plan. There is both the modesty and yet initiative of the daughters of Shu'ayb whom Moses helps. There is Moses' sense of humility and total dependence on God.

Rich and varied as they are, these comments only touch the surface of Qu'ranic narrative, within which are still many levels of spiritual meaning.

For those of us brought up in the Hellenic tradition, there is a tendency to look in a text, even a sacred text—to use Frithjof Schuon's words—for 'a meaning that is fully expressed and immediately intelligible. In the Islamic tradition, on the other hand, there is often a very highly developed love of verbal symbolism, and a capacity to read in depth. The revealed phrase is . . . an array of symbols from which more and more flashes of light shoot forth the further !he reader penetrates into the spiritual geometry of the words: the words are reference points for a doctrine that is inexhaustible.'[6]

Schuon also speaks of the role of commentaries springing from the oral tradition which accompany revelation from its beginning—intercalating missing, though implicit parts of the text, specifying in what relationship or in what sense a given thing should be understood, and explaining its diverse symbolisms, often simultaneous or superimposed one on another. In short they form part of the tradition . . . they are the sap of its continuity, even if their committal to writing, or in certain cases their re-manifestation, occurred only at a relatively late date in order to meet the requirements of a particular historical period.[7] The commentaries in fact provide the link between the revealed word and the understanding of the word in the community, which is indeed a crucial part of its meaning

There is a great tradition of Qu'ranic exegesis which has followed diverse lines of development, and explored different aspects of the Qur'an. In every case this tradition has grown out of the sayings and explanations attributed to the prophet himself and to his companions which elucidate the significance of words and phrases, sets out the context in which they are to be understood, and serves as a guide to its legal provisions and to the probing and exploration of the spiritual values implicit in it, in the events it narrates, and the personalities who have a role in it.

The Qur'anic episodes relating to the prophets have in some cases been brought together in compilations of stories about the prophets,

6. Frithjof Schuon, *Understanding Islam* (London: Unwin Paperbacks, 1979. (second impression), 59.
7. Schuon, *Islam*, 46.

in others they are scattered throughout the work of the great commentators as they explore and try to come to terms with these great heroes of the spiritual life. The living sap of the oral tradition binds them together, and discovers new dimensions of meaning.

The reputable compilers of stories make use of the scholarly apparatus of careful lines of transmission that is the basis of traditional Islamic scholarship. But story-telling too is a technique of religious instruction, an art form in its own right. al-Thaʿlabī,[8] (d 1035) for example, himself author of a major work of exegesis has, in his compilation *Qiṣaṣ al-Anbiyā'* (*Stories of the Prophets*)[9] brought together so much carefully chosen information on Moses, that his presentation of him has been called a masterpiece in its own right, and an outstanding 'novel of holiness'. Yet he can allow his imagination to rove to give an earthy realism to the story. Pharaoh for example, was so terrified at the form of Moses staff changed into a serpent, that he had forty violent bouts of diarrhoea in a day.[10]

The great twelfth century commentator Fakhr al-Dīn al-Rāzī[11] summarises much useful information as to how the Muslim community saw Moses.

He explains, for example, why this story was revealed to Muhammad: to strengthen his heart in the face of difficulties by telling him of the experience of the prophets before him, in particular Moses, because the tests and trials he endured were very great, to comfort Muhammad, and to support him in the hardships he too had to bear.[12]

At once we see a major function of the reference to earlier prophets in the Qur'an, and with it an aspect of Muhammad overlooked in the more triumphalist accounts of his life: that he was a man who suffered, and who needed the strength and consolation that the Qur'an provided.

Rāzī then takes the phrase from SūratTā Hā (20:10), 'When he (Moses) saw a fire', and sets out the background to the story, adding details that make it easier for others to understand. He tells how Moses asked permission from his father-in-law (and employer)

8. al-Nīsāpūrī. Abū Ishaq Ahmad b. Muhammad b. Ibrāhīm al-Thaʿlabī d 1035
9. *Qiṣaṣ al-anbiyā' al musammā bi'l-ʿarā'is*, al-Halabī Cairo 1347 (AH)
10. Thaʿlabi, *Qiṣaṣ*
11. Fakhr al-Dīn ʿAbd Allāh Muḥammad b. ʿUmar al-Rāzī 1149–1209.
12. Rāzī, *TK*, 22:14

Shu'ayb (Jethro in Exodus?) to return to Egypt to see his mother. Shu'ayb gave his permission, and Moses set out. On the way, his wife gave birth on a cold winter night. It was the eve of Friday, and they had lost their way. Moses tried to kindle a fire with a drill stick, but it would not light, and while he was busy with it, he suddenly noticed a fire in the distance. Suddī, one authority Rāzī cites, says that Moses thought it a fire Iit by shepherds, others say that he saw the fire in a tree, although the Qur'an furnishes no evidence of this . . . he made his way towards it.[13]

Rāzī includes a report from Ibn 'Abbās (the prophet's cousin) who says: 'He saw a tree, green from its base to its summit as though it were a white fire. He stood in wonder at the brilliant light of the fire, and the brilliant green of the tree. The fire has no effect on the green, and the abundant sap of the tree has no effect on the brightness of the fire, and then he heard the praises of angels, and saw a mighty light.[14]

Another authority he quotes says that Moses thought it a fire that someone had lit, and he gathered twigs, to light a torch from its flames. Moses looked up at its branches, and lo, there was a brilliant green in the sky, and then a light between heaven and earth, with rays that dazzled his sight, and when Moses looked at it, he put his hands over his eyes, and a voice called him 'Moses' . . . he responded 'At your service.' 'I hear your voice, I do not see you, where are you?' He replied: 'I am with you, in front of you, behind you, and totally encompass you. I am closer to you than your very self.'

Then Satan put a doubt into his mind, and said, 'how do you know that it is the voice of God you hear.' He replied: 'because I hear it from above, below and behind, from my right and my left, just as I hear it from in front of me, thus I know it is not the voice of any created thing.'[15]

al-Rāzī then gives some of the reasons offered for God's command: 'Take off both your sandals, you are in the Holy Valley of Tuwa.'

One explanation, attributed to Muhammad's cousin and son in-law 'Alī, is that as his sandals were of dead donkey skin, he was ordered take them off out of reverence for the Holy Valley. Another is that he should bestow upon his feet the blessing of the holy ground.

---

13. Rāzī, *TK*, 22:15
14. Rāzī, *TK*, 22:15–16
15. Rāzī, *TK*, 22:17

A third is that to show his reverence for the valley, he should tread it only barefoot, out of awe for it and as an act of humility on hearing the voice of his Lord.

Rāzī then gives some examples of the more elaborate interpretations evolved by the 'referential' or 'allusive' tradition of exegesis:

One is that in sleep, one's two sandals are understood as referring to wife and child, thus the order 'take off your sandals' means: have no further regard for wife and child, and let not your heart be burdened with care for them.

Another is that to remove one's sandals means to have no further heed for either this or the world to come. In other words, it is as though Moses is ordered to be totally absorbed in the knowledge of God, and not allow his mind to be attracted to anything other than He.

In this tradition, the 'Holy valley' is understood as the holiness of Almighty God, and the purity of his might. In this context the order means, once you have reached the ocean of gnosis, have no further concern with created things.

The final example al-Rāzī gives is more elaborate: Moses, having come to the holy valley has passed beyond the limitations imposed by reason on human knowledge of God. His sandals stand for the two premises on which rational argument for the existence of God is based—the necessity for a first cause and a principle of order—and he has no further need of them. Thus it is as if God is saying: you have reached the Holy Valley, and this stands for the ocean of the knowledge of God and the copiousness of His Divinity.[16]

It will be noted how the elements presented build up from common, everyday realities—a man lost on a winter's night, unsuccessfully trying to start a fire, the sight of a fire in the distance, and then suddenly the splendour of the fire in the tree which heralds the divine words: 'I, indeed I am your Lord.' There is a parallel development in the order of presentation of possible reasons for the order 'Take off both your sandals'. The first is the simple, ritual one that they were made of donkey skin, the last is that it is an order to abandon attachment to all created things, to pass beyond the limits of reason, and to plunge into the sea of gnosis. It is there that al-Rāzī stops. He explicitly resists the temptation to explore the heights and depths of mystical experience. He refers to it, identifies it, and leaves it.

---

16. Rāzī, *TK*, 22:17

This does not mean that he leaves out or understates anything of the awe or terror of the encounter, or of the solace that God brings. He comments on the words 'I have chosen you, so listen to what is to be revealed': The command 'listen to what is to be revealed' contains the ultimate in awe and majesty. It is as though God said to him: an awesome, terrifying task has been laid upon you, so prepare for it, and devote all your mind and all your thoughts to it. The words 'I have chosen you' on the other hand express the ultimate in gentleness and mercy. Thus the first expression brings to him the ultimate in hope and the latter the ultimate in fear. al-Rāzī then turns to explain God's question to Moses: 'What is that in your right hand'?

Why should God ask about the staff, al-Rāzī wonders, and answers his own question: because God can use a simple thing for extraordinary purposes. Thus, he continues Almighty God, when he intended to use the staff to show noble signs such as changing it into a snake, or using it to strike the sea and part it, or to strike the rock, so that water would spring from it, he first showed it to Moses as though to say to him: Moses, do you know what it is that you have in your hand? It is wood, that can neither harm nor help. Then He changed it into a huge snake, and by this means showed those with intelligence the perfection of his power and the extent of his might, which were such that he could display these great signs from the simplest thing that Moses had on him.[17]

Rāzī, however, has also a keen awareness of human emotions and reactions to circumstances, whether grief, joy or perplexity. Moses had undergone a great spiritual experience. God had shown him the light mounting from the tree up to heaven, had made him to hear the praise of the angels and then hear His words. He then treated him with force and gentleness. He treated him with gentleness first, by his words 'I have chosen you' and then force by imposing on him awesome responsibilities. As a result of all this, Moses was totally perplexed and bewildered, and hardly knew his right hand from his left. And for this reason. God said to him: 'What is that in your right hand, Moses', so that he would realise that his right hand was that in which he held his staff. The point of the episode then is to show that God realised that Moses was overwhelmed by bewilderment in the divine presence. and to bring him back to earthly reality, asked him about something as down to earth and commonplace as the staff, something about which he could make no mistake.[18]

17. Rāzī, *TK*, 22:25
18. Rāzī, *TK*, 22:25

This is a perception of the kindness of God for his creatures in the text of the Qur'an, his understanding of their perplexities and need for encouragement. It is an insight worthy of an experienced spiritual director.

Rāzī was not the first to put into words this insight, or to possess such skill in understanding of the human heart and its needs. Such instances of psycho-spirituality which bring us a remarkable sense of closeness with human experience across the centuries are explicitly documented in Islam from very early times.

Muqātil b Sulaymān (d 767) for example, shows how early the Qur'anic passages concerning Moses aroused in many Muslims a desire to meditate on Moses' experience as a means of access to a direct relationship with God, in such a way that later he would be seen as a prototype of the perfect mystic, called to enter into the mystery of God. Of the burning bush, Muqātil says that the fire Moses saw was the light of his Lord, and that the voice ordered him to remove his shoes because the place became holy when God revealed his presence there.[19]

A slightly later contemporary of Muqātil, Já'far b Muhammad al-Ṣādiq, gives a vivid account of how Moses was sure that his call came from God. Moses, Já'far says, is shown the light of God in the form of fire, and he was sure it was God because the light 'overwhelmed me and submerged me so that it seemed that every single one of my hairs was summoned by a call that came from all directions, and offered itself in response.[20]

Abū'l-Hasan al-Nūrī (d 907) in explaining the words—'I have given you love from myself'— Sūrat Tā Hā (20:39)—presents God as saying to Moses: Reserve your heart for my love. I have chosen it as a dwelling place for this. I have set out there a demesne of my knowledge and built a house of faith in myself. I have made to rise in your heart a sun, which is desire for me, a moon which is love for me and stars which are my visitations. I have likewise placed in your heart a cloud which is meditation on me, and made to rise a wind which is the aid I give you. Then, out of my beneficence I have sent down upon it rain. I have sown there the seed of my sincerity, and

19. Paul Nwyia, *Exégèse Coranique et Langage Mystique* Recherches 49 (Beirut: Institut de lettres orientales, 1970), 83.
20. Nwyia, *Exégèse Coranique,* 179.

made to grow the trees that are obedience for my sake. Their leaves are fidelity, and the fruits that hang from them are the wisdom born of intimate dialogue with me.[21]

This phrase 'intimate dialogue' is almost certainly a reference to the Qur'an, : Sūrat Maryam (19:52): 'We brought him close to us and spoke to him as to a friend', one of the most beautiful references to the manner in which God spoke to Moses. the Arabic word *najīyan*, suggesting a marvellous degree of intimacy.

It is striking the degree to which our authors are concerned with Moses' reactions as a man to his extraordinary experience. al-Tha'labī tells how at the sight of the burning bush 'Moses was filled with awe, and a violent fear seized him when he saw this huge smokeless fire blazing within the hollow of a green tree'. Yet it was a terror to be followed by a deep interior peace.[22]

The encounter on Mt Sinai is even more dramatic, for on that occasion, Moses made that most daring of requests to his Lord. 'Let me see you' Sūrat al-A'rāf (7:142). God's answer is like a parable in action. You (as you now are) shall not see me, unless the mountain stands firm in my presence. God reveals himself to the mountain, it shatters, and Moses collapses in a faint.

Rāzī does not touch on the mystical implications of this episode. His principal concern is to argue against those who use it to deny the possibility of ever seeing God, even on Judgement Day. He draws attention however to God's words to Moses after he had recovered from the faint: 'I have singled you out from all mankind for my message and my words (Q 7:144) so accept what I have given you, and be thankful', and adds in explanation: When God refused Moses' request to see him, he prepared for him various great favours that were His to bestow on him, and commanded him to be thankful for them. Thus it was as if he had said: I have refused your request to see me, but I have given you immense favours of such and such akind, so do not be grieved because you have not seen me. Rather, look on all the other favours that I have singled out for you alone, and be thankful. And this was to comfort Moses for not seeing Him.[23] Again

21. Nwyia, *Exégèse Coranique,* 328. (A passage quoted by Haydar Amoli in Jami' al asrār in the form of a hadīth transmitted by Wahb ibn Munabbih, V p.513),

22. Tha'labī, Qisas, 124

23. Rāzī, *TK,* 14:235

it will be noted how al-Rāzī draws attention to the kindness of God to his creatures.

The Qur'anic build up to this extraordinary scene is very brief. A striking feature is Moses preparation. He is ordered lo fast first for thirty nights, and then for another ten (Qur'an 7:142). The great mystic al-Hallaj (d 922) has developed a marvellous picture of a spiritual journey out of this period of 'forty-nights'. He gives a sublime picture of the role of Moses, and his encounter with the burning bush elaborated in his book of lyrical prose passages, al-Tawāsīn.[24] Moses, he sees as a type of spiritual pilgrim. To make his way towards Reality, he has to make himself an exile, following narrow ways, marked out by fire—and the burning bush was such a fire—alongside undulating deserts. This image of Moses as a pilgrim has a counterpart and support very early in the Christian tradition, where it is to be found in Origen and Gregory of Nyssa.[25]

Hallāj commences his meditation on Moses when 'at the predestined time', Moses concludes his service with his father-in-law—Jethro in the Judaic, Shu'ayb in the Muslim tradition—and sets out on the journey back to Egypt through narrow ways, amid rolling deserts and loses his way. Lost in the darkness of a winter's night, he sees a fire. A later commentator understands this, and the approach to the fire as Moses' entry into the mystical domain of intimacy with God. To approach the fire Moses has to leave behind his own, his wife and child, and approach the fire alone. In the rabbinic tradition too, it will be remembered, after his encounter with God in the fire, Moses led a celibate life.[26] Moses, Hallāj says, leaves his own, because the ultimate Reality wished to take him for its own. Thus the approach to the burning bush teaches the secret of the path to the mystical union, and Hallāj explains: Cast far from you created nature in order that in Reality you become He, and He becomes you. This is because it was not the bush which spoke, nor the seed from which it sprung: it was the uncreated word of God.[27]

---

24. Louis Gardet, 'L'experience interieure du Prophet Mūsā (Moise) selon les sufis' in GC. Anawati et Louis Gardet, *Mystique Musulmane Aspects et Tendances—Experiences et Techniques* (Paris: Librarie Philosophique J Vrin, 1961), 263.
25. Gardet, *Musa*, 263.
26. Wayne A Meeks, *The Prophet King Moses Traditions and the Johannine Christology* (Leiden: Brills, 1967), 207.
27. Gardet, Mūsā, 265-266.

This spiritual tradition sees the burning bush various ways. One group, the *nuzayris*, according to that extraordinary visionary Massignon, see in it the figure of Muhammad.[28] Other Sufis see in it the figure of every believer attentive to the word of God in him.

For Hallāj, the uncreated voice speaking through the created bush is a guarantee that God himself may speak on the tongue of the mystic. My role, Hallāj says is to represent the bush. The burning bush, at one and the same time flame created and voice uncreated becomes the symbol of a mystical union in which human subject and divine subject make an exchange such that one gives testimony of the other according to the reality of the one and only witness, God.[29]

A later author Ghazālī (d 1111), without the visionary intoxication of Hallāj, sees the mountain on which the burning bush is situated as a symbol of the stability and grandeur of the spirituaI world. The valleys that run through it, pathways for the dispersal of water symbolise the various levels of perfection to be obtained by those who quench their thirst in this spiritual world. The Qur'an refers to the right side of the valley, and it is from the right side of this high valley, that the beneficent waters flow to the lower valleys.

This holy valley of Tuwa (Sinai) is, Ghazālī points out (echoing Hallāj), the first stage of the entrance of the prophets into the world of holy transcendence, far from the troubles of the senses and the imagination, where they are ordered to turn the face of their souls towards the one reality, and to abandon all thought of both worlds, this, and the one to come, for this sole reality.[30]

There are various traditions which explain why Moses put his daring request: 'My Lord, let me see you.' Muqātil, the early commentator, says that when Moses had heard the word his Lord, he found it very sweet, and it was this sweetness that aroused in him the desire to see God.[31] Ja'far al-Sādiq says that Moses asks to see God because seeing the shadow of the word of God on his heart, he feels so at ease with his Lord, as to ask to see him. 'You shall not see me' replies God, because 'the perishable has no access to the imperishable'. Thus if Moses fell in a faint at the sight of the mountain become dust, what would happen to him if he saw his Lord directly.[32]

28. Gardet, Mūsā, 266.
29. Gardet, Mūsā, 266.
30. Gardet, Mūsā, 265.
31. Nwyia, *Exégèse Coranique*, 86.
32. Nwyia, *Exégèse Coranique*,.183.

In the various sources we find elaborations of God's reply, 'You shaII not see me'. Tha'labī, for example, extends the dialogue, and God's words continue: Man is not able to look upon me in the world. Anyone who looks on me dies. Moses replies: 'My God, I have heard your voice, and I yearn for the sight of you. And that I look on you and then die is better for me than that I live, and not see you.'[33]

How God spoke to him is not revealed. Abū Sa 'īd al-Kharrāz (d 899) notes that Moses was the only man called to come close to God, and remarks: God looks on His friends from behind a veil, otherwise they would be annihilated like the mountain—and thanks to the veil, the strong can receive spiritual fruits (*fawā'id*) which transform them from within, without destroying them.[34]

There are various references to God speaking to Moses from behind a veil. Tha'labī quotes Wahb as saying: Between God and Moses were seventy veils, and God lifted all of them but one, and Moses was alone with the word of God, and filled with longing, yearned to see him, so he said, 'My Lord, let me see you.'[35]

lbn Taymiyya too explains that God spoke to Moses from behind a veil. But through this veil he heard God speak to him directly, whereas the other prophets received revelation by *ihā,* God spoke to them in a dream, or by the mediation of an angel.[36]

Moses' fall in a faint is interpreted in various ways. All agree that it is the climax of an extraordinary vocation. lbn 'Abbās glosses the word *sā'iqan* as meaning simply a faint. Other authorities such as Qatāda say that Moses was struck dead, but was revived. Wahb, on the other hand, tells how all the celestial hierarchies from the first to the seventh heaven pass before Moses so that he will not collapse lifeless. Some tell him of his audacity in desiring to see God; others, by their terrifying aspect sow in him fear and terror; others make him hear the praises of the one who dies not recited by voices that ravish his heart. Lord, says Moses after this, I believe you are my master, and I am convinced no one can see you and live. If the sight of angels ravishes the heart, how much the more You.[37]

33. Tha'labi, Qisas, 140.
34. Nwyia, *Exégèse Coranique,* 254.
35. Qisas replace with *Qiṣaṣ*
36. *Risāla ba'albakiyya* in *Majmū'at al-rasā'il,* Cairo 1328 pp 402-403
37. Nwyia, *Exégèse Coranique,* 86–87.

Of special interest is the ambivalence of some of the angels towards Moses, and their resentment at his arrogance. Tha'labī quotes Wāqidi's report: 'When Moses fainted, the angels said "What right does the son of 'Imrān have to ask for a vision of God", and continues: "In one of the books it is stated that the angels of the heavens and the earth came up to Moses after his faint, and began to kick him and to say: Son of menstruating woman-kind, do you expect to look on the Lord of Might."'[38]

This animosity of the angels to this experience of Moses and his mediation of the Torah has a counterpart in the rabbinic tradition, which has them complaining, using words taken from the Psalms: 'What is man, that thou art mindful of him' and 'What is this offspring of woman who has come up on high?'[39]

Two great scenes we have described are directly related to Moses' commission on the one hand, to preach the true religion to Pharaoh, and, on the other to present the divinely revealed Law, the Torah, to the Israelites. These are essentially practical matters. But the dramatic character of their presentation in the Qur'an, and the way in which they were orchestrated in the living oral tradition deriving ultimately from Muhammad and the companions, shows in Moses a dimension which both transcends his role as law-giver and the allegorical and spiritual insights that the early Sufis attribute to him. This dimension derives from the Qur'an itself, which gives in Sūrat al-Kahf (18:65-82) an account of Moses' encounter with a mysterious figure, a saint, identified as al-Khidr, the Green One, by many recognised also as a prophet. At a superficial Ievel, this passage might he considered simply as a midrashic type of episode to show how God's knowledge is greater than that of men who know divine providence only in part. Yet it exercises an extraordinary power of attraction, and generations of exegetes have shown how deeply it is integrated into the texture of the Qur'an, and discovered in it layer upon layer of meaning.

The introduction to the story is brief. Moses vows to find his way to the meeting point of the two seas, to meet, so the commentators tell us, a wise man. He takes his servant with him. The place where they are to meet him is where they lose a salted fish that they have brought as food. They discover that the fish is missing when after a

38. Tha'labi, Qisas, 140.
39. Meeks, *Prophet-King*, 205–206.

night's sleep, they prepare for breakfast. It is at this point that Moses' servant suddenly recalls a rock, some distance back, where the fish miraculously restored to life, leapt out of the basket, and swam away. They retrace their steps to this point. The Qur'an continues the story:

65. The two of them met one of our servants to whom we had given our favours, to whom we had taught an understanding ours to give.
66. Moses said to him, 'May I follow you so that you can teach me a right understanding of what you have been taught.'
67. He replied, 'you will not be able to bear with me patiently,
68. for how can you bear it with patiently what you do not fully understand?'
69. He said, 'If God so wills, you will find me patient, I will not disobey you in anything'.
70. He replied, 'Then if you follow me, do not ask me about anything before I explain its meaning to you.'
71. So they set out. But when they were on board a ship, he made a hole in it. (Moses) said, 'Did you make a hole in it to drown those on board? You have done a terrible. thing!'
72. He replied, 'Did I not say that you would be unable to bear with me patiently?'
73. Moses said, 'Do not punish me for my forgetfulness, do not impose on me something too difficult for me to bear'.
74. Then they continued on their way until, when they met a boy, he killed him. Moses said, 'Have you killed an innocent without the excuse of retaliation? You have done an evil thing.'
75. He replied, 'Did I not say to you that you would not be able to bear with me patiently?'
76. Moses said, 'If I question you about anything after this. be my companion no longer. From my side, you have ample excuse for that.'
77. Then the two of them continued on their way until, when they came to the people of a village, they asked them for food, but the villagers refused to welcome them as guests. Then they found there a wall on the point of collapse and he shored it up. Moses said, 'If you had wished, you could have earned a wage for that'.
78. He replied, 'This is the parting of the ways between you and me. I will tell you the meaning of what you could not hear with patiently:

79. As for the ship, it belonged to some poor men who worked at sea, and I wished to damage it. Behind them was a king seizing every ship by force,
80. and as for the boy, his parents were devout believers, and we feared that he would burden them with arrogance and unbelief,
81. so we wished that their Lord would give them in place of him, one better than he, more virtuous and faithful.
82. and, as for the wall, it belonged to two orphan boys in the village; beneath it was a treasure chest belonging to them both and their father was a righteous man, so your Lord desired that they should come of age and discover their treasure as a blessing from your Lord. I did not do it of my own initiative. That is the meaning of what you could not bear with patiently.[40]

This mysterious person is identified by the commentators as (al-) Khidr, the Green One. Why did Moses wish to meet him? Rāzī explains that Moses asked God 'Who is there who knows more than I?' And God directed him to look for Khidr. Rāzī alludes to mystical dimensions in the story, but takes the matter no further, remarking that in his exegesis it was not possible to discuss them.[41]

Muqātil gives much the same information, thus indicating that this material is early. He argues, on the basis of the Qur'anic text 'one of our servants to whom we have given mercy' that Khidr is a prophet, glossing mercy (*rahma*) as a grace (*ni*ᶜ*ma*) and says that this particular *ni*ᶜ*ma* is prophecy (*nubuwwa*). For Muqātil, then, Khidr is a prophet, and if his knowledge is superior to that of Moses, it is because God has made differences between the prophets, referring Sūrat al-Isrā'(17:55): 'We have preferred some prophets over others. To some, (Muqātil says), God has spoken, to some he has put in their charge the birds and the mountains; to one he has given a great kingdom, to another the power to raise the dead and cure the lepers and the paralyzed; yet another he has raised to heaven. To each he has given something not given to the others - this is the meaning of preferring one to another.'[42]

His name, Khidr, the Green, is explained in various ways. In a saying of Muhammad, he was called Khidr because on one occasion

40. Rāzī, *TK*, 21:144
41. Rāzī, *TK*, 21:150
42. Nwyia, *Exégèse Coranique*, 90.

when he sat on a white pelt, it shook beneath him, and became green. Mujāhid reports that he was called Khidr because wherever he prayed, all around him became green.[43] It should be noted that 'He who wears green' has always been an epithet for those who live on the highest possible spiritual level—be they angels, the prophet, or Khidr himself—the guide of mystics in a very special sense.[44] Appointed as guide and mentor to Moses, he had a role in inspiring mystics on their journey, answering their questions, and investing them with the Sufi cloak, an investment regarded as valid in the tradition of Sufi initiation, and invested in it none other than Ibn 'Arabī himself'.[45]

How does Khidr perform his role, and what is Moses' relation to him? The sinking of the ship, the killing of the child, and rebuilding of the wall seem random acts, and Moses judges them at a common sense rational level—why drown the crew of a ship that has given them passage? Why kill a boy without even the excuse of retaliation (a legists' point this). Why rebuild a wall free of charge when they are desperate for food in a village that refuses them hospitality?

In each case he has broken his word to Khidr and lost sight of the larger design. He had failed the test that Khidr designed for him, although Khidr had warned him 'How can you bear with patiently what you do not fully understand', and misunderstood his mentor's actions on no less than three occasions. It is the shock of realising he has been wrong and the resulting bweilderment that is to open his mind to new levels of understanding, new, infinite perspectives, extending beyond what God had already taught him. This psychological shock at the realisation being wrong as a means of opening the mind to faith and spiritual insight occurs elsewhere in the Qur'an. In the encounter of Bilqīs, the Queen of Sheba, with Solomon, Sūrat al-Naml (27:41-44), in affairs of this world, she shows herself his equal. It is when she makes a mistake imagining that the polished glass she has to wall across to approach Solomon's throne is water, that her self-confidence is shaken, and out of the resulting bewilderment she recognises Solomon's prophetic role, and accepts his religion.

Yet this is not an end to the matter. Tha'labī shows how all three tests were related to events in Moses' earlier life, thus demonstrating

43. Tha'labi, *Qiṣaṣ*, 153

44. Annemarie Schimmel, *Mystical Dimensions of Islam* (Raleigh: University of North Carolina Press, 1975), 102.

45. Schimmel, *Mystical Dimensions of Islam*, 106.

how profoundly this episode is integrated into the Qur'an. He has Khidr saying to Moses: 'Moses, do you reproach me for wrecking the ship, fearing that those on board would drown, and forget yourself, that when you were a child, and helpless, your mother cast you into the Nile. and God preserved you! You reproached me for killing the boy, without cause, yet you killed an Egyptian without cause; and you reproached me for not taking a wage for repairing the wall, and you forget that you yourself, when you watered the herd of Shu'ayb, did so without taking a wage, counting only on a reward from the Almighty King.'[46]

The mystic Abū Saʿīd al-Kharrāz draws an important lesson from this encounter, explaining that Khidr's role is to heighten the spiritual awareness of Moses in his public role as prophet and law-giver. This is because a prophet faces a special temptation to pride just because of this public role, and has the need constantly to refer to himself as the recipient of the message, an urgent message that he has to communicate to mankind. His awareness of this vocation and personal role is a test analogous to that which Iblīs (Satan) failed when in Sūrat al-Aʿrāf (7:12) he explains why he refused to bow to Adam, saying 'I am better than he.' The saint does not fail this test, and one aspect of the role of Khidr is to alert Moses to it, as well as to awaken in him a deeper spiritual understanding.[47]

The clarity with which these spiritual directors perceived the dangers implicit in a high vocation is striking. (One might wonder whether Prime Ministers and Archbishops, not to mention professors, might benefit from such counsel.)

It is the great mystic Muhyi'l-Dīn ibn ʿArabī however, who brings the most striking psychological insights into his discussion of Moses' vocation. In examining his views, it should be mentioned that lbn ʿArabī's theosophy is unacceptable in many parts of the Muslim world. His spiritual and psychological insights however can be separated out from his theosophy, usually more to their advantage rather than the reverse.

Indeed, some of his analyses of the life of Moses are of an extraordinary poetic as well a profound spiritual beauty. One of his goals in writing on Moses, as on the other prophets in his work

46. Thaʿlabī, *Qiṣaṣ*,159

47. Nwyia, *Exégèse Coranique,* 47.

Fuṣūṣ al-Ḥikam[48] is to show that everything has a purpose and that evil has no absolute existence. His purpose is to reconcile outward appearances with inner reality, or from another standpoint to discover the inner meaning of outward phenomena. Moses was placed in a box and set adrift in the Nile. The outward act was one that could be expected to lead to death by drowning. In fact it resulted in the infant's escape from death in Pharaoh's pogrom.[49] In the same way, the outward aspect of Khidr knocking a hole in the boat, suggested that he intended to drown those on board it; inwardly it was to save the men and their means of livelihood from the depredations of an evil king.[50] Outwardly, Moses' killing of the Egyptian was an evil act, and he fled out of fear to save himself from punishment. Inwardly it was for a higher purpose. Moses' flight was for the love of life True, it meant escape from execution;[51] but it was also an act that would set in train a series of events that would lead to the rescue of the lsraelites from Egypt, the drowning, and salvation of Pharaoh, and ultimately the Epiphany on Mt Sinai.

Moses, Ibn 'Arabī says, was impelled into movement by the love of salvation, for the principle of movement is always love, no matter how the observer may be confused by outward appearances . . . The movement which is the existence of the world itself, is a movement of love, as is indicated by the divine words uttered by the prophet: I was a hidden treasure, I wished to be known, and I created the world that I might be known . . . the movement of the world from non-existence to existence is in reality the movement of love revealing itself'.[52] It is as an illustration of this principle that Ibn 'Arabī sees this inner meaning of Moses' flight.

But Moses was also a means of salvation for Pharaoh. When as an infant he was taken from the Nile, at first Pharaoh wished to kill him but his wife restrained him with the words 'a soothing of the eye to

48. *Bezels of Wisdom*, or, in view of the content, *The Wisdom of the prophets*, edited by AA Affifi al-Halabi (Cairo, 1946). A French translation of extracts from the work has been made by Titus Burckhardt, *La Sagesse des Prophetes* (Paris: Editions Albin Michel, 1955). Reference to page numbers in this translation are placed in brackets following page references in the Arabic text.
49. Ibn 'Arabī, *Fuṣūṣ*, 199 (154)
50. lbn 'Arabī, *Fuṣūṣ*, 203 (162).
51. lbn 'Arabī, *Fuṣūṣ*, 204 (164).
52. lbn 'Arabī, *Fuṣūṣ* 203 (162).

me and to you' Sūrat al-Qaṣaṣ (28:9). He 'soothed the eye of Pharaoh' because it was thanks to him that when on the point of drowning, God gave him faith, and he exclaimed: '! believe that there is no God other than the God in whom Moses and the Israelites believe, and I submit myself to him' Sūrat Yūnuf (10:9). Thus God took him, purified, without a stain of sin upon him, for he took him at the moment of his acceptance of faith, before he had committed any sin. For Islam wipes out what precedes it. He was made a sign of God's solicitude for whomever he wishes, so that no-one should despair of the kindness of God Sūrat Yūsuf (12:87). Had Pharaoh been of those who despaired, he would not all of a sudden have believed.[53]

It is the saving of Moses from the water of the Nile that Ibn 'Arabī sees as the inauguration of his career. God saved Moses from the pain of confinement in the box in which he was placed in the Nile, and rent apart the darkness of nature by what he gave him of divine knowledge, even though leaving him within nature.[54] Moses then was saved by divine knowledge, just as those who are dead in ignorance come to life by knowledge. For Ibn 'Arabi, this is the guidance (*hudā*) God gives to 'One dead whom we brought back to life' (Sūrat al-An'ām 6:122)..[55] He goes on to explain how this guidance is given: Man is led to a state of bewilderment, of confused helplessness and thus realises that existence is bewilderment . . . and that this bewilderment is instability . . . it is anxiety (tension) and movement, and movement is life. Thus there is no inertia and no death; there is existence, and no non-being. This is the way in which water brings life and movement to the earth, as the Qur'an says (Sūrat al-Hajj 22:5): 'You see the dry earth, and when we send down water upon it, it trembles, conceives and produces all kinds of species in beauty.'[56]

ln other words, just as water to the dead earth, so is bewilderment to man. It is creative. As I said earlier, it was bewilderment that brought Bilqīs (The Queen of Sheba) to accept the religion of Solomon; bewilderment that Moses experienced at the burning bush, and bewilderment that brought him to an awareness of the dimensions of knowledge beyond his experience.

53. lbn 'Arabī, *Fuṣūṣ*, 201 (156).
54. lbn 'Arabī, *Fuṣūṣ*, 202 (159).
55. lbn 'Arabī, *Fuṣūṣ*, 199 (154–155).
56. lbn 'Arabī, *Fuṣūṣ*, 199–200 (155).

These later developments might at first sight seem far removed from the literal meaning of the Qur'an, but they have roots early in the history of Islam. There is the tradition ascribed to Muhammad transmitted from from Ibn 'Abbās through Abī Ka'b, who said: 'Whenever he mentioned anyone in his prayer, he began with himself, and on that day he said: 'May God have mercy upon us, and on my brother Moses. Had he stayed with his companion (Khidr) longer, he would have seen wonder upon wonder. But he had said: If I ask you anything after this, do not accompany me any more.' This occurs in Tha'labī, but the tradition is also used by Ibn 'Arabī.[57]

Thus it is clear that the episode with Khidr has a wide range of meanings, moral, psychological and mystical. In the Ibn 'Arabī frame of reference, Khidr becomes as it were the inward aspect of spiritual understanding, to the outward aspect of divine truth expressed in the form of the Law represented by Moses.

Frithjof Schuon puts it somewhat differently: 'Moses represents the Law, the particular and exclusive form, and Khidr, universal truth, which cannot be grasped from the standpoint of the 'letter', like the wind of which thou 'canst not tell whence it cometh and whither it goeth'.[58]

This survey of Moses, while giving some idea of the importance of Moses in the Muslim tradition, has attempted to show the richness of the diverse ways in which he was understood, and in which he inspired the religious imagination in Islam. If this, in its fullness is added to the traditions he has inspired in Judaism, and in Latin and Greek Christianity, whether in story, prayer, hymn of praise or iconography, the corpus of material he has generated is staggering. What a commentary on the history of these three traditions, that in sharing such veneration for this chosen shepherd, they have found so much to quarrel about with such disastrous results! No wonder that a Sumatran poet writing in the 30's, a devout Muslim, could liken Isaac and Ismail to two shafts of light from a single jewel, Abraham. God, the master jeweller, he complains, remaining indifferent throughout the centuries to the competing claims of their respective progeny.

57. Ibn 'Arabī, *Fuṣūṣ* 205 (166), Tha'labi *Qiṣaṣ*, 157
58. Schuon, *Islam*, 81.

Rather than vex himself with the problem, to be on Sinai, close to God, like Moses, would be sufficient'.[59]

There is much for every religious tradition to share in the story of Moses. There is no need to limit its meaning or significance to the Judaeo-Christian-Islamic matrix. In almost every religious tradition, from the time of the Buddha, and before a period, exile or self-exile is required of the future teacher. Siddharta, the future Buddha, perplexed at the sight of poverty, sickness, old age and death, left home and family to seek enlightenment. Moses was lost in the mountains. He needed warmth and light. His flint and drill stick could not help him, and he looked for fire. In the fire, he found God. For, as Ibn 'Arabī puts it: God speaking to Moses, appeared to him in this form because Moses had been searching for fire. God appeared to him in the form of what he sought, so there would be no danger of his wandering astray from him. For when God brings some-one close to him, he attracts that person to him in a form that (at first) he does not recognise, just as Moses, in need of fire, through this need was drawn to God without realising it.[60] And God spoke to him.

59. Amir Hamzah, *Nianji Sunit* (Jakarta, 1954), 7.
'Alas my Beloved
For me this is all without use.
For me there is only one desire
To feel you close beside me
As did Moses on the peak of Sinai.'
60. Ibn 'Arabī, *Fuṣūṣ*, 212–213 (178).

Shu'ayb, Orator of the Prophets: Reflections on Qur'anic Narrative

A story, Dr Tom Griffiths remarks, 'is a piece of disciplined magic . . . It is the most powerful educational tool we possess. It is also a privileged carrier of truth, a way of allowing for multiplicity and complexity at the same time as guaranteeing memorability. Story creates an atmosphere in which truth becomes discernible as a pattern.'[1]

Stories of the prophets are central to the Qur'an's communication of its message. As a corollary, it is often overlooked how rich and diverse an assembly of personalities the prophets presented in the Qur'an by such narratives are, as are the varying emphases in their roles in human history from the beginning of time until the call of the Prophet Muḥammad. They are figures whose example Muḥammad himself appealed to in support of his own mission. Like him, all preached the unity of God, offered proofs of the validity of their mission, and warned of the ineluctable coming of a Day of Resurrection and Judgement. They embody different qualities, and in the challenges they face, reflect aspects of Muḥammad's own call and his experience in responding to it. The majority of them are figures that have a place in the Judaeo-Christian tradition. After Adam, the father and first teacher of humankind, there is Noah, from whom all who survived the flood are descended. Among them also are Abraham, the Friend of God; and Moses, who spoke with God; and Joseph whose story

1. Dr Tom Griffiths, 'The Humanities and an Environmentally Sustainable Australia' in *The Humanities and Australia's National Research Priorities* (Canberra: Australian Academy of the Humanities for the Commonwealth Department of Education, Science and Training, 2003), quoting Barry Lopez, 'A Literature of Place', Heat 2 (1996).

in Sura 12 overshadows all other prophetic narratives in the Qur'an in popularity. There are also David and Solomon, rulers to whom God gave gifts of wisdom and technical skills to benefit the peoples they ruled; Job, whose charism was to endure undeserved suffering patiently; and Jonah, whom God reproved for his impatience when his people were recalcitrant.

There are, however, three major figures who are associated, rather, with Arabian traditions: Hūd, Ṣāliḥ and Shu'ayb, each of whom is well attested in the Qur'an.[2] Taken together, and even individually, more verses are devoted to them than to some of the figures who have a Biblical counterpart. Each has an individual[3] character to his charism, but they have in common that they each preach to their own people, and that they figure in punishment stories. When the warnings they bring are disregarded, their people are destroyed. They have a significant place in the *qiṣaṣ al-anbiyā*[3], and each is the starting point of sublime meditations in Ibn 'Arabi's *Fuṣūṣ al-ḥikam*. By and large, however, they have not attracted much interest in their own right among Western scholars of Islam. The *Encyclopaedia of Islam*, for example, gives only succinct entries relating to each of them,' and does not suggest any particular role for them in the economy of salvation.

This reflection is based on the account of Shu'ayb in *Sūrat al-Aʿrāf* (Q 7:1–157). Shu'ayb has an established place in the Muslim tradition: Tha'labī refers to him as the orator of the prophets, *khaṭīb al-anbiyā*'[3], because of the debating skill he shows when confronting his people,[4] a quality that al-Nasafī also notes in his *tafsīr*[5] of this sura. He is distinguished by his denunciation of cheating in business and his concern for social justice and is the only prophet, apart from Muḥammad himself, whose message is explicit on this theme.

2. There are narratives about Shu'ayb in *Sūrat al-Aʿrāf* (Q 7:85–93), *Sūrat Hūd* (Q 11:84–95) and *Sūrat al-Shuʿarā'* (Q 26:176–91), and two verses referring to him in *Sūrat al-ʿAnkabūt* (Q 29:36-7); narratives about Ṣāliḥ in *Sūrat al-Aʿrāf* (Q 7:73–79), *Sūrat Hūd* (Q 11:61–68), *Sūrat al-Shuʿarā'* (Q 26:141–159), *Sūrat al-Naml* (Q 27:45–53) and *Sūrat al-Qamar* (Q 54:23–32); and narratives about Hūd in *Sūrat al-A'rāf* (Q 7:65–72), *Sūrat Hūd* - the sura bears his name (Q 11:50–60), *Sūrat al-Shucarā'* (Q 26:123–140) and *Sūrat al-Aḥqāf* (Q 46:21).

3. AJ Wensinck, art 'Hūd'; A Rippin, article 'Ṣāliḥ'; and A Rippin, art 'Shu'ayb' in *Encyclopaedia of Islam*, second edition

4. Tha'labī, *Qiṣaṣ al-anbiya'* (Beirut: Dar al kutub al-'ilmiyya), 164

5. Al-Nasafī, *Tafsīr al-Nasafī* (Beirut: Dār al-kutub al-'Arabī).

The three pericopes in which Shu'ayb has a significant role (in *Sūrat al-Aʿrāf, Sūrat Hūd* and *Sūrat al-Shuʿarāʾ*[3]) consist primarily of exchanges between himself and his people. They reject his message, and he counters their rejection with his eloquence and skill in debate. And in *Sūrat al-Aʿrāf*, when this fails to convince them, and they are destroyed, he addresses their dead bodies in the desolation of their ruined dwellings after the divine punishment of which he had warned them, has overwhelmed them.

Sūrat al-Aʿrāf presents the immense panorama of salvation history in four parts. The first is a prolegomenon (Q 7:1–58), a distillation of the divine economy of salvation for humankind, which sets out the vocation of Muhammad, his encounters with his people, and the broad themes of his message: a complex of rich variations on the great themes of Divine Unity, Prophecy, Resurrection and Judgement. The second (Q 7:55–102), is a sequence of 'punishment stories', in which that of Shu'ayb has its place (Q 7:85–93), presenting five prophets sent to 'past peoples', as examples of prophets before the time of Muḥammad, the message they preached, the objections made to them and the fates of the people who rejected them. The third (Q 7:103–157) continues the unfolding of salvation history (in the economy of the dealings of God with Man) with an account of Moses before Pharoah, his leading of the Jews into the desert, and their unfaithfulness, with an episodic account of Moses before Pharaoh and his dealings with his people on the way to Mount Sinai. In the fourth, the focus of the sura turns back to the mission of Muḥammad and issues which are contemporary with him, a unit in large measure devoted to Muḥammad's preaching to the Jewish people and others who reject him or are hypocrites, the threads of all four parts being drawn together in a resounding peroration to the sura.

The second part of the sura, Q 7:59–102, comprises narratives of five messengers whose people are destroyed because they rejected them: Noah, Hūd, Ṣāliḥ, Lot and Shu'ayb, the Shu'ayb pericope occupying a final, and so climactic, position. It presents in vivid detail the confrontation between him and his people, and, as we shall see, gains in power and authority for its message by its contextual setting, and the patterns of echoes it carries from other parts of the sura and elsewhere in the Qur'an.

The first of these messengers is Noah. He is introduced with the words, *[In ancient times] We had sent Noah to his people (la-qad arsalnā*

Nūḥan ilā qawmihi, Q 7:59). This sending of Noah marks a crucial stage in salvation history. All humankind living today are descended from him. He proclaims to his people the foundational prophetic message, '*Worship God, you have no god other than He*'. He fears the punishment that is to befall them. He denies the charge by the elders of his people that he is in error, and declares '*I am a messenger (rasūl) of the Lord of the Worlds. I preach/ declare the messages (risalāt) of my Lord; I offer counsel (anṣaḥ) to you*' (Q 7:61–62). He asks them, '*Are you astonished that a warning (dhikr) comes to you from a man of yourselves, that by it he might warn you*' (Q 7:63). The narrative concludes with the divine words, *they disbelieved in him, so We saved him and those who were with him in the boat, and drowned those who disbelieved in Our signs* (Q 7:64).

The second messenger, Hūd, is introduced with the words, *And to ᶜĀd [We sent] their brother Hūd' (wa-ilā ᶜĀdin akhāhum Hūdan,* Q 7:65). He presents to them the same foundational message as had Noah, the message of all the prophets, '*Worship God, you have no god but He*', imploring them, '*Will you not fear Him?*' The elders of his people claim that he is foolish and a liar. He denies the charge, declaring, '*I am a messenger (rasūl) from the Lord of the worlds. I bring the messages of my Lord, l am a trustworthy counsellor for you*' (Q 7:67–68). He puts to them the same question as had Noah, '*Are you astonished that a warning (dhikr) comes to you from a man of yourselves to warn you?*' and reminds them of the favours God has given them: he has made them His vicegerents *(khulafāʾ)* in place of the people of Noah who had been drowned, and has given them increase in stature; he urges them to reflect on the blessings of God *(alāʾaʾllāh)*—implicit in this appeal is that they be grateful—and so be saved (Q 7:69). The elders refuse to abandon what their fathers worshipped, and serve God alone. They challenge him to bring on the punishment he warns awaits them (Q 7:70), to which he retorts, '*Do you dare to dispute with me on the basis of names which you and your fathers have made up and to which God has given no authority?*' (Q 7:71). They were then extirpated from the earth, but Hūd and those who followed him were saved.

The third messenger to be introduced here is the Arab prophet Ṣāliḥ. He is introduced with the same words, *and to Thamūd [We sent] their brother Ṣāliḥ (wa-ilā Thamūda akhāhum Ṣāliḥan,* Q 7:73). He proclaims the foundational message, '*My people, worship God! You have no god other than He'*, and announces that he brings a proof *(bayyina)* of his message, a marvelous gift, the she-camel of God. It is theirs to pasture on God's earth, provided they do not harm it. If they harm it, a terrible punishment will befall them (Q 7:73). Ṣāliḥ reminds them of the blessings of God they have received: He has made them His vicegerents *(khulafa')* after the destruction of 'Ād, He has given them the means to move through the earth, to have castles in the plains, and to hew dwellings in the hills. Therefore, he urges them, reflect on the blessings of God *[fa'dhkurū ālā'a'llāh),* and warns them, *'do not as evildoers do harm upon the earth* (*wa-lā ta^c thaw fī'l-arḍi mufsidīn'*, Q 7:74).

The arrogant elders of his people taunt him, they kill the camel, and challenge him to bring on the punishment he has threatened if he is indeed *one of those sent (mina'l- mursalīn,* Q 7:77). They declare their contempt for those who believe in Ṣāliḥ's message, and scornfully ask them whether they really believe that Ṣāliḥ is truly one sent *(mursal).* The believers reply that indeed they do (Q 7:75), to which the arrogant elders responded that they do not, they kill the she-camel, and challenge Ṣāliḥ, *'Bring on that with which you threatened us, if you are of those sent'.* An earthquake overwhelms them, and they are left sprawling face-down, dead in their dwellings. Ṣāliḥ turns from them and says, *'My people, I have delivered the message (risāla) of my Lord. I have counselled (naṣaḥtu) you. But you have no love for those who give counsel'* (Q 7:79).

The fourth messenger is Lot, nephew of Abraham. He is introduced with a reduction of the formulaic introduction, *and Lot (wa-Lūṭan) when he said to his people, 'Do you commit debauchery (fāḥisha) that goes beyond anything perpetrated by those who went before you?'* (Q 7:81). They seek sexual gratification in men, not women, being a people that grossly goes beyond what is normal *(qawmun musrifūn,* they urge each other to expel Lot and those who follow him from their township *(qarya),* after which they are destroyed by a rain (of fire and stones from heaven). Lot and his family, apart from his wife, are saved (Q 7:84).

Shu^c ayb, the final messenger to figure in this section of the sura, is, however, introduced by the full formulaic utterance, *and to Midyan their brother Shu^c ayb* (Q 7:85). As the last of the group, he has a position of prominence and importance, an importance highlighted in a number of ways, among them the content of his message, and the rhetoric of his address. He proclaims the exclusive right of God to worship: *'My people, worship God! You have no god other than He'.* He claims to have proof of the authenticity of his mission from their Lord (for God is *their* Lord as well as his), *'a proof has come to you from your Lord'*, a proof that gives him the right to address them as God's messenger, urging them to *'Give full weight and measure'*, and continuing, *'Do not withhold from people the things that are theirs. Do not do evil upon the earth after it has been set in sound order (iṣlāḥiha) [by the prophets],'*

With that he appeals to their self-interest, modulating his commands with words of counsel that ring out like anvil strokes, *'This is the proper course for you. If you are believers [then follow what I teach]'* (Q 7:85). He warns them, *'Do not lurk in ambush (wa-lā taqᶜudū bi-kulli ṣirāt) on every highway menacing [wayfarers] trying to divert from the way of God whomever believes in it, eager to make it crooked.'* With these words a parallel is drawn between physical robbery on the highway plundering people's goods, and stealing their faith in God, through making crooked the highway of life by warping the straight lines of religious belief and practice. He gives reasons why they should comply with his teaching. First, by reminding them of their duty of gratitude to God, *'Recall when you were few and God made you many'*, then warning them of the consequences of disbelief, *'reflect on how was the punishment of those [before you] who did evil'* (Q 7:86). He concludes this address, conceding that not all will accept his message, *'If there is a group of you believing in that with which 1 was sent and a group that does not believe, then wait in patience (fa'ṣbirū) until God judges between us, He is best of those who give judgement'* (Q 7:87), thereby drawing attention away from himself, and directing it to God, for the final outcome is in His hands (Q 7:87).

Shu'ayb's message is rejected: *those who were arrogant (al-ladhīna'stakbarū) replied, 'Shu'ayb, we will certainly expel you and those who are with you from our township - unless you truly return to our faith'.* To their demand that he and those who follow him revert to the ancestral religion of the community, he puts the question, *'Even if we find it abhorrent [are we to return to it?]'* (Q 7:88), then raises the level of rhetorical intensity: *'We would thereby have perpetrated a lie against God if we returned to your faith after God has saved us from it. There is no cause for us to return to it other than were God our Lord so to wish it.'* Which would be unthinkable! He proclaims the greatness of

God (*'Our Lord has knowledge of all things'*) and expresses confidence in Him (*In God we put our trust'*) then utters the inspiring prayer, *'Our Lord, open out (iftāḥ,* that is, 'make clear a judgement') *between us and our people in truth. You are best of all who open [out]'* (Q 7:89).

The elders of his people, finding it impossible to defeat him in argument, turn on his followers, scornfully saying to them, *'If indeed you follow Shu'ayb you are then the losers'* (Q 7:90). God's punishment thereupon overwhelms them without warning: *the earthquake [that had been threatened] overwhelmed them, and they lay sprawled face down, dead in their dwellings. Those who disbelieved in Shu'ayb, it was as though they had never dwelt in them. Those who disbelieved in Shu'ayb, it was they, they who were the losers* (Q 7:91–92). And so he grieves for the death of his countrymen, turning away from their corpses, as he says, *'My people, I brought to you the messages of my Lord and 1 counselled you, yet how can I grieve for a disbelieving people'* (Q 7:93),[6] that is, I warned you of God's punishment if you disobeyed, and called you to repentance, but in vain.

The primary moral imperative of the Shu'ayb story standing at the head of his message is clear: *give full weigh t and measure in your trade and business dealings, do not withhold from people the things that are theirs* (Q 7:85). In other words, this is an element in the good ordering of society *(iṣlāḥ)* brought by the prophets. It is a statement that commercial dishonesty is destructive of the good order of society, and gives a specific example of the warning of Ṣāliḥ: *do not as evildoers do harm upon the earth* (Q 7:74). In the other two suras in which Shu'ayb pericopes appear, this message is reiterated and

6. Rāzī remarks that his sorrow for his people was intense because they were many, and he was expecting from them an acceptance of faith. And when that terrible destruction came upon them there was grief in his heart due to his kinship (with them), his proximity to them, and the extent of his affection (for them). But then, reflecting on the inexorability of divine justice, said the words 'Yet how can I sorrow for a people who are unbelievers' (Fakhr al-Dīn al-Rāzī, *al-Tafsīr al-kabīr* (Tehran: Dār al-Kutub al-'ilmiyya, nd), *TK* 14:181). Al-Nawawī al-Bantanī (in *Marāḥ Labīd* (2 volumes, Cairo: Dār Ihyā' al-Kutub al-'Arabiyya, nd), volume 1, 290) detects an internal irony: *They were left sprawled dead in their houses. Those who disbelieved in Shu'ayb, it was as though they had never dwelt in them* (Q 7:92). It was as though they had never dwelt in their township at all, that is, they were punished for their words 'We will expel you, Shu'ayb, and those who believe in you, from our township'. It was they who were expelled from the township, never to return.

further developed. In *Sūrat Hūd,* Q 11:84, he cries to his people, *'Do not give short weight and short measure'.* He adds that they have no need to cheat because they are in good circumstances, and these good circumstances are contingent on their remaining in God's favour. In Q 11:85 he urges them, *'Give full weight and measure in justice (bi'l-qisṭ), do not deprive people of the things that are theirs'.* They should be satisfied with the honest profit that God leaves for them (Q 11:86). In Q 11:87, he faces down their arrogant objection to his message, *'Does your religious devotion require you to forbid us to worship what our fathers worshipped, or to do with our wealth what we wish?'* (Q 11:87). In *Sūrat al-Shu'arā',* at Q 26:181, he insists to his people that they *'Give full measure, and not be of those who give less than is right'.* In verse 182, he urges *'Weigh with a true scale (qisṭās)',* and reiterates in verse 183, *'Do not withhold from people the things that are theirs, do not as evildoers do harm upon the earth'.*

The significance and pivotal role of this second part of the sura is not palpable until it is situated, heard and understood, within the context of the sura as a whole. The sequence of five stories appears simple, but their internal relationships within the unit they form is complex. The injunctions of all five prophets gain authority from the multi-layered structure of resonances provided by the overlapping contexts in which they are situated that give them prominence in the orchestration of the great themes of Divine Unity, Prophecy and Resurrection and Judgement that the sura provides, and highlight their role in the realisation of a properly ordered world. There is a counterpoint within and between their messages, albeit one carried by a common pulse and rhythm. They are all punishment stories, and the prophets are all of and sent to their own people. But there are variations in the ways in which their stories are told, in the continuities between them established by the use of formulaic utterances, the placing and spacing of them in the time-line that is established, and the moral imperatives they emphasise. Further, it integrates the three Arab prophets as equal participants in the line of prophecy with the figures (Noah and Lot) that have a place in the Judaic tradition.

Each has a role in calling attention to the necessary norms for the good order *(iṣlāḥ)* of society, and each highlights a different form of disobedience to the divine message disruptive of this good order. For the people of Noah, it is polytheism; for those of Hūd, it is their refusal to abandon the gods their fathers have worshipped—no more than names they themselves have made up; for those of Ṣāliḥ, it is the killing of the she-camel, in effect putting God to the test, challenging Him to punish them, if He has the power. For the people of Lot, it is sodomy. For those of Shuʿayb it is dishonesty in trading, the basis of economic life and business confidence on which the welfare of all depends. All these peoples have been guilty of doing evil upon the earth *(mufsidūn fīʾl-arḍ)* by acts which disturb the well-being of society, after it has been put right by the prophets; they have not been grateful for the blessings they have received. The injunction of Ṣāliḥ is aptly directed to each of them.

The Shuʿayb narrative stands out by virtue of its position, organisation and rhetorical power. Part of this may have been communicated by the English rendering, which shows the formal structure of his confrontation and debate with his people, but attention may also be drawn to the effective use of rhythm and rhyme. One example may suffice. The rhyme and parallel structure between the conclusion of Shuʿayb's warning to his people that if they do not accept his message, they must await God's judgment, *and He is the best of all who give judgement (huwa khayruʾl-ḥakimīn,* Q 7:87), and his call on God to exercise His power and judge between them in verse 89 contribute tremendous power to both verses, and the pericope as a whole.

There are other literary devices in the presentation of the five messengers that highlight this second part of the sura, and the position of Shuʿayb within it. One is the variation in the formulaic utterances that introduce each figure. For Noah it is *la-qad arsalnā Nūḥan ilā qawmihi ([Before this] We had sent Noah to his people,* Q 7:59). Thereafter 'We had sent' is ellipted *(maḥdhūf),* so for Hūd, it is *wa-ila ᶜĀdin akhāhum Hūdan (and to ᶜĀd their brother Hūd,* Q 7:65), and for Ṣāliḥ, *wa-ilā Thamūdan akhāhum Ṣāliḥan (and to Thamūd, their brother Ṣāliḥ,* Q 7:73). But for Lot, 'their brother' too is ellipted, leaving simply *wa-Lūṭan (and Lot,* Q 7:80), breaking the evenness of the flow. This is restored with the introduction of Shuʿayb, *wa-ilā Madyana akhāhum Shuᶜayban (and to Midyan their brother Shuᶜayb,* Q 7:85) thereby adding a renewed impulse and emphasis to the movement of the narration telling of Shuʿayb, and the message he presents. The same effect is realised by the phrase *[Before this] We had sent,* that introduces Noah, which is ellipted before the following four prophets, though its grammatical effect is sustained - all their names are *manṣūb* - and re-appears at the summation of the pericope, up to that point being heard in the ear of the mind and memory: *We have not sent any prophet to a township (wa-mā arsalnā fī qarya) [and they disbelieve in him] without disaster and harm overwhelming them, so they might become humble* (Q 7:94)[7].

Another device is the cumulative effect of themes which occur explicitly in some of the narratives, and by implication in others. There is an emotional engagement between the messengers and their peoples. Thus Noah fears for his people the disaster that is going to overwhelm them (Q 7:59), Ṣāliḥ and Shuʿayb both look in grief on the dead bodies of their people, and Hūd, Ṣāliḥ and Shuʿayb in their preaching remind their peoples of the particular ways in which God has been good to them, calling on them to reflect, be grateful—and so believe. Noah, Hūd, Ṣāliḥ and Shuʿayb present themselves as good counsellors to their peoples (Noah in Q 7:62, Hūd in Q 7:68, Ṣāliḥ in Q 7:79 and Shuʿayb in Q 7:93); all except Lot announce that they bring signs, and Ṣāliḥ, in addition to calling on them to worship the one God, brings them a test, the she-camel, gift of God, that they must not harm. All of these can be seen as contributing to a heightened sense of the presence of Shuʿayb, the message he brings, and the emotion he feels at the death of his people.

To return to the Shuʿayb pericope in *Sūrat al-Aʿrāf:* the significance of this part of the sura, and the role that Shuʿayb plays in it, is also reinforced by its position within the broader architecture of the sura. It is given depth by Q 7:1-10, which are in effect an exordium to part one of the sura. These verses set out the centrality of revelation, the human condition, and the pathway for humankind to negotiate its way through life. They offer a concentrated distillation of the themes and lessons presented so vividly and with such detail in the narratives of the five messengers in part two. In verse 2, God assures Muḥammad that a Book is indeed being revealed to him, that by it he is to warn, and that it is a reminder *(dhikrā)* to those who believe. In verse 3, He warns humankind that they should follow what is revealed to them, and reproves them, *how little you reflect!* In verse 4 He tells of past townships *(qurā)* that have been destroyed in punishment for their sins—as had been the townships of the messengers in part two. Brought to judgement, their inhabitants can only confess, '*We have indeed been evildoers*' (Q 7:5).

7. A number of commentators regard the bracketed words as ellipted ʿayns

God will question those to whom Messengers had been sent, and those sent to them (Q 7:6)— as would be the case with the five Messengers and their peoples. This verse is echoed by Shu'ayb, who speaks of those who believe and do not believe *in that with which I have been sent* in Q 7:87. In Q 7:8, God tells of 'the weighing' *(al-wazn)* of human deeds to come on Judgement Day, which will be meticulous, accurate and just. Shu'ayb's message, in similar vein, calls on his people to be correspondingly just in their business dealings in this world, *'Give full weight and measure (fa-awfū'l-kayla wa'l-mīzān) and do not deprive people of the things that are theirs'* (Q 7:85).

In Q 7:9, there is the assurance that *those whose scales are light are those who have brought about loss to themselves (khasirū anfusahum) due to the wrong they have done to Our signs*—as had the peoples of the five messengers. Shu'ayb's people who reject him, sneer at those who follow him, saying to them *'you will be the losers' (al-khasirūn,* Q 7:90). Yet it is these unbelievers who meet the fate of those referred to in verse 9, who are the losers *(al-khasirīn,* Q 7:92). In Q 7:10, God reminds humankind in general terms that He has *given you power over the earth, and given you your livelihood in it.* Ṣāliḥ and Shu'ayb, in their addresses to their peoples, remind them of specific instances of God's goodness to them (in verses 74 and 86 respectively). Yet—the exordium concludes—*How little do you give thanks!*

The sura continues with an account of the creation of Adam, God's command to the angels to bow in before him, and Satan's arrogant refusal to join the angels in this act of homage and subsequent expulsion from the Garden, following which he swears to God, *I will lurk in ambush for them [humankind) on Your right path (la-aqᶜudanna lahum sirāṭaka 'l-mustaqīm), I will come upon them from before and behind, from their right and from their left - You will not find most of them grateful* (Q 7:16–17). What Satan swears he will do, Shu'ayb calls on his people to desist from in Q 7:86, echoing Satan's very words: *'Do not lurk in ambush at every roadway, menacing wayfarers' (wa-lā taqᶜudū bi-kulli sirāṭin tuᶜidūna).* Satan deploys his guile against Adam and Eve, persuading them to eat from the forbidden tree (Q 7:20), claiming to be a true counsellor to them (Q 7:21). Adam and Eve then disobey God, just as the peoples of the five messengers disobeyed them. And a chiasmus is established between Satan's temptation of them, and the call of the messengers. Satan claims to be a true counsellor to them. He lies, but they believe him. Four of the five Messengers claim to be giving counsel. They speak the truth, but their peoples reject their message.

Likewise, verse 7 tells how, in the hereafter, when people are before Him for judgement, God Himself will narrate to them what they had done, for He too had been present when His messengers preached to them. This verse sets sounding the word *wazn,* the concept of a balance on the Day of Judgment. But it also, when counterbalanced with Shu'ayb's warning to his people to *give full measure and weight* in Q 7:85, adds a particular weight and dimension to Shu'ayb's message: as God is just, so should human beings be just in their dealings with each other. If the people of Shu'ayb use different scales and measurements for buying and selling to defraud those with whom they deal, the judgement of God is utterly just. The exordium concludes with a summation of God's good deeds to humankind (Q 7:10), which concludes with an appeal filled with yearning, *how little you give thanks* which echoes *how little do you reflect.*

The messengers share a compassion for the fate that will befall their unbelieving peoples. Noah fears for his people the punishment of an Awesome Day (Q 7:59), Ṣāliḥ mourns that his people have no love for those who give counsel (Q 7:79), and Shu'ayb grieves that he has given good counsel to no avail (Q 7:93). Yet this compassion on the part of the messengers is but a reflection of the compassion of God for those who persist in rejecting them: after their narratives God declares in Q 7:96, *if only the peoples of the townships (qurā) had believed [their prophets] and had been devout, We would have opened (fataḥnā) for them blessings from the heavens and the earth, but they disbelieved.* The word *fataḥnā,* here used of God bestowing His blessings, carries echoes of other aspects of God's power revealed in this root. In particular it has resonances of Shu'ayb's call to God in Q 7:89 to lay open the truth between him and those who disbelieve, appealing to Him as *the best of those who open out [blessings and the truth] (khayru'l-fātihīn).*

Further, God asks, *how could the peoples of these townships have thought themselves safe from Our anger that could come upon them at night as they slept? How could the peoples of these townships have thought themselves safe from Our anger at bright day as they amused themselves]* (Q 7:97–98), verses that echo the exordium of verse 4 in part one, *how many townships [of unbelievers] have We destroyed, for Our wrath came upon them at night, or as they took their noon-day rest.*

The role of Shu'ayb as a prophet of social justice also requires further reflection. In his call for honesty in trading and social justice, he seems to prefigure Muḥammad. Social justice is one of the great themes of the Qur'an. It is at the heart of the revelations put on the Prophet Muḥammad's lips to address to his Meccan contemporaries, attested in the earliest suras of the Qur'an, and is reiterated time and again.[8] Fair trading, based on the observance of proper weight and measure, justice, go beyond the way in which faithfulness to them is realised in this world. They have a cosmic dimension that extends beyond time, for God Himself is just, and humankind are called on to be just likewise. This is why on the day of Judgment, the weighing of human deeds will be exact (Q 7:8–9).

In *Sūrat Hūd* (Q 11:85), Shu'ayb reiterates his cry to give full weight and measure with justice *(bi'l-qisṭ),* taking up and re-presenting the words Muhammad is commanded to utter in *Sūrat al-Aʿrāf* (Q 7:29), *'My Lord demands justice'*. This association of true weight and measure with a universal principle of justice *(qisṭ)* is one of the great themes of the Qur'an, presented in a number of attestations.[9] It is by this scale that humankind will be judged in the hereafter, according to the measure of their good and their evil deeds. They may cheat in the measure they use, God does not. He will judge according to His absolute scale of justice: *We have set a just scale for the Day of*

8. For example, *Woe to those who defraud, those who when they take a measure from others demand it in full, Yet when they measure or weigh out to them cause them loss. Do those who do such not reflect that [after death] they are to be resurrected to face an awesome Day* (Q 83:1–5). It goes beyond cheating in trade, and includes the oppression of the poor, as in Q. 107, *Have you reflected on the one who rejects religion, he's the one who rebuts the orphan and does not urge the feeding of the poor*. This moral imperative is presented from a different perspective in *Sūrat al-Isra'*, Q 17:34, in which Muḥammad is commanded to say to the Meccans, *Do not approach the property of orphans except in such a way as to add to it. Give full weight and measure with justice–We do not burden anyone beyond his capacity–If you give your word, then be true to it, even if a kinsman be disadvantaged. Be true to God's covenant with you.*
9. For example, Give *true weight and measure in justice* (Q 6:152); *Establish the measure in justice, and do not give short weight* (Q 55:9); and, *We sent our messengers with convincing signs. Through them We revealed the Book and the Balance, so that humankind might act with justice* (Q 57:25). This is vividly expressed in *Sūrat al-Raḥmān*, Q 55:7–9, *He has raised up the heavens and set the scale of justice [so firmly] that you cannot play it false. Apply this scale with justice, you must not give short measure by this scale.*

Resurrection, and no one will be done any wrong (Q 21:47). As God is exact in His judgements, so should humankind be: in obedience to the divine law, in their business dealings with each other, and in their care for the oppressed.

There are, then, multiple layers of related meanings in the Qur'anic narratives of Shu'ayb, which add to the force of his denunciation against giving false weight and measure. The context in which the story told of him is situated and the demotic character of the exchanges between himself and his people, creates a dramatic tension that adds to the power of the imperatives he preaches. This is part of the rhetorical dynamic of the Qur'an, and it is aspects of this dynamic that this reflection explores both within and across the suras in which he is mentioned. In this sura, the strength of Shu'ayb's message is amply attested. It is set in a context of past and present. It juxtaposes time and eternity. In each attestation he shows himself as *khaṭīb al-anbiyā',* and through his oratory appealing for honesty in trading and social justice.

Narrations such as these on the 'big screen' of Qur'anic *balāgha,* addressed on the lips of Muḥammad to the Meccans of his time, present situations in the past with which they could identify, involving people like themselves, who had experienced trials of various kinds. They have reason to be grateful to God for delivery from them, and yet in rejecting Muḥammad, they are ungrateful. The narrative in *Sūrat al-A ʿrāf* gives a picture of an Arab prophet, Shu'ayb, preaching to Arabs like themselves, guilty of sins such as they themselves were guilty of—idol worship, and cheating in their trading practices, facing arguments levelled against him of the same kind as those levelled against Muḥammad, and the punishment that befell them. Punishment was threatened if the Meccans rejected Muḥammad's message. Shu'ayb's people, like those of Muḥammad did not believe it would befall them. Muḥammad's people too then should realise that if they continue to reject his warnings and deny his mission, just as their predecessors, the people of Shu'ayb, they are destined for punishment in this world and the next. In presenting his message, Shu'ayb had used eloquence and skill in debate, the skill of the Arabs par excellence. The story, communicating this debate, carries specific values and moral imperatives. It has a rhetorical dynamic within the structure of the sura, as a component in a unitary structure, and can properly be understood as 'a privileged carrier of truth' in the message it presents.

In the Qur'an, literary form is inseparable from ethical message. Thus, in modem times the Lebanese Amal leader Muḥammad Ḥusayn Faḍl Allāh (1935–2010) in *al-Ḥiwār fī'l-Qurʾan* has made a study of dialogues and altercations in the Qur'an, between whom they take place, and the issues that are debated.[10] He presents a composite account of the preaching of Shu'ayb, and the objections his people make to his teaching. Clearly he sees the accounts of Shu'ayb's preaching in all four suras in which he appears, as forming a unity. He presents the teaching of *Sūrat al-Aʿrāf,* and then observes that in *Sūrat Hūd,* Q 11:85, it is made explicit that to give full weight and measure is a matter of justice *(qisṭ);* that Shu'ayb's people are in good circumstances (verse 84) which are contingent on their remaining in God's favour. *Do not act wickedly on the earth* is a refrain that sounds through all the Shu'ayb pericopes. His vocation is that he established good order *(iṣlāḥ)* upon the earth. He advises, *'The honest profit that God leaves for you is what is best'* (Q 11:86). *'Do not withhold from people what is theirs',* is reiterated. Faḍl Allah diagnoses the arrogance and selfishness in Shu'ayb's people when they reply objecting to his teaching, *'Does your religious devotion require you to forbid us to do with what is ours what we wish?'* (Q 11:87). His people should not cause loss and harm to others (Q 26:181).

In the narratives of Shu'ayb he finds one of the fundamental principles of a global ethic: economic security. Shu'ayb's preaching, he writes, condemns economic freedom in the capitalist sense of the words.[11] By this Faḍl Allāh means a freedom not bounded by ethical and human values. Freedom in monetary activities has to be restrained within a framework of human well-being and a sense of social responsibility. The principles that Shu'ayb presents, he shows are designed to permit what is appropriate to this, and forbid whatever goes beyond it in every time and place. Freedom can never be unfettered. It carries with it obligations. That this is an Islamic ideal is of course widely recognised, but perhaps there is something to be learned from the fact that a basic argument for such an awareness of economic responsibility is to be found in the preaching of the Arab prophet Shu'ayb.

---

10. Muḥammad Ḥusayn Faḍl Allāh, *al-Ḥiwār fī'l-Qur'ān* (Beirut: al-Mu'assasa li'l-Dirāsa wa'l-Nashr wa'l-Tawzī ', 1985/1405).
11. Faḍl Allah, *al-Ḥiwār fī'l-Qur'ān*, 305–309.

Narrative, Intertext and Allusion in the Qur'anic Presentation of Job

A recurring theme in the Qur'an is the constancy of God's care for His creatures from the beginning of time by the sending of prophets. In presenting a record of these divine interventions in human affairs, the Qur'an establishes the framework of a salvation history.

These prophets are a specially chosen community, many of them known by name, others whose names were not divulged even to the Prophet Muḥammad (al-Nisā' (4):163). A number of them, notably Abraham and Moses, have a commanding authority and self-evidently major role, others such as Joseph and Noah appear in fully fledged narratives, yet others such as David and Solomon are presented in a number of vividly etched pericopes. Others, however, are referred to comparatively briefly, their role and character defined and identified by a minimum of narrated information about them and the words God addresses to them, or sets on their lips as direct speech.

These 'lesser' prophetic figures include Idrīs (19:56–57 and 21:85); Dhū'l-Kifl (21:85 and 38:48); al-Yasa' (Elisha) (6:87 and 38:48); Ilyās (Elias) (6:85 and 37:124–30, and possibly referred to 18:65); Ayyūb (Job) (4:163, 6:84, 21:83–84, 38:41–44) and Yūnus (Jonah)—also referred to as Dhū 'l-Nūn and Ṣāḥib al-Ḥūt -(4:163, 6:86, 10:98, 2 I: 87–88, 37:139–48, 68:48–50).[1]

They appear as vignettes, and have to the great figures of prophecy a role comparable to that of predella to major paintings in the visual arts. Assessed by the criteria of the number of episodes in which they play a role, frequency of mention and the length and detail of the pericopes devoted to them, they are subsidiary to the great figures.

1. 'Lesser' in relation to the space devoted to them, not to their importance.

Yet they preach the same message and present individual aspects of revealed truth, and are integrated into the prophetic structure of the Qur'an by a variety of intermeshing literary conduits and devices. Frequency of mention and length of pericope does not, however, always coincide with the hierarchical order in which some traditions place them. When the Prophet was taken up to the seventh heaven on the night of the *miʿrāj*, at each stage of his ascent he met one of his predecessors. At the fourth heaven he met Idrīs, who, with only two attestations, was ranked above Adam (at the first), Jesus and John (at the second), and Joseph (at the third),[2] notwithstanding the multiple and extensive references to each of these and the entire chapter devoted to Joseph.

Although these six 'lesser' prophets are well represented in *qiṣaṣ al-anbiyā'* (Stories of the prophets—the title is generic) and are popular as personal names among male Muslims, outside the world of Islam they have attracted only minor interest. The pericopes in which they occur have not received much positive comment from western scholars. Lemmata dedicated to them in reference works, including the *Encyclopaedia of Islam* (both editions), are brief, and often more concerned with their identification in the Judaeo-Christian tradition than with their significance in the context of the Qur'an and the spiritual values they exemplify.

By way of example, Arthur Jeffrey in his entry Ayyūb in *EI 2* regards the references to Job as 'confused' and, by implication, of little interest.[3]

This essay is structured around Job (Ayyūb) as one of these 'lesser' prophets. Of four pericopes in which he is mentioned, only two give narrative information about him, one in the space of four verses, and the other of two. The other two simply include his name among an assembly of prophets. Nevertheless, despite the brevity of

2. A Guillaume, *The Life of Muhammad* (London: Oxford University Press, 1955), 185–186.
3. 'Job is mentioned twice in the Qur'an in lists of those to whom Allah had given special guidance and inspiration (iv, 163/161; vi, 84), and fragments of his story are given in xxi, 83-84; xxxviii, 41/40–44. In the story of the miraculous spring by which he was healed there seems to be a confusion with the Naaman story of II Kings V, and in the obscure verse about his taking a bundle in his hand and striking with it, there may be a similar confusion with the story in II Kings xiii, 14 ff.' EI2 s.v. Aiyūb, volume I, 795–796.

these Qur'anic references, they have made a major contribution to the religious imagination and spirituality of the Muslim community documented in *tafsīr,* in *qiṣaṣ al-anbiyā* ', and in the mystical tradition.

They are discussed in order of revelation, that is Ṣād (38):41–42, al-Anbiyā' (21):83–84 (both of which give narrative information), and al-An'ām (6):83–87 and al-Nisā' (4):163 (which present him only as a member of an assembly of prophets).

I
Sūrat Ṣād (38)

A suggested rendering of the Ṣād pericope is as follows:

41. And tell of Our servant Job,
    when he called his Lord,
    'Satan has indeed touched me with hardship and pain.'
42. 'Scuff [the earth] with your foot.' 'This
    is [a spring] a cool place to bathe, and
    [it is] drink.'
43. We gave [back] to him his kinsfolk and the like of them
    with them as a mercy from Us
    and as a lesson to those with understanding.
44. 'Take in your hand a sprig [of leaves]
    and strike with it!
    Do not break an oath.'
    Indeed We found him patient. How excellent a servant!
    He was turned constantly [to Us].

These verses may be regarded as a core statement of the prophetic experience of Job which the other Qur'anic references to him complement or re-present. It is highly dramatic. God instructs Muḥammad to tell of when Job called out in pain, presenting Job's words in direct speech. God's response to his call, in the form of a command, also in direct speech, follows immediately. Job's obedience to it is understood. God, switching to narrative mode, then tells a wider audience what He has done for Job and why God then addresses Job with a second command. Again Job's obedience to it is understood. God, switching again to narrative mode, praises him, indicating the qualities by which he is distinguished.

The Qur'anic language is condensed and allusive, and the extent and depth of meanings that the exegetical tradition discovers within it are not self-evident. The pericope is confronting, and presents a challenge which could be perplexing, particularly since Job does not at first sight fit into the general prophetic mould. There is no account of his call, of divine words by which he is commissioned, the giving to him of a Book, the people to whom he preached, their acceptance or rejection of him, or the punishment that would follow such a rejection. In fact it is his example in bearing undeserved suffering that is his message.

Despite, indeed because of, its brevity and allusiveness, there is a tautness and dramatic power in the language, deriving from the tension of undisclosed information. Who was Job? What led him to cry out in anguish? How did Satan bring hardship and pain upon him? Why was he told to scuff the ground? Why did he need the water? When and how was his family taken from him? Why was Job ordered to take a sprig of leaves to strike someone or something? What was the oath it is incumbent on him to keep? What is the connection between the two apparently unrelated parts of the pericope? And finally, why does God praise him so highly at the conclusion of the verse?

Such questions raise the issue as to how the first hearers of these verses understood them, profoundly conscious as they were that the words they were hearing were divine words. For the answer that they had for them, it is necessary to turn to the reports of the Companions and Followers as they have been passed on by the *muḥaddith* and the *qaṣṣās*'.[4]

These answers are given in their fullest form by Ṭabarī in his *Jāmiʿ al-bayān* in three narrations, two deriving from Wahb b. Munabbih and one from al-Ḥasan al-Baṣrī, that he includes in his exegesis. The information they provide may be summarized as follows. Satan, speaking to God, claims that Job who is faithful to Him in prosperity will not be faithful when he encounters adversity. God accordingly allows Satan to put Job to the test by destroying his property, by killing his livestock and members of his family, and then afflicting him with painful and repellent disease, so that all apart from his wife abandon him. Satan attempts to make Job waver in his faithfulness to God through his wife. Playing on her pity for him in his misery, he persuades her to urge him to sacrifice a kid to Satan. Job realizes that she has

4. As for example in Ibn al-ʿArabi's *Fuṣūṣ al-ḥikam*. See RWJ Austin, translator, *Ibn al-ʿArabī The Bezels of Wisdom* (New York: Paulist Press, 1980), 21–27.

allowed herself to be taken in by Satan. He swears an oath to punish her with a hundred lashes if he recovers and tells her to leave him. Totally alone after she has left, he cries out to God in anguish, uttering the words: 'Satan has indeed touched me with hardship and pain' (v 41).

Ṭabarī, by putting together these reports has established a context for the events mentioned or referred to in the verses, identified the *dramatis personae,* and clarified their spiritual and moral message.

In the light of the background he provides, the compact language of the Qur'an presents with deft strokes a vivid picture of how Job, a prophet put to the test by the loss of his possessions, livestock, family and the physical suffering of disease, remained as faithful to God in hardship as he had been in prosperity without questioning God's wisdom. When he calls out in pain and loneliness after dismissing his wife who has unwittingly been deceived by Satan, God answers him. He relieves his suffering with a spring of water to heal him and quench his thirst; out of His mercy He restores to him his family, and in addition. the like of them with them. By His answer to Job's cry, He makes of Job's patience and endurance a lesson 'for those with understanding' (v 43). He instructs him to take into his hand a sprig of a hundred leaves so that by one blow with it he would have struck his wife with the hundred lashes as he had sworn to do on his recovery, warning him not to break the oath he has made. He then praises Job.

With this background, the sense of the pericope is clear. It does not present serious lexical difficulties, although, for example, it is difficult to find a situationally convincing English equivalent for the word *urkuḍ*. Pickthall renders it 'Strike (the ground with your foot') Bell renders it 'Stamp'.[5] On the basis of Ṭabarī's gloss of *urkuḍ birijlika ['l-arḍa]-harrikhā wa-idfa'hā bi-rijlika,*[6] that is, move the earth and press it with your foot, 'scuff' seems an acceptable English equivalent.

The pericope is exquisitely structured. Not a word is wasted, and even the interstices of silence between the utterances are implicit with meaning. Notwithstanding its brevity, the literary design is complex. It is in two parts: one Job's calling on his Lord for relief from the pain with which Satan has afflicted him, the other God commanding him to take a sprig of leaves and to strike one blow with it.

5. Muhammad Marmaduke Pickthall, *The Meaning of the Glorious Qur'an,* numerous printings, sv and Richard Bell, *The Qur'an Translated* (Edinburgh: T&T Clark, 1939), volume 2, 454.
6. Ṭabarī *Jāmi' al-bayān fī tafsīr ay al-Qur'an* (Bulaq, 1905) *ad* Ṣād. Volume 23, 95 ff.

Each includes a mix of narration and direct speech. In part one, Job cries aloud (direct speech); God responds giving an order (direct speech); God then speaks in narrative mode. In part two, God gives an order (direct speech) then speaks in narrative mode. A binary structure informs both parts. In part one, there are two components to God's response to Job, and each has likewise two parts. The spring is cleansing, it is also drink; Job's family is restored *and* the like of them with them; God's response is represented as a mercy *and* a lesson.

But within these complementary binary structures, there are antitheses. Job suffers hardship and pain, the water brings cleansing and quenches thirst. Something harmful is removed, something beneficent put in its place. Job's kin have been taken away (understood), they are brought back. There are parallels in the structure of part two. God's second command is likewise binary. Job is to do one thing (take a sprig and strike) he is to avoid doing another (break an oath).

The unity between the two parts is established in a number of other ways. In each there is a tension to be released. In part one the tension occasioned by Job's pain, in part two the possibility of the sin of a dishonoured oath. Another is the chiasmus between the two commands, 'scuff with your foot' *(urkuḍ, bi-rijlika)* (v 42), in part one, and 'take in your hand' *(khudh bi-yadika)* (v 44) in part two. Further, there is a symmetric distribution of double bipartite ellipses. In part one, Job's obedience to God's command to scuff the earth is understood, and likewise the healing that the water brings him. In the second, what is to be struck (his wife), and his obedience to the command are ellipted.

The closing formula, 'Indeed we found him patient. How excellent a servant! He was turned constantly [to us]' *(innā wajadnāhu ṣābiran, ni'ma'l-'abdu, innahu awwāb)* (v 44), is imbued with a verbal music that carries melodic tones of other formulae in praise of the prophets throughout the Qur'an.

The appearance of the spring is especially significant. It carries echoes of other references in the Qur'an to the appearance of springs with life-giving water, and the death and disintegration that follows drought. God's order to Job to scuff the ground with his foot may be seen as a counterpart to His order to Moses 'Strike the rock with your staff' in al-A'rāf (7):160—the water that quenched the thirst of the Israelites. Indeed the appearance of a spring, and the image of a cleansing, healing stream it evokes, dominates the scene. It is difficult not to see a reference to Job and the healing spring that burst from the ground when he scuffed his foot at the divine command in the ecstatic line of Rumi, 'Whenever the lover touches the ground with his dancing feet, the water of life will spring out of the darkness', quoted by Annemarie Schimmel.[7]

These Job verses have in addition as their immediate context a pericope presenting him as one of an assembly of prophets. His place in such a context presenting him as a prophet among prophets, demonstrates that he is important not simply as an individual but as a member of a community of prophets who, while sharing a common role and election, are distinct from one another in their personalities and individual charisms. The variety of perspectives from which they are presented shows the richness of their vocation, which, with the varying emphases of the divine messages they preach, demonstrates and justifies Muhammad's own role and vocation.

The assembly of prophets with whom he is associated comprises Noah, Hūd, Moses (v 12) Ṣāliḥ, Lot and Shu'ayb (v 13); David (vv 17–26) Solomon (vv 30–40), Job himself (vv 41–44) Abraham, Isaac and Jacob (vv 45–47) Ishmael, Elisha, Dhū'l-Kifl (v 48). This company is not given in a chronological order, but ranges from the most frequently mentioned to the least, from Abraham and Moses, to Elisha and Dhu'1-Kifl.

This assembly is symmetrically structured into three groups: The first of six, (sub-divided into two groups of three), the second of three, and the third of six (also sub-divided into two groups of three). Of the first group, no narrative information is given other than that all the peoples to whom they were sent were destroyed. Only two are mentioned by name, Noah and Lot. The others are identified by the peoples to whom they were sent, 'Ād, to whom Hūd was sent, Thamūd, to whom Ṣāliḥ was sent; in the case of the Egyptians, by their leader Pharaoh, to whom Moses was sent, and by residence, the people of the thicket, that is, Midian, to whom Shu'ayb was sent. Emphasis is here on the peoples destroyed for rejecting their prophets, rather than on the prophets sent them.

The second forms the core group. It consists of David, Solomon and Job. Narrative information is given of each of them. Each has

7. In *Mystical Dimensions of Islam* (University of North Carolina Press, 1975), referring in a footnote (183) to Rumi, *Rubā'iyyāt* ms Esat Ef. No. 2693, fol. 322 a 5.

a different charism. They differ from the first group in that none of them is named as sent to a particular people with a specific message, no one rejects them and is destroyed in punishment. They likewise differ from each other.

David is presented as one 'endued with strength', he was constantly turned [to Us] *(dhā'l-aydi innahu awwāb)* (v 17), as one with whom the hills and birds were made to join in singing the praise of God (vv 18–19). His kingdom was made secure, he was given decisiveness in speech *(faṣl al-khiṭāb).* He is put to the test by two disputants who intrude into his sanctuary.[8] For a fault revealed by, or committed in the course of facing that test, he repents/turns again to God. He is given a reward: 'Indeed he is close to Us, and has a beautiful dwelling place' *(innahu 'indanā la-zulfā wa-ḥusnā ma'āb)* (v 25). He is appointed vicegerent, and commanded to rule with justice.

Solomon is presented as David's son. He is described thus: 'How excellent a servant! He was constantly turned [to Us]' *(ni'ma'l-'abdu innahu awwāb)* (v 30). On one occasion, when fine horses were paraded before him, he forgot the performance of a prayer. As soon as he realized this fault, he had them slaughtered so that never again would they distract him from his Lord. He was then put to the test by a figure placed on his throne.[9] For a fault that this test discloses, he repents, addressing God, 'My Lord forgive me, and give me a kingdom such as none may have after me, you indeed are the Bestower *(al-Wahhāb).*' He is rewarded: the winds are made subject to him and the demons *(shayāṭīn)* put in servitude and made subject to him. This is God's gift. Of him too God says, 'Indeed he is close to Us, and has a beautiful dwelling' *(innahu 'indanā la-zulfā wa-ḥusnā ma'āb)* (v 40).

Job is presented without any introduction. Muḥammad is told directly to tell the words Job uttered when he called out in pain, what God said to him, and how he obeyed. God says of him, 'Indeed We found him patient *(ṣābiran).* How excellent a servant! He was constantly turned [to Us]' (v 44).

---

8. See AH Johns, 'David and Bathsheba: A Case Study in the Exegesis of Qur'anic Storytelling'. MIDEO, 19 (1989) pp 225–266 for a discussion of this scene.
9. A common interpretation of this verse is that Solomon captured the daughter of the king of Sidon, and that since she grieved for her father so much, he had the demons at his service to make an image of him to which she and her maid-servants paid homage, leading unwittingly to the tolerance of idolatry under his roof.

The pericope closes with a panorama of a further six prophets, divided, like the first periscope, divided into two groups of three: Abraham, Isaac and Jacob who are 'possessed of strength and perception' (*ūlī 'l-aydī wa'l-abṣār)* (vv 45–46), and Ishmael, Elisha and Dhū'l-Kifl also 'of the elect', thus bringing the pericope to an end with a resounding hymnodic close.

Although grouped together, there are marked differences between these three prophets. David and Solomon are father and son, but have different charisms. Only David has mountains and hills sing in praise of God with him. Unlike Solomon, he does not address God directly with a request. He exchanges words only with the intruders who confront him. There is a difference in the tests to which he and David are put, likewise there is a nuanced variation in the statement of their personal qualities. David is 'endued with strength, he was constantly turned [to us]' *(dhā'l-aydi innahu awwāb).* Solomon is 'How excellent a servant! He was constantly turned [to us]' *(ni'ma'l 'abdu, innahu awwāb)* (v 30).

The contrast with Job could hardly be greater. There are no introductory phrases to identify him or to highlight his qualities. His words are a cry of pain. In contrast to Solomon he makes no request, unlike David he does not repent of any sin. God answers his cry with two commands, his obedience to both of which is ellipted. The laudatory formulae bestowed on him follow, not precede, the account given of him.

Notwithstanding these differences however, there are common elements in the vocabulary that define their qualities and rewards that stress their community. David is 'endued with strength' *(dhā'l-aydī)* and Solomon is 'How excellent a servant!' *(ni'ma'l- 'abdu)* but of both God says, 'he was constantly turned [to Us]' *(innahu awwāb).* They both receive the same reward, God saying of each of them, 'Indeed he is close to Us, and has a beautiful dwelling' (vv 25 and 40). By the same token, Abraham, Isaac and Jacob echo David's quality of being *dhā'l-aydī* by being ūlī*'l-aydī wa'l-abṣār.*

Job is honoured by the same laudatory phrase as Solomon: 'How excellent a servant! He was constantly turned [to Us]' *(ni'ma'l-abdu, innahu awwāb),* the second half of which is also said of David. He is distinguished from the others in this pericope because of him alone God says, 'Indeed We found him patient *(ṣābiran)'* (v 44). Further, the phrase 'for those with understanding' *(li-ūlī'l-albāb)* (v 43) describing those for whom God's design stands as a lesson, is perhaps a cue to the qualities exemplified by Abraham, Isaac and Jacob, numbered among those 'possessing strength and perception' *(ūlī 'l-aydī wa'l-abṣār)* (v 45).

The pericope is still to be heard in the wider context of the sura. The sura opens presenting a scene of the arrogance and dissension of those to whom the prophet Muḥammad is preaching, and the divine warning directed to them: 'How many of [former] ages have We destroyed before them! They cried out [when destruction fell upon them] but then was no time for deliverance' *(kam ahlakna min qablihim min qarnin fa-nādaw, wa-lāta ḥina manāṣin)* (v 3). It presents some of the objections they make to the vocation of Muḥammad, answered by God's words of scorn as He says to the prophet, ' . . . do they have [charge of] the treasure chests of the mercy of your Lord, The Mighty, *(al-'Azīz)*, the Bestower *(al-Wahhāb)*?' This is followed by warnings made from the examples of past peoples who had rejected the prophets sent to them and who had been destroyed.

In this early part of the sura there are two words that establish themes developed later. The first is *nādaw* in 'They cried out [when destruction fell upon them] but then was no time for deliverance' *(fa-nādaw wa-lāta ḥina manāṣin)* (v 3). This word does not occur again until Job's call, presented with dramatic suddenness in the phrase *idh nādā rabbahu* (v 41), presenting a message with stark clarity: If the unbelievers cry out when punishment overwhelms them, their cry is in vain. When a prophet (or a believer) enduring suffering cries out, he is heard at once. Thus when Job calls he is given a healing spring, and what had been taken from him when he was put to the test is restored.

The second is the designation of God as *al-Wahhāb* (v 9). The Meccans reject Muḥammad because they refuse to believe that a revelation be given to one of themselves. They are astonished that a warner, one of their own should come to them—*wa-'ajibū an jā'ahum mundhirun minhum* (v 4). God proclaims that He is *al-'Azīz,*the Mighty, *al-Wahhāb,*the Bestower. In other words it is in His nature to give, and He can give the gift of prophecy to whomever He wills. This quality of God as Bestower is reiterated through the sura. God *gave* David Solomon—*wa-wahabnā li-Dāwūd Sulaymān* (v 30). Solomon asks *to be given* a kingdom—*hab lī mulkan.* When addressing God with a request, he appeals to Him as *al-Wahhāb* (v 35). Power over the wind and the demons, God says, is *Our gift* to Solomon—*'atā'unā* (v 39). God *gave* back to Job what had been taken from him—*wa-wahabnā lahu ahlahu wa-mithlahum ma'ahum.*

A feature of the structure of the sura is the alternation of passages referring to the Meccans, Mubammad's contemporaries, with passages relating to former prophets. Thus after an account of the fate of past peoples who have been destroyed—the people of Noah, the tribe of 'Ād, and others (vv 12–13), the Qur'an tells of the mockery of Mubammad's contemporaries when warned of the coming of a day of reckoning: 'Lord of ours, give us our requittal now, before the day of reckoning' *(rabbanā, 'ajjil lanā qiṣṭanā qabla yawmi'l-ḥisāb)* (v 16), concerning which God commands the prophet 'Be patient in the face of what they say' *(iṣbir 'alā ma yaqūlūna)* (v 17), telling him to recall/tell of David, the first of the group of three prophets to which Job belongs. It is this word, *iṣbir,* which is picked up in the words in praise of Job, 'Indeed We found him patient *(ṣābiran)*' (v 44), for Patience/Endurance is Job's special charism as a supreme model for Muḥammad as he faces rejection by his people.

II
Sūrat al-Anbiyā' (Q 21)

The pericope from al-Anbiyā' may be rendered as follows:

83. And [tell too of] Job when he called his Lord
 'Hurt has indeed touched me
 though You are most merciful of the merciful.'
84. We thereupon heard him, so removed what of hurt was upon him.
 We brought [back] to him his kinsfolk and the like of them with them as a mercy from Our presence
 and as a lesson to [Our] servants.

Like the previous pericope in Sūrat Ṣād (Q 38), it is introduced by the ellipted command to the prophet—*udhkur yā Muḥammad*—to tell of Job when he called to his Lord. Job's words are given in direct speech. He calls, 'Hurt *(ḍurr)* has indeed touched me,' and continues 'though You are most merciful of the merciful' *(wa-anta arḥamu'l-rāḥimīn).* God then tells of his response to Job's cry: 'We thereupon heard him *(fa'stajabnāhu)* so removed what of hurt was upon him' (v 84), and tells how He brought [back] to him his kin and the like of them with them as a mercy and a lesson.

It is briefer than the corresponding pericope in Ṣād. It echoes it, and the key words and phrases it repeats reinforce and enrich the hearer's memory of Job in the earlier (in order of revelation) pericope, and thereby heightens awareness of the presence of Job as a personality in the Qur'an. Heard together with the earlier pericope, it gives the episode a stereophonic, and indeed stereoscopic, dimension.

Nevertheless it has its own character established by variations that occur at word and phrase level. They may be summarized as follows:

(i) 'Hurt has indeed touched me' *(annī massanī al-ḍurr)* in place of 'Satan has indeed touched me' *(annī massanī al-shayṭān).*

(ii) 'with hurt' *(bi-ḍurrin),*in place of 'with hardship and pain' *(bi-nuṣbin wa-'adhāb).*

(iii) Additional phrase: 'though You are most merciful of the merciful' *(wa-anta arḥamu'l-rāḥimīn).*

(iv) Omission of 'Scuff with your foot' *(urkuḍ bi-rijlika).*

(v) Additional phrase: 'We thereupon heard him, then removed what of hurt was upon him' *(fa' stajabnāhu fa-kashafnā mā bihi min ḍurrin).*

(vi) 'We brought [back] to him' *(ataynāhu)* for 'We gave him' *(wahabnāhu).*

(vii) 'from Our presence' *(min 'indinā)* for 'from Us' *(minnā).*

(viii) 'to [Our]servants' *(li-'ibād)* for 'to those with understanding' *(li-ūlī'l-albāb).*

(ix) Absence of second command.

(x) Absence of laudatory formulae.

So closely are the two presentations of the scene bonded, that variations at phrase level, the absences and additions, may be regarded as ellipses in the one and complements in the other. Thus the juxtaposition of the additional phrase, 'though You are most merciful of the merciful·, not occurring in Ṣād, is not inconsistent with the tone of the cry in Ṣād, and may well be considered as a complement, realizing an ellipsis. At the same time its presence in al-Anbiyā' suggests a different perspective to Job's cry, investing it with an element of reproach. For how or why should the 'most merciful of the merciful' allow 'hurt' to touch His servant?

Likewise the divine command 'Scuff with your foot' (38:42) may in al-Anbiya' be regarded as ellipted, whereas God's words, 'We thereupon heard him *(fa'stajabnāhu)* and lifted the hurt that was upon him' may be regarded as a complement, as He continues the narrative in al-Anbiyā', supplying what is ellipted in Ṣād. So just as the command 'Scuff with your foot' is present in the minds of hearers of al-Anbiyā' who know the Ṣād presentation, so 'We thereupon heard him' is present in the minds of listeners to the Ṣād presentation of the scene. In other words, in Ṣād, the emphasis is on the means by which God removed the 'hardship' *(nuṣb)* and 'pain' *('adhāb)* suffered by Job, that is, by providing the spring, whereas in al-Anbiyā', it is on God's removing the hurt—*fa-kashafnā mā bihi min ḍurrin.*

The word *ḍurr* when added to *nuṣb* and *'adhāb* generalises and internalises the degree of Job's agony. In addition it has a particular resonance in Qur'anic discourse, and evokes an association with other verses which have to do with the power of God, and the helplessness of idols as in '. . . *min duni'llāhi* mā *lā yanfa'ukum shay'an wa-lā yaḍurrukum*' (21:66).

Job's cry 'Hurt has touched me' in place of 'Satan has touched me . . .' shifts the agency of the act from Satan, but, without accusing God of causing the pain, recognises that only God can lift it. This opens the way for a different perspective on Job's suffering, and God's relationship to it.

Part two of the corresponding verses in Ṣād is not repeated, and the passage concludes with a nuanced reprise of the significance of the restoration of Job's kin. The lesson it teaches being 'for [Our] servants', a variation leaving open the possibility for a different perspective and shift of emphasis.

As in Ṣād, the immediate context of the Job verses is provided by an assembly of other prophets. They are Moses and Aaron (v 48) Abraham (vv 51-71), Lot (v 71) Isaac and Jacob (vv 72–73), Lot (vv 74–75), Noah (vv 76–77), David and Solomon (vv. 78–79), David (v 80), Solomon (vv 81–82), Job (vv 83–84), Ishmael, Idrīs and Dhū'l-Kifl (vv 85–86), Dhū'I-Nūn/Jonah (vv 87–88), Zechariah and John (vv 89–90), and Jesus son of Mary (91). This assembly can be divided into two groups, those of whom God speaks directly, and those whom He commands Muhammad to tell of. They may also be divided between those concerning whom narrative information, or at least an allusion to an event in their lives, is given, and those mentioned only by name, but honoured by laudatory formulae either as a preamble or a conclusion.

God Himself speaking in narrative mode introduces the assembly of prophets. He tells first of Moses and Aaron. He celebrates them for His gift to them of *al-furqān* to guide the children of Israel (v 48), but does not here allude to any events in their prophetic careers which are copiously attested elsewhere in the Qur'an.

He next tells of Abraham, presenting in narrative form a central episode in his career as a prophet (vv 51–71). Abraham having been given the right path to fol1ow *(rushdahu)* (v 51), thereupon challenges his father and kin: 'What are these images to which you devote yourselves?' (v 52), and proclaims to them, 'Your Lord is the Lord of the heavens and the earth. He created them' (v 56). They spurn him. He smashes their idols, and when they protest, he defeats them in argument, asking 'Do you then worship in place of God what can neither help you *(yanfa'ukum)* nor hurt you *(yaḍurrukum)?'* (v 66). To vindicate the honour of their gods they attempt to burn him, but God intervenes, commanding the fire: 'Be cool' (v 69), and, speaking in narrative mode. declares, 'We saved him *(najjaynāhu).*' He tells of Lot, that he was brought with Abraham 'to the land We have blessed' (v 71), of Isaac and Jacob, that 'We gave them to him (Abraham)', and that 'all [of them] We made righteous' *(wa-ja'alnā'l-ṣāliḥīn,)* (v 72). Here no information is given concerning them. They are mentioned only in association with Abraham.

From here on (v 74), there is an extended parade of prophets, Job among them, their names grammatically *manṣūb,* each being introduced by an ellipted *udhkur yā Muḥammad* ('Tell of/recall, Muḥammad').

A summary of each is as follows:

Lot. We gave him wisdom *(ḥukm)* and understanding*('ilm).* He preached against the wickedness of his people. They threatened him. We saved him *(najjaynāhu* v 74). His reward is that 'We took him into Our mercy. Indeed, he is of the righteous' *(wa-adkhalnāhu fī raḥmatinā, innahu mina'l-ṣāliḥīn)* (v 75).

Noah. He called *(nādā)* to his Lord (when his people rejected him). God replies, 'So We heard him' *(fa'stajabnāhu),* and saved him *(najjaynahu)* and his kin from the awesome disaster, when his people were drowned (vv 76–77).

David and Solomon. First they are mentioned together (vv 78–79). They were asked to give judgement in a case brought before them concerning sheep that had had strayed into and damaged a vineyard.[10] Each gave judgement, but the judgement given by Solomon was the wiser. God says, 'We gave each of them wisdom (*ḥukm*) and knowledge (*'ilm*).' Then they are spoken of individually.

David. The hills and the birds were made to celebrate God's praise with him (v 79), God teaches him the making of mail armour for protection in war (v 80).

Solomon. The tempestuous wind is made subject to his command (v 81), the demons are compelled to obey him. Solomon rules the wind, and directs the demons (*shayāṭīn*) to secure wealth and engage in construction (v 82).

Job. He called *(nādā)* to his Lord, 'Indeed hurt *(ḍurr)*has touched me, though You are most merciful of the merciful' (v 83). God replies, 'So We heard him *(fa'stajabnā lahu)* and removed what was of hurt from him' (v 84).

Ishmael, Idrīs and Dhu'l-Kifl. No narrative information is given, but God praises them, 'All were of the patient' *(kullun mina'l- ṣābirīn)* (v 85) and tells of their reward 'We took them into our mercy. Indeed they were of the righteous' *(wa-adkhalnāhum fī raḥmatinā, innahum mina'l-ṣāliḥīn)* (v 86).

Jonah. He departs in anger, thinking We have no power over him. He called out *(nādā)* in the darkness, 'There is no God but You. Glorious beyond compare are You!' *(lā ilāha illā anta, ṣubḥānaka).* God answers 'So We heard him *(fa'stajabnā lahu)* and saved him *(najjaynāhu)* from oppression' (v 87). God adds 'In like manner so We save *(nunjī)* those who believe'.

Zechariah. He called out *(nādā)* to his Lord 'Do not leave me alone when you are the best of inheritors'. God replies 'So We heard him *(fa'stajabnā lahu)* and gave him John' (v 90).

John. He vied with his father and mother in the performance of good deeds, they supplicated Us in fear and longing, they were devoted to us (v 90).

---

10. The components of this judgement are as follows: I. Sheep damage a field of corn/vineyard at night. 2. Leading to a dispute between owner of the sheep and the vineyard. 3. The matter is brought before David and Solomon. 4. David judges that the owner of the vineyard should take the sheep in compensation for the harm done. 5. Solomon judges that the owner of the field should take only the product of the sheep—milk, lambs, wool, etc, until the shepherd has repaired the damage done, and then the sheep are to be returned. David agrees that this is the wiser judgment.

Jesus son of Mary. He with his mother are made a sign to all the worlds (v 91).

The pericope exhibits a variety of structural devices. One already mentioned is the bipartite division between those prophets told of directly by God, and those by the words Muhammad is commanded to utter. Another is the distribution between those of whom narrative information is given, and those marked only by laudatory formulae. It is a device with considerable literary effect.

An example is in the narrative verses relating to Job (vv 83–84) and Jonah (vv 87–88) separated by the verse in praise of lshmael, ldrīs and Dhū'l-Kifl (v 85). Job and Jonah both cry out in anguish, and the verses devoted to each of them are of great emotional power. The intervening verse, one in praise of three other prophets, offers a brief relaxation of tension, and so doing adds to the impact of both. This verse however has an additional function. Ishmael, ldrīs and Dhu'1-Kifl are praised as being 'all of the patient' *(mina'l-ṣābirīn).* In this sura, the Job verses make no mention of his patience, so evident in Ṣād (38:44): 'Indeed We found him patient *(ṣābiran).*' The phrase *mina'l -ṣābirīn* occurring in the following verse serves as a cue to God's praise of Job's patience in Ṣād, and so, by proxy associates it with him here too. This may be compared with the reference to the demons *(shayāṭīn)* made subject to Solomon, and diving for him (v 82). The word *shayāṭīn* may likewise be heard as a cue to the role of Satan in Job's cry in Ṣād: 'Indeed Satan has touched me . . .' *(annī massanī al-shayṭānu . . .)* (38:41), thereby drawing attention to the role of Satan in Job's suffering.

The prophets in this assembly differ from one another in personality and the situation in which they are set. Moses and Aaron are given the *furqān* as a light and a reminder to the people of Israel; Abraham confronts the worship of idols; Lot condemns the wickedness of his people; David and Solomon play a role as judges; Job is touched by hurt; Jonah is in darkness; and Zechariah is distressed because he has no son.

Typologically Job, Jonah and Zechariah form a group. They have in common that they are not prophets who preach, are rejected, and vindicated when punishment falls on those who rejected them as are Lot, Noah, Abraham and Moses. They are not prophet-rulers like David and Solomon, they do not play a role in a grand scheme of reconciliation and the righting of wrong like Joseph. They are prophets who suffer. Yet they suffer in different ways, and for different reasons. Even though each gives a call in direct speech, each cry appeals to God in relation to his own needs. Job calls for relief from the hurt that has touched him - loss of property, family and physical affliction, Jonah is in darkness frustrated that his people had rejected him, and Zechariah appeals out of longing for an heir because otherwise, without a child of his own, his evil nephews would inherit from him, and destroy his spiritual patrimony.

Despite their diversity, however, the prophets are marked as a community sharing formulae of praise distributed among them within the pericope, and across sub-groupings within the pericope. Lot, David and Solomon are given *ḥukm* and *'ilm*. Lot, together with Ishmael, Idrīs and Dhū'l-Kifl have the reward expressed in the formula 'We took them into Our mercy' *(fa-adkhalnāhum fī raḥmatinā)* (vv 75 and 86). In addition, individuals among them have difficulties they endure. Noah, Job, Jonah and Zechariah all cried out *(nādā)* to their Lord, and God answers, saying of each of them, 'We heard him' *(fa'stajabnā lahu)*. Of Abraham, Lot, Noah and Jonah, He says, 'We saved *them'(najjaynāhum)*.Of Job, He says, 'We removed from him what of hurt was upon him' *(kashafnā mā bihi min ḍurrin)*. Of Zechariah, He says, 'We gave him John', *(wa-wahabnā lahu Yaḥyā)* (v 89).

Further the pericope is held together as a unit by parallelisms in its internal structure. Thus when God tells of prophets, He speaks first of Moses, and then of an earlier prophet, Abraham. When, at the next stage of the pericope, He commands Muḥammad to continue telling of them, the first to be mentioned is Lot, and then an earlier prophet, Noah.

The first narrative in the pericope is of Abraham, a prophet to whom an unexpected child is born in old age. The final narrative is of Zechariah, likewise, a prophet who begets a child in old age. Jesus, the final prophet mentioned, represents the ultimate miracle, being born of Mary by divine decree without a human father.

This pericope too is an organic part of the sura in which it is set, and the meaning of the pericope is enhanced and a further dimension disclosed when it is heard in this wider context. It opens with a warning of the coming of an eschatological moment (v 1), and the disregard of humankind for such warnings (v 2). It tells of the insults of those who reject the prophet: 'Is this other than a human being like yourselves?'(v 3),

And ' . . . he has made it up, he is a poet, so let him bring us a sign as did those who were formerly sent' (v 5). It answers the objections made to Muḥammad, telling of the destruction of previous peoples who had rejected the messengers sent to them, affirming that all these messengers too had been human, and as humans had needed food to live by, and that none of them were immortal (v 8).

From such points of departure, the sura articulates a number of general themes that are individualized in the prophets presented in the pericope. It proclaims that the message God has revealed to Muhammad and to every messenger before him is 'We have not sent any prophet before you without revealing to him that there is no God but I, so worship Me' *(annahu Iā ilāha illā ana, fa'budūnī)* (v 25), and the testimony to this is the cry of Jonah in the great fish, 'There is no god but You. Glorious beyond compare are You!' by virtue of which God saves him from the triple darknesses (v 87).

It proclaims God as 'The Merciful'. The unbelievers are denounced because they claim the Merciful has taken a son (v 26), and because they 'disbelieve what is said of the Merciful' (v 36). In rebuttal, Muhammad is commanded to warn them: 'Who can guard you by day or night from the Merciful' (v 42). And a proof of God's mercy is His answer to Job's call for relief from hurt *(ḍurr)* as soon as he addresses God as 'most merciful of the merciful'. God's mercy is realized and proved by this response to Job, thereby highlighting the example Job gives of how one should appeal to Him, and his consequent status among the prophets.

Yet another theme is that humankind are put to the test. God addresses humankind, 'We try you, putting you to the test, by evil and by good *(wa-nablūkum bi'l-sharri wa' l-khayri fiṭnatan)* and to us you shal1 be returned' (v 35). Job is the ultimate example of a prophet put to the test, and the Ṣād pericope tells how David and Solomon too were put to the test (38:24 and 34).

Yet although God puts individuals to the test, He is a saving God. When His prophets are in difficulties or danger, He saves them. This is enunciated clearly, God proclaiming, 'We were true to Our promise to them, so We saved them *(anjaynāhum)* [from those who rejected them] together with whomever We willed [to save], and We destroyed the wicked' (v 9). This word *anjaynā* establishes a perspective of the divine economy of revelation that has a specific place here. The verse makes the general statement that God is faithful to His promise (to his prophets). In the pericope in which Job has his place are individual examples of God acting as faithful to His promise to save. He saves Abraham (v 71), Lot (v 74), Noah (v 76) and Jonah (v 88). He lifts the hurt from Job (v 84), and He gives Zechariah a son (v 90).

There are numerous links between the earlier part of the sura and the prophetic pericope, both direct and indirect. Another example is to be seen in two verses telling how the evildoers react when they feel God's punishment: Behold, they scuff *(yarkuḍūna) the* ground in flight from it' (v 12), and God orders them with biting sarcasm, 'Do not scuff *(la tarkuḍū)* the ground in flight . . .' (v 13). The Job verses in this sura do not present the divine command to Job in Ṣād 'Scuff with your foot' *(urkuḍ bi-rijlika),* which may be regarded as ellipted in this more concentrated presentation of the scene. This phrase may be taken as a cue to this ellipsis. The negative command to the evildoers—'Do not scuff' *(lā tarkuḍū)*—suggests the positive command to Job—'Scuff with your foot' *(urkuḍ bi-rijlika)*—being sufficient to realize the ellipsis in the minds of hearers of the Qur'an, highlighting the different destiny of the good and the wicked by the dichotomy between those who scuff the ground in flight, and are told it will avail them nothing, and Job who is commanded to scuff the ground, who obeys, and whose hurt is relieved by the water of the spring.

The sura tells of the touch of *'adhāb* that may come from God to the evil doers, thereby highlighting the paradox that Satan can touch Job with *nuṣb wa-'adhāb,* and that *ḍurr* can touch him. The punishment is so terrible that 'the unbelievers if touched by a breath of God's punishment cry out, but there will be no relief for them.' It tells that Muhammad warns them by an inspiration given to him, albeit they are deaf to his warning (v 45): 'Yet if even a breath of the Lord's punishment were to touch them, they would say "Woe are we, indeed we have been sinners"' *(wa-la-in massathum nafhatun min 'adhābi rabbika la-yaqūlunna yā waylanā innā kunnā ḥālimīn)* (v 46). Harm touches Job—he is put to the test by what is evil, he calls out, and is saved.

III
Sūrat al-An'ām (6)

The pericope from al-An'ām may be rendered as follows:

83. Thus was Our argument
We gave it to Abraham to convince his people.
We raise in rank whom We will
-Your Lord is indeed Wise, Knowing.
84. We gave to him Isaac and Jacob.
each of them We guided.
And before them We guided Noah,
and of his posterity We guided
David, Solomon, Job
Joseph, Moses and Aaron
-thus We reward those who do good-
85. together with Zechariah and John, Jesus and Elias,
-each of them was one of the righteous -
86. and Ishmael and Elisha, Jonah and Lot
-each of them We favoured above all others -
87. and of their forebears and posterity and brethren
-We chose them and guided them to a straight path.
88. Thus is the guidance of God
He guides with it whom of His servants He will
Yet were they to put aught beside Him,
all they have done would fall from them.
89. It is these to whom We have given
the Book, Wisdom and Prophecy
yet if these were to disbelieve in it,
then We would give it to a people who would not be faithless to it.
90. It is these whom God has guided,
So [Muḥammad] follow the guidance given them.

Here too, Job is included in an assembly of prophets, although after Jacob the chronology is structured to emphasize their commonality and community, showing Job as a member of this community, with his own place and charism.

The pericope is addressed to Muḥammad. From one standpoint its words are of comfort and support addressed to him, telling him that just as these were prophets, so is he. But equally important, it is a hymnodic celebration of God's providence. It celebrates God for His wisdom in choosing them—'Your Lord is indeed Wise and Knowing'; it tells of the guidance and blessing given to them, their kin and their families—'thus do We reward those who do good'. It emphasises their virtues—'each of them was righteous', and how they had been raised to a rank above all other humankind—'each of them We favoured above all others.' It gives the reminder, however that if they had failed to lived up to their calling and the guidance they had been given, they would be as nothing. Muḥammad is urged to follow the guidance given them.

There is no narrative component, but the pericope is far more than a list of names. Central to its theme are the opening words 'Thus was Our argument *(ḥujja)'*. This argument is that given by God to Abraham, and by which He guided Isaac and Jacob and the subsequent prophets such as David and Solomon, Job and Joseph, Moses and Aaron (v 84), Zechariah, John, Jesus and Elias (v 85), Ishmael, Elisha. Jonah and Lot, as prior to them He had guided Noah, and finally Muḥammad. Of them He says. 'We chose them and guided them to a straight path' (v 87).

It states that God, in choosing them, does so with wisdom and knowledge, for as He says of Himself, 'Your Lord is indeed Wise *(ḥakīm),* Knowing *'alīm)'* (v 83). This verse indicates the qualities God reveals in choosing these prophets, His closeness to them and them to Him, giving them the wisdom *(ḥukm)* and knowledge *('ilm)* by which they are qualified to implement their calling as prophets.

The bestowal of these gifts on Lot (21:74) serves to establish a thread in the skein that binds this pericope with the others in which Job is mentioned. Alongside it are formulae such as 'each of them was of the righteous' (21:75 and 21:86) and rhyming phrases of complementary meaning, for example 'thus do We reward those who do good' *(wa-kadhālika najī 'l-muḥsinīn)* (v 84) which suggests 'thus do We save those who believe' *(wa-kadhālika nunjī'l-mu'minīn)* (21:88). Within the pericope then is a network of acoustic and semantic relationships with the other pericopes presenting the assemblies of prophets among whom Job is celebrated.

It has however a distinctive character and perspective. This character derives from the immediately preceding verses (vv 74–83) that tell what the argument *(ḥujja)* given to Abraham was, why it was given to him, how it was given to him, and the use to which it was put.

It was given to Abraham to confront his father and his people with the challenge. 'Do you regard your idols as gods?' (v 74). God had guided him to it by showing him the kingdom of the heavens and the earth in which to search for his Lord. Abraham accordingly looked for his Lord in the heavens. First he chose a star. But the star set. and he said, 'I cannot love what sets' (v 76). He then turned to the moon when he saw it rising. But that too set, and he exclaimed, 'If my Lord goes not guide me, *(la-in lam yahdinī)* I will surely be of those who go astray' (v 77). So he turned to the sun when it rose, exclaiming, 'This is my Lord, this is most great' (v 78). But when the sun in its tum set, he realised they were finite, impermanent, and contingent, and so turned from them to the eternal God who had made them. He declared himself innocent of the polytheism of his people, and uttered his profession of faith: 'Indeed I tum my face to the one who created the heavens and the earth, pure in faith' *(innī wajjahtu wajhiya li'l-ladhī faṭara '/-samāwāti wa'l-arḍa ḥanīfan).* That the stars, moon and sun set, but God does not set, is the argument *(ḥujja)* (v 83), to which God guided Abraham, and by which He had given him his superiority.

This argument then, that all natural phenomena set but God does not, is God's guidance to Abraham, 'We gave him Isaac and Jacob, all (three) of them We guided—We guided Noah before him, and all of his descendants', also guided by the argument, and 'thereby strengthened with it Noah, David, Solomon, Job and Joseph . . . (v 84)'

When his people argued *(ḥājjūhu)* against his rejection of their idol-worship he replied to them with it, asking 'Do you argue with me concerning God, when he has guided me?' *(hadānī)* (v 80) God's guidance to him, leading him to realize the truth through his experience of gods that failed, is the ultimate argument, is indeed *al-ḥujja al-bāligha* (v 149).

The point is emphasised in 'Thus is guidance. By it God guides whomever of [the Prophets] His servants that He wills (v 88) . . . those are they to whom We gave the Book, Wisdom and Prophethood' (v 89).

The wider context of the sura further orchestrates and enhances this great scene, for it is rich with words and phrases carrying resonances that contribute to the dramatic effectiveness, and the celebratory power, of these verses.

The sura opens with a majestic exordium in praise of God 'Creator of the heavens and the earth, and of darkness and light (v 1), Who created humankind from clay' (v 2). Yet humankind, despite the blessings given them, refused to accept His messengers, and were destroyed in punishment (vv 4–6). Yet despite this wicked rejection of His Messengers, God is Merciful (v I 2).

These verses set out the themes central to the Islamic revelation: the unicity and power of God, the role of the prophets, and the coming of a Day of Judgment. In the presentation of these themes there is discernible and perceptible the tension between the prophet and those who disbelieve. There are the objections of the unbelievers, the words given to Muḥammad to rebut them, as well to encourage him and comfort him in the face of rejection. Underlying these tensions is a basic rhythm of predication, rejection, riposte, and reassurance, presented in real time as it depicts the experience of the prophet Muḥammad, and in virtual time, with the focus on Abraham's confrontation with his father, coming to a climax in the argument *(ḥujja)* given to Abraham and to which to all the prophets were guided.

The verses carrying these tensions are rich and diverse in the themes and continuities they establish, and include words and phrases which, to use a musical term, if 'leaned' on, reveal an underlying theme. Alongside their role in their individual contexts, they establish resonances that draw attention to and underline these themes in the other periscopes discussed.

The opening verse 'Praise be to God who created the heavens and the Earth' *(al- (ḥamdu li'llāhi'l-ladhī khalaqa'l-samāwāti wa'l-arḍa)* sounds a chord that proclaims the majesty of the Creator. The phrase 'the heavens and the earth' *(al-samāwāti wa'l- arḍa)* becomes a leitmotif through later verses triggering echoes of the opening doxology, and preparing the ground for the apotheosis. Its path can be followed through the sura: 'He it is who is in the heavens and the earth' (v 3); 'Say, "To whom belongs what is in the heavens and the earth?"' (v 12); 'and Say, "Should I take as my protector any other than God, Creator of the heavens and the earth?"' (v 14); 'And it is He who created the heavens and the earth in truth' (v 73); and yet again when God shows Abraham 'the kingdom of the heavens and the earth' (v 75), leading to both a resolution and climax when Abraham having seen star, moon and sun set, turns to the one who created 'the heavens and the earth' (v 79).

God's mercy is another theme carried through the earlier part of the sura. If this word is 'leaned' upon, then the mention of Job in the assembly of prophets draws attention to the mercy he has received, told of in Ṣād and al-Anbiyā'.

This mercy is presented from a number of aspects. God defines Himself by His mercy: 'He has written mercy *(raḥma)* of Himself' (v 12). God commands Muhammad to tell those who believe that their sins will be forgiven, saying to them, 'Peace be with you, for Your Lord has written mercy *(raḥma)* of Himself' (v 54). God celebrates the exercise of His mercy, 'If a person is spared the punishment of a terrible day, God has had mercy on him' *(fa-qad raḥimahu)* (v 16). Only God can save from harm. God is 'pardoning, merciful' *(ghafūrun raḥīm)* (v 54).

It is in the light of such references to God's mercy, and of course they are not limited to this sura, that Job's appeal to God in al-Anbiyā' for relief from his anguish is to be heard, as he addresses Him, 'You are most merciful of the merciful' (21:84), and God's response to him, when addressed by this appellative, healing him and restoring to him his family and the like of them with them, in Ṣād 'as a mercy from Us' *(raḥmatan minnā)* (38:43) and 'as a mercy from Our presence' *(min 'indinā)* (21:84). Such mercy is not for Job alone. It is also given to Job's fellow prophets on whom God bestows it, and to all who ask for it. The word *raḥma* serves as a cue to the words said of Lot, 'We took him into Our mercy' *(fī rahmatinā)* (21:75), and of lshmael, Idrīs and Dhū'l-Kifl, 'We took them into Our mercy *(fī raḥmatinā)*. Indeed they were of the righteous' (21:86).

Job is suffering because hurt *(ḍurr)* has touched him (21:83), and Satan has touched him with hardship *(nuṣb)* and pain *('adhāb)* (38:41). Human pain as a consequence of divine punishment for disbelief is another theme in the sura. God, speaking in narrative mode, warns, 'those who disbelieve in Our signs are deaf and dumb in darkness' (v 39). He commands the prophet to say to the unbelieving Meccans, 'If the pain *('adhāb)* of God comes upon you, or the Hour overwhelms you, do you call on other than God' (v 40)? 'Those who deny our signs, pain *('adhāb)* will touch them for their disobedience' (v 49), and 'Are we to call on something other than God that can neither help us nor hurt us' (v 71)? God punishes with the infliction of pain *('adhāb)* and only God can remove it. Only God can help or hurt.

But the prophets too suffer pain. Satan touched Job with hardship and pain (38:41), hurt touched him (21:83). The inclusion of Job among the assembly of prophets in this pericope is a cue to the verses telling of his suffering. Muḥammad too suffers hurt because his people reject him. So God addresses him, 'If God touches you *(yamsaska)* with hurt *(ḍurr)* there is no one to remove it other than He' (6:17).

And Job, recognizing that there is no remover *(kāshif)* of hurt *(ḍurr)* other than God, calls to Him, 'Hurt *(al-ḍurr)* has indeed touched me' (21:83), and God, in narrative mode, tells how He answered this cry: 'So We removed *(kashafnā)* his hurt from him' (21:84). In effect, Job is shown as a role model for the prophet Muḥammad in this sura, just as he was in Ṣād when God told him when the unbelievers mocked him to be 'patient *(iṣbir)* in face of what they say' (38:17), and said of Job, 'Indeed, We found him patient *(ṣābiran)*' (38:44). There is an internal aspect of the hurt afflicting Job brought out by the use of the word *kashafnā,* when Job's hurt is removed, instead of *najjaynā* which tells of rescue from physical danger, as was the case with Abraham from the fire (21:71), Lot from an attack by his people (21:74), Noah from the great disaster (21:76) and Jonah from the darkness (21:87).

Yet another theme articulated by the"leaning' on such key words is guidance. 'God, had He willed, could have gathered them all [that is, the Meccan unbelievers] under Guidance *(al-hudā)*' (6:31). Were the prophet to join those who worship false gods, he is told to say, 'I would not then have been one of those guided' (v 56). He is to say to the unbelievers, 'Indeed the guidance *(hudā)* of God is guidance indeed.' Abraham was guided to the argument he needed to confront his father and his kin (6:71). When the moon he has taken as his Lord fails him, Abraham declares: 'Unless my Lord guide me . . .' (v 77). God indeed declares of all the prophets mentioned here 'We guided them' (v 87); in leading them to Abraham's argument 'such is His guidance' (v 88), and 'the prophets are those God has guided' (v 90).

This guidance is given to each according to his situation and needs. In the case of Abraham it had been for the argument to confront his father and his kin. In the case of Job, it was in relation to his particular trial, to call to God as the Merciful.

IV
Sūrat al-Nisā' (4)

The fourth pericope, al-Nisā' (4), vv 163–165, may be rendered as follows:

163. We have made a revelation to you as We made it
to Noah and those succeeding him,
and we made it to Abraham, Ishmael, Isaac, Jacob
and his descendants Jesus, Job,
Jonah, Aaron, and Solomon,
-to David We gave the psalms! -
164. and to messengers We have told you of previously,
and to messengers of whom We have not told you
to Moses God spoke directly! -
165. messengers giving good tiding and warning
that humankind might have no claim *(ḥujja)* against God once
messengers [had been sent them],
God being mighty and wise.

Here again, Job has a place among an assembly of prophets largely coinciding with those named in the other pericopes, but extended to include prophets of whom Muḥammad has not been told, a phrase which adds a universalistic dimension to the pericope. These prophets are presented as messengers giving good tidings and warning without reference to any of their words or deeds. There are no laudatory formulae, they are presented solely as recipients of revelation. David and Moses are indeed distinguished by parenthetic statements, but only to articulate and stress this emphasis: 'to David We gave the psalms' indicating the Book given to him, and 'to Moses God spoke directly' indicating the mode of revelation made to him.

Again, not all of them are presented in chronological order. After Jacob, they are arrayed not according to era, but in a patterned constellation, that places Jesus before Job and Jonah, Solomon before David, and separates Aaron from Moses.

The pericope in al-An'ām was primarily celebratory in character, praising the guidance and the argument given to Abraham and the prophets stemming from him, to which line Muḥammad too belonged. In these verses the emphasis is a justification of the divine economy by which God made revelations to His prophets, and the continuity through time of these revelations from Noah to Muḥammad the final prophet: that humankind might have no argument *(ḥujja)* against God by being able to claim ignorance of His will. Messengers had been sent to them.

It has a number of associations with the other suras in which Job has a place and with the prophets whose company he shared, in particular Abraham, David and Moses. The parenthetic phrase 'to David We gave the psalms' brings to mind the scene of the hills and the birds singing with David told of in Ṣād (vv I 8–19) and al-Anbiyā' (v 79) The parenthetic phrase relating to Moses 'to Moses God spoke directly' carries resonances of what God said of Moses and Aaron in al-Anbiyā': 'We gave Moses and Aaron the *furqān,* a light and a reminder' (v 48). The climax of the pericope however is the divine declaration as to why all such messengers were sent: that humankind might have no argument *(ḥujja)* against God when they face His judgement. This declaration derives its power from the the associations of the word *ḥujja.* God gave Abraham an argument *(ḥujja)* (6:83) by which he was able to confront the idol-worship of his father and his people, and this *ḥujja* that God gave to Abraham, and is passed from him to the prophets who follow him, including Job, is incontrovertible. There is however no argument *(ḥujja)* humankind can bring against God when He judges them.

AI-Nisā' is a Madinan sura, and as such has an important role as a source for the bases and principles of Islamic Law, in particular family law and the position, rights and responsibilities of women. Nevertheless it resounds with the great themes of the Islamic revelation epitomized in a verse such as 'God, there is no God but He! Most surely He will assemble you on the Day of Resurrection, there is no doubt of it' (v 87). Indeed, alongside its legal provisions, the sura offers a kaleidoscope of doxology, prophetology and theodicy. There are however two verses which give a special place to Abraham, and as such relate directly to the pericope under discussion, and through it to the Abraham scene presented in al-An'ām and the guidance passed on to Job.

The first is 'For We gave the descendants of Abraham the Book and Wisdom, and We gave them a mighty kingdom' (v 4:54).

The second is 'Who is better as to his religion than one who submits his face *(wajhahu)* to God, he being one who follows the religion of Abraham in total sincerity *(ḥanīfan)*
[or as a *ḥan*īf. Now God took Abraham as a friend (v 125).'

The first establishes the position of Abraham, and prepares the way for the naming of some of his prophetic progeny in this pericope. The second, by its reference to 'one who submits his face *(wajhahu)* to God', and 'who follows the religion of Abraham . . . *ḥanīfan*', by the placing of the two words *wajhahu* and *ḥanīfan* in close proximity here, trigger in the mind an association with Abraham's profession of faith, 'I indeed, I tum my face to Him who created the heavens and the earth in total sincerity *(ḥanīfan)*' (6:74), after God had given him His *ḥujja* by showing him the setting of star, moon and sun (6:76–68).

But there is yet another thread to the skein. The wonderful phrase 'God took Abraham as a friend' has a direct association with the phrase in the pericope 'to Moses God spoke directly' (*wa-kallama'llāhu Mūsā taklīman)* (v 164). These two prophets have titles that place them above all others except Muḥammad. That of Moses, *kalīm Allāh,* the man with whom God spoke, and that of Abraham *khalīl Allāh,* God's friend.

Conclusion

In a very real sense, this essay is experimental. It has selected a 'lesser' prophet, Job, and examined the verses in which he is named in an attempt to explore how in the Qur'an he is nevertheless presented to such powerful effect. It does not claim to be comprehensive, but tries to show something of the vitality and moral passion concentrated in so few verses.

Each of the four pericopes in which he occurs either contributes information about him or reveals a perspective of his position within the community of prophets, and his relation to the prophetic experience of Muḥammad. Viewed synoptically, they provide a model in miniature of the rhetorical genius of the Qur'an, especially when illumined by the intertextualities within them uncovered by Ṭabarī in his exegesis of the Job episode in al-Anbiyā'.

A closer study, however, immediately involves the student in the broader context to which these attestations of Job belong. For it then becomes clear that his profile as a prophet is achieved not simply because he is an individual referred to only four times, but the way he is integrated into the community of prophets, individuals various in their vocations and styles, but sharing a common vocation and a common reward.

As a result, the richness of their vocation, and the varying emphases of the divine messages given them is revealed, and the account they give of themselves shows and justifies Muḥammad's role and vocation. For the prophets complement each other, and references to and narratives about them establish an echoing grove in which the distinctive features of Job's prophetic charism are highlighted are brought into focus.

It has been shown that the pericopes themselves display Job and his prophet companions from varying perspectives, and emphasise different themes.

In the Ṣād pericope a leading theme is that belief is a prior condition for a call to God to be answered. Thus Solomon first asked pardon for a fault, and then asked God for a kingdom such as that possessed by none other, addressing Him as *al-Wahhāb,* the Bestower. He was given power of the Winds and the Demons (38:35–38). Job called for relief from hardship and pain. His call was likewise answered, and God gave back to him the kin that had been taken from him, and restored his health (38:41–43). But when the time came for the unbelievers who rejected the prophet to call for relief, with their punishment about to overwhelm them, their call would be in vain (38:3).

In al-Anbiyā', a dominant theme is of God being true to His word to His prophets, hearing them when they call, saving them from physical danger, removing from them oppression *(al-ghamm),* and bestowing on them what they ask.

In al-An'ām, emphasis is on the argument that God gives to His prophets to enable them to answer those who reject His message, and the assurance that they will be guided to the argument *(ḥujja),* that they need.

In al-Nisā', a predominant theme is the continuity and consistency of God's sending messengers sent to numbers of peoples, some of them known, some unknown, to numerous communities ensure that His will is known, and that accordingly humankind cannot claim ignorance as an excuse for their sinfulness.

All four pericopes are interrelated, acoustically, conceptually and thematically; often the essence of a wide range of associations being concentrated in a single word, which if 'leaned on' discloses a richness and diversity of meanings at a number of levels.

In each, Job is shown from a different perspective, one which throws an individual light both on himself, and the other prophets with whom he is associated, in accordance with the character of the pericope. Thus in

Ṣād, he is placed with David and Solomon at the core of a symmetrically structured pericope. The difference between him and them (David and Solomon are prophet-kings), draws attention to the special character of his prophetic vocation, as one who suffers and whose message is preached by his endurance of undeserved suffering. God says of him, 'Indeed We found him patient *(ṣābiran)'* (38:44). As such he is presented as a role model for Muḥammad in the face of rejection, to whom God says, 'Be patient *(iṣbir)* in face of what they say' (38:17).

In al-Anbiyā', among a more extended panorama of prophets, he is associated in particular with two of them, Jonah and Zechariah, whose calls to God, like his, are given in direct speech. All three are in torment, but for different reasons. Job, because of the hurt that is upon him (loss of family and the pain of disease); Jonah, in the darkness of the great fish after his outburst of anger, and Zechariah in anguish at his childlessness.

Each of them addresses God in his own way. Job calls on Him as 'Most merciful of the merciful' *(arḥamu'l-rāḥimīn)* Jonah calls on him in a formula of recognition and praise 'There is no God but You. Glorious beyond compare are You!' *(lā ilāha illā anta, subhānaka)* and Zechariah calls on Him as 'Best of inheritors' *(khayru'l-warithīn).* God answers each of them). The hurt is taken from Job, Jonah is saved from the darkness that oppresses him *(al-ghamm),* and Zechariah is given a son.

As in Ṣād, Job then is one of a core group of three prophets which forms a focus of tension in the pericope dominated by Abraham's rejection of all gods but God, Abraham the very model of those rescued from danger when God saved him from the fire (2I:7I).

In al-An'ām, Job's inclusion in the assembly of the prophets, in addition to his place among those to whom God has given guidance, serves as a reminder that just as Muḥammad suffered one kind of hurt because those to whom he preached the Qur'an rejected him, so too did one of his predecessors, Job, a brother prophet, who was touched by hurt *(ḍurr),* and whom Satan had touched with hardship and pain. Yet without complaint he called to the 'Most merciful of the merciful'.

In al-Nisā', Job is included in a celebratory concourse of prophets eulogizing God's providence in the sending of prophets. It is marked by a striking reversal of context in the use of the word *ḥujja.* God sent the prophets so that man may have no *ḥujja* against God. And this is sufficient to trigger a memory of the *ḥujja* that God gave to Abraham (6:83) that no human opponent could refute.

Together these four pericopes show Job as a member of the community of prophets with a distinctive place and a special charism: that he should suffer without knowing why, and, instead of despairing, cry to God for relief, trusting in God as the Merciful. This is what makes him, and God's answer to him, a lesson *(dhikrā)* 'to those with understanding' (38:43).

This discussion has barely touched the surface of the richness, complexities and shared intertextualities within these four pericopes. It is sufficient however to show how elaborate is the intertext sustained and informed by the exegetic tradition, and the network of themes and verbal echoes that are one aspect of the unity of the Qur'an. They yield spiritual meanings and disclose some of the aspects of the literary dimension of the Qur'an once the relevant reference points that point to its internal structure have been discovered. It may therefore bring to light hitherto unexplored aspects of the literary and religious dynamics of the Qur'an.

It has also drawn attention to some of the ways in which the Qur'an as Divine Revelation plays its role in the religious life and imagination of the Muslim world. It prompts reflection on the varying responses to revelation in different, albeit related, religious traditions. Divine revelation presents an image of a spiritual rhythm which both clashes and harmonizes with the human rhythm of everyday life. In the Western tradition, memories of the exemplars by which this rhythm is carried are presented visually through a complex iconography that serves as an emotional trigger to activate and so realize these rhythms. In the Islamic tradition, however, which largely rejects the role of visual images, such emotional triggers are provided by the language of the Qur'an, which in its own way presents vivid verbal images of natural phenomena, of heaven and hell, of the confrontation of good and evil, and the human situation in general, without the need to depict the physical characteristics of any individual. It is the language itself which constitutes the iconic tradition. Not a single word can be taken or heard in isolation. All represent nuclei of meaning that are cumulative and cohere, serving as triggers to activate the profoundest depths of religious consciousness.[11]

---

11. These ideas are suggested by a paragraph in *History of Italian Art, Volume Two,* translated by Claire Dory (Oxford: Polity Press, 1994), 129, brought to my attention by Dr AD Street.

Jonah in the Qur'an
An Essay on Thematic Counter-point

Jonah, along with Idrīs, Ilyās (Elias), al-Yasaʿ Dhū'l-Kifl and Ayyūb (Job)[1]. may be reckoned among the 'lesser' prophets presented in the Qur'an. He is mentioned in only six pericopes, and in all, only eighteen verses, in which he is variously identified as Yūnus, Dhū'l-Nūn or Ṣāḥib al-Ḥūt, have a place for him. In *Sūrat al-Nisā'* (4:143) he is named amid a panorama of the prophets as *one to whom God sent a revelation*, in *Sūrat al-Anʿām* (6:86) likewise he has a place among his fellow prophets as *one of those guided*, and in whose footsteps Muhammad was sent. In four other suras however there are verses that give narrative information. *Sūrat Yūnus* (10:98) tells of the repentance of his people, *Sūrat al-Anbiyā'*(21:87) proclaims the doxology he utters in the great fish (Q 21:87–88), *Sūrat al-Ṣāffāt* (37:139–48) gives an account of the salient events of his mission and *Sūrat al-Qalam* ((68:48–50) presents him to Muḥammad as an example from which to take heed. All these attestations are integral to the sura in which they occur, and have a strategic place within it.

They present Jonah from different perspectives, and as such are the principal concern of this essay. An accepted order of revelation

1. See AH Johns, 1999, 'Narrative, Intertext and Allusion in the Qur'anic Presentation of Job' in *Journal of Qur'anic Studies*, Volume I, Issue I, Centre of Islamic Studies, SOAS, University of London, 1/1 (1999): 1–25.

of these suras is Q 68:48–50, 37:139–148, 21:87–88, and 10:98.[2] While recognising that there are incongruences between the order of revelation and that of the *muṣḥaf*, the discussion follows this order—taking *Sūrat al-Qala*m as the earliest—and is set within the parameters and insights of the 'classical' tradition of exegesis established by Muqātil b Sulaymān.[3] Even when short, they resonate with each other, within and across the suras in which they occur, and contribute to teachings central to the Islamic tradition.

Few scholars outside the Muslim tradition have reflected on these Qur'anic attestations of Jonah. An entry in the *Encyclopaedia of Islam*[4] (sv 'Yūnus b Mattai') for example, after pointing out that a prophet swallowed by a fish would naturally be of interest, is devoted for the most part to accounts given of him in *qiṣaṣ al-anbiyā'* (stories of the prophets—the title is generic), without reference to his role in the Qur'an. Yet in fact he has a status rooted in the Qur'an itself. His place in Muslim life and devotion reflects this, and his name is popular among Muslim men. This essay suggests some of the ways in which his presence, personality and charism are embedded in the texture of the Qur'an, and show him with a role that goes far beyond what a simple verse count might suggest.

The narrative information in these suras may be summarised as follows: Revelations were made to Jonah as they were to Muḥammad and the other prophets in whose company he is named. He was sent to a people. They rejected him. He departed from them in anger on board a heavily laden boat, thinking God would not hold him to

2. Proposed orders of revelation of these suras (N - Noeldeke, B - Blachere C - Cairo [Khedival muṣḥaf]

sura		N	B	C
4	al-Nisā'	100	102	90
6	al An'ām	89	91	55
10	Yūnus	84	86	51
21	al-Anbiyā'	65	67	73
37	al-Ṣāffāt	50	52	56
68	al-Qalam	18	51	2

3. Muqātil b. Sulaymān (d 767 CE) In *al-Asbāḥ wa'l-nasā'ir fī'l-Qur'an al-karīm*, ed. 'Abd Allāh Maḥmūd Shiḥāta. (Cairo, al-Hāya'a al-misriyya al-'āmma li'l-kitāb, 1975. (Reference to verse).

4. *Shorter Encyclopaedia of Islam* (Leiden: EJ Brill, 1953).

account. Identified by the drawing of lots, he was thrown overboard and swallowed by a great fish, as one deserving of blame (*mulīm*, *cf* Q 37:139–142). Within the fish he called out to God, 'There is no God but You, Glorious beyond compare are You' (*cf* Q 21:87). Had he not done so he would have remained within the fish until the Day of Resurrection (*cf* Q 37:144). His call was heard (*cf* Q 21:88). He was cast on the shore, sick (*saqīm cf* Q 37:145). But for a grace of his Lord, he would have been 'in disgrace' (*madhmūm cf* Q 68:49). God made a gourd grow over him (to the height of a tree) to give him shelter (*cf* Q 37:146). God chose him (*cf* Q 68:50) and sent him to a city of a hundred thousand or more (*cf* Q 37:148). They believed (*cf* Q 37:148). The pain of shame in this world was lifted from them (*cf* Q 10:98).

The Jonah pericope in *sūrat al-Qalam* may be rendered

48 *So, [Muḥammad], await in patience the judgement of your Lord,*
Do not be as the Man of the Fish.
[Recall] when he called [his Lord]
burdened with heavy sorrow.
49 *Had a grace of his Lord not come upon him,*
he would have been cast on the barren shore in disgrace.
50 *But his Lord then chose him,*
and set him among the righteous.

The information given is succinct but lucid. The words are addressed directly to the Muḥammad. He is enjoined to be patient until his Lord gives judgement (*ḥukm*). He is not to be as was the 'Man of the Fish', a *laqab*, that both identifies Jonah, and serves to evoke the events of the Jonah story. Yet in it there are paradoxical elements. One is that Jonah. a fellow prophet, is presented to Muḥammad as a man whose example he should *not* follow. It implies that if Muḥammad does not *await in patience* the judgement of his Lord, he, like Jonah may be in *disgrace*. How could Muḥammad have been in need of such a warning? In what respects was the experience of Jonah appropriate to Muḥammad, and how might it offer a lesson to him?

This pericope then, while at first sight straightforward, has built into it a number of complexities which are resolved only when it is considered in the context of the sura as a whole: a sura in which Jonah is the only prophet named, and the pericope in which his name occurs is in the final verses (Q 68:48–50)

For our purposes, the sura may be seen as comprising an Introduction, three distinct but inter-related episodes and a Conclusion. Together they make a seamless unit

The Introduction (vv 1–16) is an intense and highly charged address to the Prophet, prefaced in v. 1 by the resonances of the Arabic letter *Nūn*, followed by the oath

By the Pen, and what they inscribe

Leading to the words directed to the Prophet,

You, by the grace of your Lord are not possessed (*majnūn* Q 68:2).

He is assured that he has a great mission and will receive a great reward. Time will show who it is who is possessed (*cf* Q 68:6). He is not to compromise with anyone who rejects the Qur'an or asks him to modify its content. In a glittering cascade of rhetoric, God enjoins the Prophet

Do not give in to a contemptible swearer of oaths
a slanderer bearing calumnies,
an obstructor of good, a perpetrator of evil -
violent and wicked in his false claims (Q 68:10–13).

The individual in question, by some identified as Ibn al-Mughīra, is one who takes pride in his wealth and sons, one who when verses from the Qur'an, are recited to him, dismisses them as *tales of ancient times* (Q 68:15). Using a demotic language register, God declares,

We will smite him on the snout (*sa-nasimuhu 'alā'l-khurṭūm* Q 68:16).

***

The first episode is the refusal of the unbelieving Meccans to leave remnants of their harvest to be gleaned by the poor. The lesson they should learn is presented as a parable. It tells how their forebears had been punished for their wickedness as had been the owners of a plantation (*aṣḥāb al-janna*)[5] in the Yemen. One evening, they decided to harvest their crops the following morning (*muṣbiḥina*

5. To reproduce the play on words in English, *janna* should be rendered garden. The exigencies of English render plantation, which is within the semantic spread of *janna*, more appropriate.

v17). They did so *without making an exception* (*yastathnūna* v 18). As a punishment, while they slept, their crops were destroyed by a fiery whirlwind and the plantation became (*aṣbaḥat* v 20) as though harvested. As they set out in the morning (*muṣbihīna* v 21) they called aloud to each other, 'Let us go to harvest our crops', and as they moved towards the plantation whispered, 'Let no poor man gain anything from our plantation today'.

When they arrived, they found it blackened and bare. Startled, they thought they had come to the wrong place, that they were astray (*ḍāllūn* v 26) When they realised that it was indeed their field, they exclaimed 'We have been deprived (*maḥrūmūn*)[of our harvest]'. The wisest of them said to them, 'Did I not urge you to glorify the incomparability of your Lord (*tusabbiḥūna* v 28) [before setting out]?'. In other words, they had both neglected their duty to God, and planned to defraud the poor of their right. They recognized this, and thereupon exclaimed, *Glorious beyond compare is our Lord* (*subḥāna rabbinā* Q 68:26)'.[6] They blamed themselves for the wrong they had done. They yearned for their Lord, asking His pardon, and prayed that what had been taken from them as punishment would be restored on their repentance. The ending draws a further lesson from the parable. The punishment they had received was in this world; punishment in the hereafter would be far more painful. However they should remember that for those who fear their Lord, are gardens of delight (*jannāti'l-na'īm* v 34).

The story is multi-layered, and presented with a vividness that gives it a gem like character. There are a number of features that enhance its message. Among them is economy in the use of language, and dramatic shifts from narrative to direct speech:

19 *A fiery whirlwind from your Lord*
swept over the plantation as they slept.
20 *It became (aṣbaḥat) as though harvested [black and bare].*
21 *They called to each other as morning came (muṣbiḥīna)*
'Get early to your plantation if you intend to harvest it'
22 *As they set out they whispered to each other,*
'Let no poor man enter it today at your expense'.

6. 'Declare, Glorious beyond compare is God'. (Not, be it noted, 'Why did you not say *bi'smillāh*, or *in shā' Allāh*' At this they say, *subḥāna rabbinā innā kunnā ḥālimīna*.

The direct speech with the antithesis between shouting and whispering, highlights the contrast between the openly proclaimed good act, of going to harvest, and the concealed wicked intention of depriving the poor of their right to glean. It likewise heightens the impact of their shock at the sight of their plantation, when they exclaim,

> *We are astray* (*ḍāllūn* v 26)

An exquisite effect is achieved by the close paronamasia between the *ṣ.b.ḥ* and *s.b.ḥ.*, between *muṣbiḥīn, aṣbaḥat muṣbiḥīn* and *subḥān Allāhi* (*tusabbiḥūna*). The difference between *ṣād* and *sīn* creates a dissonance which heightens the distinction between their evil intentions, as they set out bent on defrauding the poor of their traditional rights, and the redemption of the wrong they had intended. Another device is the final vowel contrast in two structurally identical verses to highlight a contrast in idea. After their 'conversion' the owners of the plantation confess they have been evildoers *(ḥālimīn* v 29), oppressors (*ṭāghīn* v 31) of the poor. But having repented of their wrongdoing, they are now yearning (*rāghibūn* v 33) for their Lord. Up to the moment they uttered it, their intentions had been evil. Their utterance of this prayer (which has a thematic role through the entire Jonah story) shows they have realized that they have done wrong.

There is a double-entendre in the owners' exclamation, *innā la-ḍāllūn* (v 26)—*We are astray*—They have not come to the wrong place. But they are *ḍāllūn - astray* in that they were intending to do wrong. And there is an irony in their declaration that they have been deprived (*maḥrūmūn* v 27) of their harvest. For (as Muqātil puts it) they had intended to deprive the poor of the fruits of their right to glean, to take up 'what the eye has missed, the sickle passed over, and been blown by the wind'[7]

The phrase *wa lā yastathnūna* is significant. It is the only occurrence of this form of the root *th.n.y.* in the Qur'an. Literally it means, 'Without making an exception'. Muqātil b Sulaymān, understands it as declaring the intention to do something without saying *in shā' Allāh—If God wills.*[8] There are however other interpretations, among them 'Without leaving aside remnants of what they had harvested for

7. Muqātil *al-Asbāḥ* 4:405
8. Muqātil *al-Asbāḥ* 4:406

the gleaners,'[9] noted by Rāzī, although he does not give weight to this view.[10] The highlighting of this wicked act implies that the Meccans the pericope addresses were guilty not only of rejecting Muḥammad, but of oppressing the poor, and for this too they will be punished.[11] Finally, there is a delicate cue to marking the beginning and ending of the parable. It opens with the word *janna* in *aṣḥāb al-janna* (v 17) and closes with *jannāti'l-na'īm* (v 34),

***

The second episode presents questions Muḥammad is to put to the unbelieving Meccans (vv 35–43). The first of these is central to Islamic theodicy,

> *'Would We then treat those who submit themselves [to God]*
> *as [We do] those who do evil ?* (Q 68:35)

refers back to the lesson of of the parable, and confronts the Meccans' rejection of the resurrection with the question, 'Does God treat the good and the evil alike?' Since denial of the resurrection would entail the answer 'Yes', God presents further questions for Muḥammad to put to them,

> *What is it with you*
> *How can you so judge (taḥkumūn* v 36)*?*
> *Is it that you have a Book you study*
> *in which you find such a doctrine].*
> *Can you find in it anything you choose]?*
> *Do you have an oath by which to bind Us*
> *[valid] until the Day of Resurrection:*
> *that whatever you judge (taḥkumūn)*
> *to be the case [is so?])* (v 39)

---

9. Rāzī, TK 30:88.
10. Professor Mustansir Mir suggests that this is a counterpart to the injunction in Leviticus 19:9, noting that the requirement to say *in shā'Allāh* prior to any formulation of intention, was not introduced until a sura later in order of revelation.
11. As in *Sūrat al-Mā'ūn* (107): vv 1-2 *a rayta'l-ladhī yukadhdhibu bi'l-dīn.*

Further Muḥammad is to challenge them to say what allies they have to support them in their claim. Treatment of the issue concludes with an account of what will befall them on Judgement Day, when

> *Their eyes will be cast down (khāshiʿatan abṣāruhum* v 43)
> *shame will overwhelm them*

***

The third episode (which is central to the whole Joah story) concerns Muhammad's response to the rejection of his message and the Qur'an, and God's counsel to him. (vv 44–50),

> *Leave Me with those who deny this revelation.*
> *We will take them step by step*
> *from where they do not know* (Q 68:44)

assuring him

> *I will give them respite for a while!*
> *My design is firm* (Q 68:45).

Two rhetorical questions follow:

> *Are you asking a payment from them* (Q 68:46)
> *and so are a burden to them?*
> *Is it they who own the unseen world*
> *so can write of it [what they will]?* (Q 68:47)

building up to the climactic verses,

> *Leave me then with those who disbelieve* (Q 68:44) . . .
> *I will give them respite for a while* (Q 68:45) . . .
> *So then, [Muhammad] await in patience* . . .
> *Do not be as the Man of the Fish* (Q 68:48),

The conclusion (vv 51–52) is brief, bringing the sura to a triumphal close, reminding the Prophet that God knows the hatred the Meccans have for him,

> *Those who disbelieve—the hating*
> *glare in their glances (abṣārihim)*
> *could set you sprawling!* (v 51)

> *When they hear the Qur'an recited*
> *They say he is indeed possessed (majnūn* Q 68:51)

But God responds with the ringing reassurance

> *It is nothing less than a Recitation for all the worlds* (68:52).

*****

Although the treatment of the content of each episode is distinctive, the sura has a seamless continuity, illumined and enhanced by a variety of stylistic features. One is its name, *al-Qalam*, 'The Pen'. It is taken up and re-iterated in the oaths of the first verse, *By the Pen, and by what they inscribe* (*wa'l-qalam wa mā yasṭurūn* v 1). Those who inscribe are the angels who write as God directs them. The verse contrasts their humility and obedience with the arrogance of the unbelievers of whom God scornfully asks,

> '*Is it that they own the unseen world* (*al-ghayb*)
> *so can write of it [what they will]?*' (Q 68:47)

Another is the repetition, echoing or paraphrasing key words and phrases at strategic points in the sura. Among them are:

I Nūn (v1). This is one of the 'isolated letters' (*muqaṭṭa'āt*) that introduce a number of suras. Among the meanings the exegetic tradition proposes here is the lexical meaning, 'fish'. Muqātil explains it as the cosmic fish in the ocean beneath the lowest of the seven earths.[12] But it might equally be an allusion to the great fish that swallowed Jonah, 'Man of the Fish' (v 48) given that in *sūrat al-Anbiyā'* (21:86), Jonah is referred to as Dhū'i-Nūn, a synonym for *Ṣāḥib al-Ḥūt*.

ii *Bi ni'mati rabbika* (*by the grace of your Lord* v 2). It is '*by the grace of your Lord*' that you, Muḥammad, are not possessed (*majnūn*). By this phrase, Muḥammad is associated with Jonah, for it is because Jonah received *a grace (ni'matun) from his Lord* (v 49) that he was not cast onto the barren shore 'in disgrace' (*madhmūm*). This association is further strengthened by virtue of the rhyme between *majnūn* and *madhmūm*, that indirectly draws attention to a parallel between the two prophets: Muḥammad is *not possessed*, Jonah is *not in disgrace*.

12. Muqātil *al-Asbāḥ* 4:403.

The recurrence of the word *majnūn* in v 51 recalls the same insult in v 2, and its rhyme with *madhmūm* again evokes this parallel.

iii *Ajran (ghayra mamnūn)* (v 3). Muḥammad is promised *a reward* (*without limit*) for his faithful preaching. Later God asks the Prophet, pained by his people's rejection of him, *Are you are asking a payment (ajran) from them and so be a burden to them*? (Q 68:46)

iv *Man ḍalla ʿan sabīlihi* (*Whoever strays from His path* v 7). From discussion of the first issue, it is clear that the Meccans believe that Muhammad is astray, possessed. God's reply is that He knows best who has strayed from His path. The root *ḍ.l.l.* occurs in the exclamation of the owners of the plantation at the sight of their ravaged field—*indeed we are astray* (*ḍāllīn* v 26) thinking they have come to the wrong field.

v *Fa sa-tubṣiru wa yubṣirūna* (v 5) *Then you will see and they will see [the divine punishment]* v 5). This draws attention to the implied question that haunts Muḥammad, and gives occasion for the Meccans to jeer at him: When will the threatened punishment come? Only God knows the answer. But when it comes, the eyes of the unbelievers will be cast down *khāshiʿatan abṣāruhum* (v 43). And this has a chiastic relationship the words describing the scorn of the unbelievers,

> *Those who disbelieve—the hating*
> *glare in their glances (abṣārihim)*
> *could set you sprawling!* (v 51)

vi *Mannāʿin liʾl-khayr* (*an obstructor of good* v 13). This phrase is widely understood as 'one who hinders the acceptance of Islam'. Rāzī however gives as the first meaning, 'one stingy with his property.[13] The *Jalālayn* however take it further as meaning, 'One miserly with his property towards those who have a rightful claim on it, *bakhīl biʾl-māl ʿaniʾl-ḥuqūq*, thus foreshadowing the crime of the owners of the plantation who intended to deprive the poor of their gleanings,[14] thereby emphasizing this aspect of the lesson of the parable.

vii *aṣḥāb al-janna* (*owners of the plantation* v 17). This phrase cues the later reference to Jonah as *Ṣāḥib al-Ḥūt* (v 48) and draws

13. Rāzī, *TK* 30:84
14. Jalāl al- Dīn Muḥammad b. Aḥmad al- Mahalli & Jalāl al-Dīn ʿAbd al-Raḥmān b. Abī Bakr al-Suyūtī, *Tafsīr al-Jalalāyn*, Dār al-Shaʿb p, 503.

attention to the parallelism that just as these owners (*aṣḥāb*) formed an evil intention, but repented of it, so do the people to whom Jonah preached.

viii *Kayfa taḥkumūn* (*How can you so judge?* v 36). The root *ḥ.k.m.* has an important role in the buildup to the climax of the sura, *Await with patience the judgement of your Lord* (v 48). The unbelievers of Mecca make the arbitrary judgement that God treats good and bad alike as though whatever you judge (*taḥkumūna*) to be the case is so'(v 39). The word 'judge' here is used sarcastically, and so juxtaposed to the wisdom of the judgement (*ḥukm*) of his Lord that Muḥammad is urged to await.

Such internal continuities within and between the episodes could be elaborated further. More important than these individual points however is the pulsating resonance of the sound of *Nūn* with which the sura opens. The sound is established in verse 1 *Nūn . . . wa mā yasṭurūna*, continued in v 2 *mā anta bi ni'mati rabbika bi majnūn* in which the letter *nūn* is articulated four times thus heightening the impact of the insult *majnūn* (possessed), and extended into v 3, saying of the Prophet's reward that it is *ghayra mamnūn*. It continues through the sura like a 'drone' in music lying behind and pervading the individual points of continuity already mentioned. Of the sura's 52 verses, 42 end in *-n*, and the remaining ten with the homorganic sound *-m*. ringing the changes with the contrasting final vowels *ū* and *ī*. (Twenty eight final long vowel endings are *-ū*, the remainder *ī*.

In view of the continuity and acoustic dominance of the sound *nūn* in the sura, one might have expected that Jonah in v 48 would have been referred to as *Ṣāḥib al- Nūn,* which lexically would be appropriate. Instead he is *Ṣāḥib al-Ḥūt*. Given the phonetic environment, this is unexpected. The effect however is to highlight his importance in the sura, an importance further underlined by the triple repetition of the sound *ḥ* in verse 48 . . . the judgement of your Lord –(*li ḥukm rabbika) . . . like the Man of the Fish* (*ka Ṣāḥib al-Ḥ*ūt). The contrast between the final vowel of the last verse—*īn* in *dhikrun li'l-'ālamīn* with *ūn* in *innahu la majnūn* in the penultimate verse, adds significantly to the power of the ending, driving home the message that the owners of the plantation and the people of Jonah, the unbelievers of Mecca still have time to repent.

The essence of God's message is that Muḥammad should endure rejection patiently until his Lord makes His judgement. Jonah is presented to Muḥammad as a prophet offering an example he is not to follow. As Muqātil puts it, 'Do not ask for things to be brought on swiftly, as did Jonah, do not be angry, as he was, for if you are, you will be punished as he was, when he called on his Lord from the belly of the fish, as told of in *Sūrat al-Anbiyā'*.'[15]

*****

al-Sāffāt (37)

The pericope in *sūrat al-Ṣāffāt* may be rendered

139 *Indeed Jonah was one of the messengers!*
140 *[Tell of] when he fled on the heavily laden ship.*
141 *He took part in the drawing of lots. He was condemned.*
142 *The great fish swallowed him, he was deserving of blame*
143 *Had he not been of those praising the incomparable glory of God*
144 *he would have remained in its belly until the day all are to be raised.*
145 *Then We cast him onto the barren shore, sick.*
146 *We made grow over him a gourd tree.*
147 *We sent him to [a city of] a hundred thousand or more*
148 *and they believed, so We gave them lee time for a while* (vv 139–148).

It comes at the end of a sequence of prophets who have testified to te resurrection, the punishment in hell of those who deny it, and the rewards in Paradise for those who believe. It begins with Noah (75), and extends through Abraham, Ismail, Isaac, Moses and Aaron, on to Elias and Lot, over 63 verses, coming to its conclusion and climax with Jonah (See below).

The pericope complements and renders explicit much that is implicit in *al-Qalam*. It answers the question, why is Jonah referred to by the *laqab* 'Man of the Fish'? A great fish swallowed him. Why he was oppressed with sorrow? He had fled on a heavily laden ship. Why did the mercy of the Lord touch him so that he was not cast on the shore in disgrace (*madhmūm*)? Because he was of those who praised the incomparable glory of God (*min al-musabbiḥīn* v 143). For what did his Lord choose him? To send him to a city of a hundred thousand or more, whose inhabitants believed, and whose belief would be accepted.

15. Muqātil, *al-Asbāḥ* 4:412

The narrative is succinct and its sense clear. But there still remain questions that need answers if the full sense of the pericope and the lessons it teaches are to be fully understood. What were the circumstances of his flight? Why was there a drawing of lots? How did he come to be swallowed by a great fish? Why was he blameworthy (*mulīm*) when swallowed by it? What were the words of his prayer? Why was he sick on the barren shore? What is a gourd tree (an oxymoron)? What was the city to which he was sent?

The answers to some of these questions are in the Qur'an itself. Others are supplied from extra-qur'anic sources by the exegetic tradition. From the Qur'an we learn that Jonah had departed [from his mission] in anger, *mughāḍiban* (*Sūrat al-Anbiyā'* (21:85) and that within the Fish he had cried *Subḥānaka—Glorious beyond compare are You* From the exegetic tradition we learn that he fled because his people refused to believe, and the punishment threatened did not descend upon them, and that he did so without leave from his Lord; that lots were drawn because the ship was caught in a violent storm, and its mariners decided there was a runaway slave among those on board, and drew lots to decide which of the passengers it was. The drawing of lots discovered him, and he was thrown over-board; that he was cast on the barren shore, sick after his experience in the sea and in the fish, 'like a plucked fowl'. As a sign of God's care for him after his great prayer *Glorious beyond compare are you*, the gourd-plant grew up like a tree to shelter him, and a she-goat came to give him milk twice a day. Some say that this tree was a probative miracle for him. The city to which he was sent was Nineveh. When its people saw the punishment that threatened them, they repented and were spared.[16]

The literary shape of the pericope merits mention. It consists of brief verses, each presenting a vivid verbal picture. Each verse has a caesura: Jonah flees—to the heavily laden ship; he draws lots—he is condemned; the great fish swallows him—he is blameworthy, (*mulīm*). There is a shift in pace in verse 143 in which there is no caesura. The first part of the sense unit, a conditional clause '*Had he not been . . .*' fills the verse, and thus receives emphasis. The mid-verse caesura recurs in the following verse '*he would have remained in its belly - till the day all are to be raised* (v 144)). We cast him on the bare

16. For a convenient summary See Rāzī *TK*, 26:163–166, and *Jalalāyn*, 399.

shore—and he was sick; We made a tree to grow over him—a tree supporting a gourd; We sent him to one hundred thousand—or even more; then they believed—so We gave them lee time for a while.

Further, it is in two parts. Verses 139–144 tell of Jonah. But in verses 145–148 God speaks in the first person, indicating his decisive role in each stage of the action: We cast him on a barren shore, *nabadhnāhu* (v 145), We made to grow over him . . . *anbatnā 'alayhi* (v 146), We sent him . . . *wa arsalnāhu* (v 147). We gave them a lee-time of life *fa matta'nāhum* (v 147) This last verse is the climax of the pericope. But the pericope and Jonah within it, gain an enriched significance when set in the context of the sura as a whole, highlighting the thematic counterpoint it articulates in the other suras in which Jonah is mentioned.

The sura itself has two parts. The first (Q 37:1–4) presents in various forms of discourse the great themes of the Islamic revelation, prophecy, the divine unity, and the resurrection. The second, (Q 37:75–182), presents six prophets, (of whom Jonah is the last), who over the centuries before Muḥammad, have been sent to teach these doctrines.

It opens with a passage of blazing intensity:

By those arrayed in rows
By those who drive the clouds,
By those who recite the Qur'an
Your God is indeed one (37:1–2).

The pronoun 'those' is widely understand as referring to angels, and Muqātil, paraphrases the two verses 'By the angels standing in ranks, By the angels who scatter and guide the clouds, by the Angel who recites the counsel [that is the divine revelation to those who are sent]'.[17]

Q 37:1–10 is a prologemenon. In it angels play a crucial role: they stand guard over the stars, and keep at a distance the *jinn* who try to overhear the deliberations of the high council in heaven, driving off with a searing flame those who venture close.

It prepares the ground for a great question Muhammad is to commanded to put to the Meccans who deny God's power to restore the dead to life.

17. Muqātil, *al-Asbāḥ* 3:601

So *ask them then [Muḥammad]*
'Are they the mightiest of creation
or those [the angels] We have made?
Them We made merely of malleable clay '(Q 37:11).

The Meccans are arrogant. They glory in their wealth, and their sons (Q 68:14). This prologemenon shows them how puny they are in the great scheme of things. They should look at God's power manifest in the creation of the heavens, and reflect on the humility of the angelic beings who are so much greater than they.

The following verses rebut the accusation that the Qur'an is self-evident sorcery (*siḥr mubīn* v.15). And as the sura continues, it presents the reality of the resurrection through vivid pictures of events in heaven and hell, telling how those in hell quarrel with and blame each other for their fate, and reporting what those in heaven say to each other about the unbelievers (*cf* Q 37:27–30:50–58).

Part two presents a panorama of six of the prophets preceding Muḥammad referred to earlier. It is introduced by a bridge passage that gives a vivid account of the torments of Hell, tells how those in it are there because they found their fathers doing evil deeds, and followed their example,

71 *Before them,* [*i.e. the Meccans who reject Muḥammad*]
most of their forebears had gone astray
72 *even though We had sent among them warners.*
73 *So look on how those warned are punished,*
Apart from those who devoted themselves to God.

These prophets, (Jonah among them) all endured rejection, called on God for help, and their prayer was answered. The first is Noah (v 75). His call was heard. All who disbelieved in him were drowned, but he and his family were saved and, after the flood, his posterity repopulated the earth. The Noah pericope ends with the refrain,

'A blessing [from Us] rests on Noah throughout all the worlds' (Q 37: 79).

Abraham follows. He denounced the idol (and star) worship of his father and his people, and put to them the question,

'What do you think then

of the Lord of all the worlds'(*rabbi'l-'ālamīn* v 87).

He cast a glance at the stars [they worshipped] and said,

'Indeed, I am sick (*saqīm* v 89).

He went into their temple while they were absent, and smashed all their idols except the biggest. Realising that it was Abraham who had done this, they tried to burn him, but God saved him. He thereupon left his home and his people saying,

I am going [in search of] my Lord. He will guide me! (Q 37:99).

God then puts Abraham to the test, commanding him to sacrifice his son. The boy declares himself ready to accept God's will,

Do what you are commanded. You will find me,
if God so wills, of those who wait in patience (*min al-ṣābirīn*
Q 37:102).

At the last moment the son is saved from sacrifice, and a victim provided in his place (v.107). The episode closes with the formula that honored Noah,

A blessing [from Us] rests on Abraham' (v109).

In the same way God chose and cared for Moses and Aaron, saving them, as he had Noah, from the great disaster (v 115). This episode too concludes with the refrain,

A blessing [from Us] rests on Moses and Aaron' (Q 37:120).

The next prophet is Elias. Like Abraham, he puts a question to his people,

Do you call on Baal and abandon the best of creators,
God, your Lord, and Lord of your fathers? (Q 37:126).

But they rejected him, and were taken to judgement. It too concludes with the refrain,

'A blessing [from Us] rests on Elias (Q 37:125).

The story of Lot follows. He too with his family was saved from the destruction that overwhelmed his people. And by way of emphasis Muhammad is commanded to warn the Meccans of the fate of Lot's people,

> *You pass by them as travellers by morning* (*muḥbiḥīn* Q 37:137) *and by night* (Q 37:138).

This paves the way for Jonah, and the pericope devoted to him, apart from that of Abraham, is the longest. His appearance here marks a climactic point in the sura. He is set apart from his predecessors in relation to the tests to which they were put, the dangers from which they were saved, and the fates of the peoples to whom they preached in vain. Of them, he is the only one who turned aside from his call, was described as *mulīm*, and the only one whose people eventually heard his message, and were saved. All preached the coming of a Day of Resurrection and a punishment for disbelief. They taught the answer to the question Muhammad was ordered to put to the Meccans, Noah's people had rejected his message and were drowned. Abraham's father and people rejected his teaching, and attempted to burn him. Abraham set out to go to his Lord to be put to the test. Inevitably this draws attention to Jonah, for Jonah, on rejection by his people, attempted to flee from his commission. Abraham's son was ready for the sacrificial knife, the son who declared himself among those who wait in patience [for whatever God wills]. Moses and Aaron preached before Pharaoh. They were saved from him, and from the waters that drowned him and his armies. Elias warned his people against the worship of Baal. They rejected him, and were brought to judgement (*muhdarūn* v 127). Lot denounced the sinfulness of his people. They rejected his warning and threatened him. He and his family were saved from them, and from the punishment of fire from heaven that destroyed their people. All of these prophets were faithful, enduring in patience the tests to which they were put. All were saved from danger. The peoples who rejected them were destroyed by fire or water.

Only Jonah shirked his responsibility. Of them, he is the only one who turned aside from his mission, who is described as *mulīm* yet he too was saved from terrible dangers. Of them he is the only to have his fault redeemed by being one of those who proclaim the incomparable glory of God; he is the only one whose people eventually believed, whose belief availed them, and who were saved from disaster. His success is resoundingly expressed in the divine words, *We sent him [to a city of] 100,000 . . . They believed, so We gave them lee time for a while*(vv 145–148).

These prophets, including Jonah, all preached the coming of a punishment for disbelief, and the reality of the resurrection and judgement. They taught the answer to the question Muhammad was to put to the Meccans,

> '*Are they the mightiest of creation*
> *or those [the angels] We have made?* '(Q 37:11).

And it was these prophets too who provided the great NO to what is the second great question put to the Meccans who deny the divine unicity, when the prophet is commanded,

> *So ask them [Muhammad]*
> *Does your Lord have daughters but they have sons?*
> *Were they watching*
> *when we created the angels female?* (Q 37:149–150).

And if they persist in this claim, he is to ask them,

> *What is it with you?*
> *How can you decide (taḥkumūn) in this way?*
> *Will you not then reflect?* (Q 37:154–155)

The divine response to their blasphemy is

> *Glorious beyond compare is God (subḥāna'llāh)*
> *[exalted] above what they say of Him* (v 159),

the prayer by which Jonah was saved from imprisonment in the great fish until Judgement Day.

Finally, when the Meccans jeer at Muḥammad, asking why the threatened punishment for disbelief does not come, God counsels him,

> *Turn aside from them for a while*
> *and watch [what will befall them them]!*

For soon they will see [what is to come upon them]! (Q 37: 175–175),

and asks,

Is Our punishment something they can ask
to be brought down more swiftly upon them? (Q 37:176)

then reiterates the counsel of vv 174–175

Turn aside from them for a while
and watch [what will befall them them]!
For soon they will see [what is to come upon them!] (Q 37:178–178)

The sura comes to a triumphant conclusion with the same great prayer

Glorious beyond compare is your Lord
the Lord of Might (Q 37:180)

followed by the recurring refrain within the panorama of prophets,

A blessing [from Us] rests on the Messengers [We have sent] (Q 37:181),

and ends with the sublime laudation

al-ḥamdu li'llāhi rabbi'l-'ālamīn (Q 37:182)

As with *Sūrat al-Qalam*, there are links between the various parts and personalities in the sura which establish themes and serve as cues to a perception of its unitary character. It opens with the oath *wa'l-ṣaffāti ṣaffan By those arrayed in rows* (v 1), that is, as Muqātil interprets it, 'By the angels standing in ranks'.[18] These angels, great spiritual beings, reject the semi-divine status attributed to them by the unbelievers of Mecca. Later in the sura they are to say of themselves,

'We, we indeed stand in rows (ṣaffūn)
'We, we indeed are those

18. Muqātil, *al-Asbāḥ* 3:601.

> *who celebrate His incomparable glory* (*musabbiḥūn* Q 37: 165–166),

uttering the prayer of Jonah within the great fish (*cf* Q 37:143).

Muhammad is then commanded to put a question to the Meccan unbelievers to try to make them understand God's power to effect the resurrection. 'Which is the greater, themselves, made of clay, or the angels and firmament of the heavens? (v 11).

After the panorama of prophets and their teaching, he is commanded in identical words to ask these same Meccans (*fa'stiftihim*), Does God have daughters, whereas they prefer sons? Did they watch God making the angels female? (vv 149–150).

The refrain of praise, '*A blessing from Us rests on . . .*' follows the names of Noah (v 79), Abraham (v 109), Moses and Aaron (v 120), and Elias (v 123). It is part of the penultimate verse, contributing to the majesty of the conclusion of the sura '*A blessing [from Us] rests on the messengers We have sent* (Q 37:181).

Abraham, when he looked at the stars exclaimed '*Indeed I am sick*' (*saqīm* v 89), serving to draw attention to the role and experience of Jonah, when cast '*on the barren shore sick* (*saqīm*' v 145).

When Abraham told his son he was to be sacrificed, the son replied that if God so willed, he would have the patience to endure it (v 102). Patience was the quality Jonah needed in face of the rejection by his people and the delay in coming of the punishment he had threatened them. It is the quality enjoined in Muḥammad, when God says to him, *Turn aside from them for a while* (Q 37: 175, 179). In other words, *Await in patience the judgement of your Lord* (Q 68:48) that is, allow time to pass. And it is not far-fetched to see in the imperative *abṣir* (vv 175, 179) a paranomasia by metathesis of the radicals of *isbir*, as in *sūrat al-Qalam, fa'ṣbir li ḥukmi rabbika* (Q 68:48).

Abraham's question to his father and people *What then is your thinking of the Lord of the Worlds* (*fa mā ẓannukum bi rabbi'l-'ālamīn* v 87) receives its triumphant answer in the final verse *al ḥamdu li'llāhi rabbi'l- 'ālamīn* (Q 37:182)

In the story of Lot, there is an exquisite echo of the paranamosia that was noted in *sūrat al-Qalam*. This Lot pericope concludes with a reference to the ruins of the people of Sodom, reminding the Meccans, *You pass by [vestiges of] them as travellers by morning (muṣbiḥīn* v 137) *and by night* (v138). It is a cue to the appearance of Jonah, one of the *musabbiḥīn* (v143), those who praise the incomparability of God as the next prophet in the sequence. In Sūrat al-Qalam this imperfect paranamosia draws attention to the wickedness of the owners of the plantation who had set out in the morning (*muṣbiḥīn*) and found it destroyed because they had not uttered the laudatory prayer *subḥān Allāh—Glorious beyond compare is God.* Jonah was saved from confinement in the great fish until the Day of Resurrection because he was of the *musabbiḥīn,* those who utter this prayer.

Finally, the command to Muḥammad to leave the matter to God highlights a point of comparison with Jonah. Jonah had been frustrated and fled in anger because the punishment he threatened did not occur. Yet in the lee-time that God gave his people, they repented. Muḥammad is ordered to stand aside and wait. His people too may repent.

*****

al-Anbiyā'

The pericope in *sūrat al-Anbiyā'* may be rendered,

87 *[And tell of] Dhū'l-Nūn, when he departed enraged,*
thinking We would not exercise [Our] power over him.
Yet then he called in the darknesses [covering him]
'There is no God but You!
Glorious [beyond compare] are You!
I, indeed I have been of those who do wrong',
88 *and We answered him. We delivered him from the anguish [he was in].*
Thus do We save those who believe.

This pericope is distinguished by the intensity of its focus. The scene is of great power, though invoking a larger narrative. It provokes the questions: From where did Jonah depart? Why was he enraged (*mughāḍiban*)? Why should he imagine God would not exercise His almighty power over him? What were the darknesses within which he found himself? How could he have been of those who do wrong?

Answers to most of the questions are in the *Sūrat al-Ṣāffāt* pericope. He had fled on a heavily laden boat. In fleeing he thought that God would not exercise His almighty power over him, thus he had been blameworthy (*mulīm* Q 37:142) when swallowed by the great fish. He was trapped in the triple darkness of fish, sea and night. Yet his heart-rending call, *There is no God but You! Glorious beyond compare are You!* (v 87) penetrates these layers of darkness as he confesses that he is of those who have done wrong. His call is alluded to in *Sūrat al-Qalam* (Q 68:48) and *Sūrat al-Ṣāffāt* (Q 37:143) when he is numbered among those who proclaim the incomparable glory of God (*min al-musabbiḥīn*). This call and prayer illumines virtually every Qur'anic reference him.

The commentators raise and discuss a number of questions as to why he had this anger, and from whom he fled.[19] In a sense the answer is not important. The crucial point is that God answered his call and saved him from affliction (*al-ghamm*). In this, the pericope offers a distinctive aspect of God's providence. He saves His prophet even from a difficulty of his own making, once he calls on Him for help. And so He does for all who believe.

In *Sūrat al-Qalam*, Jonah is the only prophet named. In *Sūrat al-*Ṣāffāt his name concludes a sequence of six prophets. In both cases, his appearance is at a climactic point in the structure of the sura. In this sura (*al-Anbiyā'*), he is amid a panorama of prophets, in a way perhaps imaging his place in the huge fish. There are however, a number of other distinctive features about him and the ways in which he relates to other prophets.

In it, fifteen prophets are named: Abraham, and his son and grandson, Isaac and Jacob (Q 51:73); Lot (Q 21:74-5); Noah (Q 21:76–77); David and Solomon (Q 21:78-82); Job (Q.21:83–84), Ismael, Idrīs and Dhū'l-Kifl (Q 21:85–86), Jonah (vv 87–88); Zachariah and John (Q 21:89–90),and finally Jesus (Q 21:91–92). Of them, there are four who *called* (*nādā*) God: Noah (Q 21:76), Job (Q 21:83), Jonah (Q 21:87), and Zakariah (Q.21:89); four of whom God says *We answered him* (*fa'stajabnā lahu*): Noah (Q 21:76), Job (Q 21:84), Jonah (Q 21:88), and Zakariah (Q 21:90); five of whom God says *We saved him* (*najjaynāhu*): Abraham (Q 21:71), Lot (Q 21:74), Noah (Q 21:76), Job (periphrastically v76), and Jonah (Q 21:88); and three the words of whose call are given in direct speech: Job (Q 21:83). Jonah (Q 21:87) and Zakariah (Q 21:89)

Jonah, then, is one who calls, the words of whose call are presented in direct speech, whose call is answered, and who is saved from danger. His placing is significant. He is set between Job, who exclaimed, *Hurt has indeed touched me, though you are most merciful of the merciful*

19. Rāzī, *TK* 22:212-213

(Q 21:83) and Zachariah who called, *Do not leave me childless, when You are the best of inheritors* (Q 21:89). After the two verses telling of Job (Q 21:83–84), Ismael, Idrīs and Dhū'l-Kifl are mentioned in a single verse. It is said of them:

> *All were of those who endured in patience* (*min al-ṣābirīn* Q 21: 85).

Job is proverbial for his patience. There is thus a delicate emphasis on the fact that patience, when Jonah *departed enraged* (*mughāḍiban* Q 21:87), was a quality in which Jonah had fallen short.

Like Sūrat al-Ṣāffāt, this sura comprises two parts, the first focusing on the experience of Muḥammad and his encounters with the disbelieving Meccans, and the second on the prophets who preceded him. As the sura develops, it presents a dialectic of tension between objections to Muhammad's message, and the divine responses to them. And as with *Sūrat al-Qalam* and *Sūrat al-Ṣāffāt*, there is a complex articulation of motifs and personalities that resonate within it, and offer clues to its unity.

One such theme is the period of lee time between the threat of divine punishment and its execution, leading unbelievers to regard the threat as as empty. This was as much a challenge for Muḥammad as it was for Jonah. Thus the sura begins with the proclamation,

> *The Day of Reckoning for mankind draws near* (Q 21: 1)

But it has not yet come, hence the Meccans' contempt for Muhammad's warning, as they demand that it come quickly. So God says of them,

> *Humankind is formed of haste!*
> *I will show you My signs [in My own time]*
> *so do not ask that they be brought to you in haste* (Q 21:37).

Yet still they ask

> *When will be this threat be carried out*
> *if you speak the truth* ? (Q 21:38)

In part two of the sura, it is told that the messengers sent before Muhammad, were also mocked, but punishment nevertheless destroyed them (Q 21:41). The warning in Q 21:1 is sounded again in Q 21: 97, *This threat is true and is drawing near*. Nevertheless Muḥammad is commanded to say to them,

> *I do not know whether that with which you are threatened*
> *is close at hand or far off* (Q 21:109)

Since it fails to eventuate, the Meccans insult the prophet with impunity. They say his revelations are muddled dreams, that he is making the Qur'an up, that he is a poet. If he is a true prophet, let him bring a miracle (v 5). For,

> *When those who disbelieve see you,*
> *they take you as nothing but a joke* (Q 21: 36).

The demotic style of the utterance is savage and scarifying. Yet God reassures him,

> *The messengers sent before you were also scoffed at* (Q 21: 41),

to which Muqātil adds, 'Just as you Muhammad are scoffed at'. He comments that God is comforting His Prophet so that he will be patient and steadfast in face of their disbelief.[20]

The Meccans insist that *the Merciful has taken a son* (Q 21:36.) and the angels are daughters of God.

Yet the angels themselves

> *do not shrink from His service,*
> *and they do not falter [in their praise of Him]* (Q 21:19).
> *Night and day they proclaim*
> *His incomparable glory (yusabbiḥūnahu),*
> *they do so without faltering* (Q 21:20)

Further

> *They are His honoured servants*
> *They never utter a word before He speaks,*
> *They carry out His command* (Q 21:27).

They serve the God who had revealed to every prophet:

---

20. Muqātil, *al-Asbāḥ* 3: 80–81.

> *There is no God but I, so serve Me* (Q 21:25).

It is this divine self-proclamation that received its fitting acknowledgement in Jonah's great prayer from within the fish,

> *There is no god but You,*
> *Glorious beyond compare are You* (*subhānaka* Q 21:87)

God Himself reaffirms it,

> *I am your Lord, so serve Me* (Q v 92)

The celebration of God by the proclamation of His incomparable glory sounds through the sura. It is the prayer of the angels night and day, it is the phrase that God uses of Himself to declare His transcendence of what the Meccans say of Him (*cf* Q 21:22), it is given a cosmic dimension by the paranomasia (*yasbaḥūna—yusabbihuna*) in the verse,

> *He it is who created night and day, the sun and the moon,*
> *each follows its course in its own orbit* (*yasbaḥūna* Q 21:33)

It is the prayer that David sings in praise of his Lord, and which the hills and the birds sing with him (Q 21:79). And the expression *subḥānaka*—'Glorious beyond compare are You', is the prayer which lifts from Jonah the epithet *mulīm* of being blame-worthy, and ensures that he will not be cast on the barren shore in disgrace.

*****

Yūnus

The Sūrat Yūnus Pericope (Q 10:98) may be rendered:

> *There was no community (qarya) that believed*[21],
> *and its belief availed them*
> *other than the people of Jonah.*
> *When they believed*
> *the pain of shame in this world was lifted from them,*
> *and they were given*
> *a lee time of life in this world* (Q 10:98).

21. Rendering *law lā* as *mā*, the first option offered by Rāzī, *TK*, 17:164.

It is the briefest of the Jonah pericopes, just one verse of the 109 that make up the sura. Thus it is at first sight paradoxical that his name be given to it. The prose sense of the verse is clear: The people of Jonah were the only one of the *umam khāliya, the past peoples* who believed, and whose belief availed them. This fact alone is sufficient to give the verse special significance in the message of the Qur'an, in the preaching of Muḥammad, in his relationship to the people to whom he preached, and the timing of the punishment that would befall them if they rejected him.

The sura mentions three prophets: Noah (Q 10:71–73), Moses (with Aaron) (vv 75–93) and Jonah (v 98). All have in common that they were saved from death by water: Noah from the flood, Moses from the Red Sea, and Jonah from the ocean when he was thrown overboard.

Yet there is diversity in the destinies of those to whom they were sent. The people of Noah disbelieved and were drowned; Pharaoh professed belief as he was about to drown, but his belief did not avail him; Jonah's people at first disbelieved, but took advantage of the lee-time God gave them, believed, and their belief was accepted.

Such a patterning of the figures of these three prophets, and the destiny of those to whom they were sent, raises the profile of Jonah in the sura. It is raised further by the allusion to him in Q 10:94, in which God instructs Muḥammad that if he is any doubt about what is revealed to him, he should ask those who recite the Book (the Torah) that is the Jews. They know that Jonah, a prophet sent (like Muḥammad) to a non-Jewish people, was the only prophet sent to one of the *umam khāliya* (past peoples) who believed, as Q 10:98 testifies.

Q 10:98 presents the dialectic of debate between prophet and unbelievers. It defends the authenticity of the Qur'an, establishing themes directly relevant to the experience of Muḥammad. In so doing, it foreshadows the experience and role of the prophets it presents in the second part. In its turn, the second part adds historical depth and authority to the mission of Muhammad, as his experienced is imaged in the prophets of earlier times.

The sura opens with a declarative theme:

1 *Alif Lām Rā'*
These are verses from the Book that stands in Judgement!
2 *Is it bewildering to mankind that We should reveal to*

one among them [the message],
'Warn mankind
and give a good tiding to those who believe
that they stand on a footing of truth with their Lord'?
(Q 10:1–2)

These two verses announce the role of the Qur'an, question the response of the Meccans to it, and reassure those who believe. The succeeding verses answer objections to the Qur'an. They tell of the unity and power of God, the truth of His promise, with the justice (*qist*) of His rewards and punishments, and the authenticity of the Qur'anic revelation. They present a mix of argument, threat, promise and reproach. But strikingly, they also tell that God may defer punishment in this world, if He so wills, to a time that He alone determines.

Within the constraints of this essay it is possible only to draw attention to a selection of the continuities that bind the two parts of the sura together, and in so doing highlight parallels between Muḥammad and Jonah.

The phrase *al-kitāb al-ḥakīm* (v 1) establishes a theme that continues through the sura. The word *al-ḥakīm* is protean in its significances,[22] and as one of the names of Gosd, it carries with it a resonance that sounds through the sura. As a qualifier for *al-Qur'an*, it presents it as a dynamic entity. It is a Book that takes charge, has authority, is imbued with wisdom. It stands in judgement. Judgements made by the unbelievers lack a sound foundation. They follow entities incapable of giving guidance. Only God can guide to the truth, and so Muhammad is commanded to ask them

Who is more worthy to be followed,
One who guides,
or one who cannot find the way unless he be guided
What is it with you?
How can you judge (taḥkumūn) anything else to be the case?
(Q 10:35)

22. Rāzī, *TK* 17:4–5 gives an account of the semantic spread of *ḥakīm*. This rendering follows what he states is the majority view, that is *al- ḥakīm –fa'īl* in the sense of *fa'īl* (the majority view). The Qur'an is, as it were *al- ḥakīm* of beliefs, to distinguish those that are true from those that are false, and of deeds, to distinguish those that are correct from those that are erroneous etc.

God's judgement is to be seen both in His punishment of the people to whom Noah is sent and of Pharaoh, but equally in the mercy bestowed on those to whom Jonah preached. This is why at the conclusion of the sura It is in the light of such judgements that at the conclusion of the sura Muḥammad is commanded,

> *Follow what is revealed to you,*
> *Await in patience until God gives judgement,*

and the sura ends with the exultant doxology

> *He being best of all who give judgement* (Q 10:109).

The perpetual call on the lips of those in gardens of delight, 'Glorious beyond compare are you O God' (Q.10:10, identical with the prayer uttered by Jonah in the great fish (Q.21:85) rings through the sura. The perpetual call on the lips of those in gardens of delight—*jannāti'l-na'īm*—(Q 10:9) is,

> *Glorious beyond compare are you, O God* (Q 10:10)

identical with the prayer uttered by Jonah in the fish (Q 21:85) rings through the sura. As for those entities whom the Meccans say

> *These are our intercessors with God*

God says of Himself

> *Glorious beyond compare and exalted is God*
> *above what they associate with Him* (Q 10:18)

i.e. the intercessors they presume can influence Him.

In face of their claim that God has taken a son, He tells them,

> *Glorious beyond compare is He,*
> *He is the Self-Sufficient,*
> *His is whatever is in the heavens and the earth* (Q 10:68).

Set against the celebration of God's glory are the sneers of the unbelievers, who because they go unpunished, imagine that the punishment threatened them will never come. They say,

> *When will this judgement be*
> *if you are speaking the truth?* (Q 19:48)

They say of the Qur'an,

> *He has made it up!* (Q 10: 38)

Insult is added to insult. They say,

> *This man is self-evidently a sorcerer* (v 2).

The scorn that Muḥammad faces was faced by Moses

> *This is self-evidently a sorcerer* (Q 10:76)[23]

yet the sneer is turned back on Pharaoh himself (*cf* Q10:77–82). Noah too suffered scorn from his people, challenging them to do their worst to him (*cf* Q 10:71). Jonah did not escape the common experience of the prophets, and it was surely said to him

> *When will this judgement be*
> *if what you say is true?* (Q 10:48)

The Qur'an presents arguments for the coming of a Day of Reckoning. It points out how fragile human prosperity is, even when mankind have most confidence in themselves, whether at sea or on land,

> *It is He who gives you to travel*
> *over land and sea,*
> *so that when you are on board ship,*
> *and ships sail with them swiftly,*
> *blown by a fair wind, they rejoice.*
> *When a storm wind descends upon them,*
> *and waves come upon them from every side,*
> *and they fear they will be overwhelmed,*
> *they call on God* (Q10:22)

23. Following the Nāfi's recitation *saḥir*. Ḥafs recites it *siḥr*.

It will be recalled that in part two, God's providence provided safety against the dangers of sea and flood for Noah, Moses and Jonah.

And on land,

> *The life of this world may be compared*
> *only to the rain We send down from the sky.*
> *The plants of the earth,*
> *which mankind and their cattle eat*
> *commingle with it.*
> *Yet when the earth has put on its ornaments*
> *and is decked [in greenery],*
> *and its inhabitants presume they are its masters,*
> *Our decree will descend by night or day*
> *and We will render it as reaped,*
> *as though the previous day it had never been* (v 24)

a lesson that is vividly imparted in *Sūrat al-Qalam*, (Q 68:17–34)

Then there is the evidence of the punishment inflicted on past peoples. God says to Muḥammad,

> *We destroyed the peoples who came before you*
> *When they did evil,*
> *Our messengers having come to them*
> *with clear proofs* (Q 10:13).

and in the stories of Noah and Moses there are clear examples of unbelievers who were destroyed (*cf* Q10:71–94).

And of the Meccans who reject him, Muhammad is ordered to say,

> *Can they expect, [due to their disbelief]*
> *anything other than the fate*
> *of those who went before them* (Q 10:102*)*.

Their punishment will come,

> *The time set for them will not be set back an hour*
> *or put forward an hour* (Q 10:49).

Perhaps the Meccans will believe only when the punishment is upon them, and then there is no denying its reality. And God will say to them,

So when it has come, now you believe in it?
What? now! (a'āl'āna !) and you were asking
that it be brought on more swiftly! (Q 10:51).

The scorn and power of the phrase *a'āl'āna* is difficult to replicate in English. Their faith at that moment will not avail them now.[24]

The lesson is presented with an even greater force when Pharaoh declares he believes in the God of Moses in exactly these circumstances, and as he sees the waves towering over him, cries out,

I believe that there is no god
other than that in whom the children of Israel believe,
and I am of those who submit to Him (Q 10: 91)

and God replies with words that were uttered in threat to the Meccans,

What? Now!
and previously you disobeyed,
and were of those who do evil (Q 10:91).

Pharaoh's protestation of belief did not avail him. His body alone was preserved to be a sign (like the ruins of Sodom), of God's exercise of His power to punish the wicked! (10:92). But, and this is emphasized by the fate of Pharaoh, the belief of the people of Jonah *did* avail them. The period of respite allowed them had been put to good use.

Muḥammad continued to suffer insults and rejection. Throughout the Qur'an there are numerous verses telling of the pain he endured. In this sura too, are a number of verses in which God assures him that He knows his situation.

Among them are some who believe in it (the Qur'an)
and among them some who do not believe in it.
Your Lord knows full-well those who are evil-doers (Q10: 40).

He should not necessarily even expect the punishment threatened them to come in his life-time,

Whether We show you anything of what We threatened them

24. The same warning is given in *Ṣād* (Q 38:3), How many of [former] ages have We destroyed before them! They cried out [when destruction fell upon them], but then there was no time for deliverance'.

> *or We take you in death [before their punishment comes].*
> *In either case to Us is their return,*
> *God being a witness*
> *to what they are doing* (Q 10:46)

Moreover God says to him,

> *Let not their words grieve you* (Q 10: 65)

And finally,

> *Were God so to will,*
> *then all on earth would believe,*
> *but can you alone compel*
> *all mankind to believe*? (Q10:99)

the prophet being warned that, in the last resort, belief comes from God.

As mentioned above, it is perhaps a paradox that the sura should be called Yūnus, on the basis of a single verse.

Nevertheless the story of Jonah and the fact that his people believed, is embedded in the sura as a sub-text, underpins it, and is a key to its structure. Thus that a human individual can be chosen as a prophet to warn and give good tidings (v2), inevitably calls to mind Jonah as one such individual; every reference to the celebration of God's incomparable glory (*cf* Q 10:10 *et passim*) evokes Jonah's prayer in the fish. Muhammad's declaration that he fears the punishment of a terrible day if he disobeys his Lord (v 15) hints at Jonah's flight from God's command in *Sūrat al-Ṣāffāt* (*cf* Q 37:140). The reference to mariners in terror at a storm (*cf* Q10:22) arouses memories of Jonah in the darknesses of the great fish, sea and night (*cf* Q 21:87). The words addressed to Muhammad, *Do not let their words grieve you* (*cf* Q 10:65) relate directly to Jonah, for it is clear that the words of his people, when they rejected him, did grieve him, and he left them *enraged* (*mughāḍiban*) (*cf* Q 21:87).

The exegetic tradition highlights the uniqueness of Jonah in that his people believed. Ṭabarī comments on this verse, 'There was no people who believed after they had been singled out for punishment due to their disobedience of their Lord and their faith availed them . . . other than the people of Jonah'.[25]

For Ṭabarī, a central point in the sura is the contrast between the destinies of the people of Jonah, who had at first rejected their prophet and then believed, and Pharaoh, whose faith did not avail him. This is a more important element in the story than the sensational circumstance that Jonah was swallowed by a great fish. Rāzī too develops this point. He sets his remarks against the background that the stories of the three prophets in this sura are told to comfort the prophet. He points out that just as Muḥammad suffered the pain of rejection, so had the prophets before him. He sums up God's care for His prophet in this way by the neat and highly humanistic apothgem, *al-muṣīb*a *idhā 'ammat khaffa*t—Disaster if shared is lightened.[26]

A cue to his sensitivity to this sub-text is in the story he transmits of the people of Nineveh, and the events prompting their belief: 'Awesomely black clouds appeared in the sky. Smoke billowed out of them, a smoke that descended and settled on the city and blackened the roofs of its inhabitants.[27] . . . They then showed clear signs of their belief and repentance . . . It is said that they went out to an elder of one of the few religious scholars remaining, and said to him, 'Punishment is descending upon us. What is it we should do?' He said to them, cry out,

> O Living One, When there was no life,
> O Living One, Bringer of Life to the dead,
> O living One, There is no God but you'

a prayer which is in respons to the question in this sura,

> *Who is it who brings forth the living from the dead,*
> *and the dead from the living?* (Q 10: 31),

and

> *He brings to life and He slays,*
> *and to Him you will be returned* (Q 10, v:56)

25. Abu Ja'far Muhammad b. Jarīr al-Ṭabarī, *Jāmi' al-Bayān*, al-Ḥalabī Cairo 1954/1373, Volume 11, 170 (abridged).
26. Rāzī, *TK*, 17:135
27. Rāzī, *TK*, 17:165.

Is there perhaps concealed within this sura a yearning that this people of Muhammad might be as the people of Jonah, who after first rejecting their prophet, accepted him, and were spared the final punishment. There is still time for the Meccans to believe, and their faith to avail them.

*****

The primary goal of this essay has been to explore the role of Jonah in the Qur'an. The discussion of Q 10:98 however raises a different though allied issue, the relation between a sura and its name, it being generally accepted that the name is not part of the revelation. Among scholars outside the Muslim tradition, Watt's remark, 'As a rule, the name has no reference to the subject matter of the sura, but is taken from some prominent or unusual word in it. Usually this word occurs near the beginning, but this is not always so,[28] generally passes as received wisdom. At the very least, it can be countered that this is not always the case. And in the analysis of *Sūrat Yūnus* it has been argued that although Jonah is referred to explicitly in only one verse out of the 109 that comprise the sura, a Jonah sub-text informs it as a whole, and this, combined with the commanding position of the Jonah verse (v 98), is more than adequate reason for its being so named. Attention has already been drawn to the thematic importance of The Pen, in *Sūrat al-Qalam*. The same consideration applied to the name of sura 37, *al-Ṣāffāt*. If the oath with which the sura opens *Wa'l-ṣāffāt* is understood as meaning, 'By the angels standing in rows,' then the title draws attention to and establishes a theme running through the sura, the humility of the angels and their obedience to God's command, a role far removed from the status attributed to them by the Meccan idolaters. It is a theme accentuated by the recurrence of the root *ṣ.f.f* also in the sense of angels, as the hosts of angels say of themselves

> *We, we indeed stand in rows,*
> *We, we indeed are those*
> *Who celebrate His incomparable glory* (vv 165–166)

28. WM Watt & R Bell, *Introduction to the Qur'an*, Islamic Surveys 8, (Edinburgh: Edinburgh University Press 1970, Reprint 1990), 58–59.

Sūrat al-Anbiyā' virtually names itself by the variety of prophetic models that it presents, in which the great prayer of Jonah has a central place.

There are good grounds then to explore further the relevance of the names given to the suras. In the cases mentioned above, there is evidence of an integral relationship, be it thematic or symbolic, which highlights threads of its meaning. At least one should recognize the wisdom and understanding of the *muṣḥaf* that gave them these names. One of the conclusions from this is that a simple name count does not necessarily give a reliable idea of the importance or the nature of the presence of prophetic figures in the Qur'an.

Conclusion

The four pericopes discussed present Jonah from different perspectives and with varying *foci* of emphasis. The first in *Ṣūrat al-Qalam* (Q 68: 48–50), is a command to the prophet Muḥammad, *Do not be as the Man of the fish*. Its focus is on Muḥammad: he is not to act as did Jonah. The second, in *Sūrat al-Ṣāffāt* (Q 37:139–148), is a narrative account of the principal events of Jonah's career; the third, in *Sūrat al-Anbiyā'* (Q 21: 87–88) has as its focus, Jonah's prayer within the fish; and the fourth, in Yūnus (Q 10:98) is concerned with the people to whom he was sent, a people who believed. Each is brief. The longest, that in *Sūrat al-Ṣāffāt*, consists of only ten verses, that in *Yūnus*, of only one, yet implicit in each of them is an awareness of the Jonah story as a whole. Taken together they complement each other, and such a synoptic view shows how they enrich each other, and establish Jonah as a significant actor in the drama of salvation history that is the Qur'an.

An encounter with the four pericopes from this perspective not only enhances their significance, but opens up a picture of the dynamics and emphases of the suras in which they occur, and sets sounding echoes from one to the other. The presentation of different aspects of Jonah's career in each of these pericopes, has then a rhetorical function both within the sura and the Qur'an itself. It therefore follows that Qur'anic storytelling is not susceptible of the application of any redactionist or other theories of literary analysis such as with that proposed by Wanbrough.[29]

Each of these attestations of Jonah has been situated within the broader context of stories of the prophets presented in the Qur'an, and the role this story-telling has within the wider context of divine revelation. It is often overlooked how rich and diverse an assembly these prophets were, or what their role in salvation history was, from the beginning of time up to the call of Muḥammad. Each refracts an aspect of Muḥammad's experience. They are his brothers in salvation history. Hs teaching is what they taught. His experience is what they experienced. His pains and frustrations are also theirs. There is pain in being a prophet. Such was the experience of all the prophets, and there are many Qur'anic references to the pain Muhammad endured at the apparent lack of success of his preaching. God recognizes this pain saying to him,

> *You may indeed torment yourself in anguish*
> *sorrowing, over their actions,*
> *that they do not believe in this revelation* (Q 18:6)

and reassures him that the revelation of the Qur'an to him is not to cause him pain,

> *We have not revealed the Qur'an to you*
> *that you should grieve* (Q 20:2)

reminding him

> *Whatever We relate to you of the stories of the messengers*
> *is that by it We may strengthen your heart.*
> *And in this is truth, warning, and counsel to those who believe*
> (Q11:20)

It is this pain of rejection that Muḥammad shares with Jonah, and the reason why God says to him,

> *So then [Muhammad] await in patience*

29. J Wansbrough, *Quranic Studies Sources and methods of scriptural interpretation*, Oxford University Press, London Oriental Series Volume 31, in chapter 1, 'Revelation and Canon', in particular 20–27.

the judgement of, your Lord,
and do not be like the Man of the Fish (Q 68:48.

Jonah's enraged departure (*cf* Q 21:87) has a counterpart in the biblical Book of Jonah. The rabbinic commentators remark that he was angry because the punishment he had threatened would befall the Ninevites did not come to pass, and he was laughed at. He felt that he and his deity had become the objects of taunting abuse.[30] This was certainly the experience of Muhammad. He too was the butt of the jeering question, 'When is it going to be?' And one of the bitterest sneers of his opponents is the parody they make of a prayer in *Sūrat Ṣād,*

Lord of ours, give us our requittal now,
before the Day of Reckoning (Q 38:16)

and God urges restraint on him, just as He had in *Sūrat al-Qalam*,

Endure in patience (iṣbir) what they say (Q 68:17)

But there is another parallel between Jonah and Muḥammad. God cared for Jonah after he had been cast on the barren shore sick (*saqīm*). He says,

We made grow over him a gourd tree (Q 37:146).

and from it, gave him shade and nourishment. Rāzī remarks that this gourd growing on a trunk to give him shelter was a probative miracle.[31] The *Jalālayn* and add that a she-goat was sent to him morning and evening to give him milk.[32] Thus Jonah was given the means to recover his strength before he was sent to preach. *Sūrat al-Duʿā* (Q 93) gives an eloquent and moving account of the care God gave to Muhammad before his mission.

There is however a third parallel. The people of Jonah, although at first they disbelieved, were given time to repent. Accordingly the message to Muḥammad is that if his people are not yet punished, there is a reason for it: There is still time for them to believe, and their faith to avail them. Muḥammad is not to give in to frustration as did

30. *The Literary Guide to the Bible,* Robert Alter and Frank Kermode, editors (London: Collins, 1987), 240 in 'Jonah' James S Ackerman.
31. Rāzī, *TK*, 26:166.
32. *Jalālayn*, 399.

Jonah. In the experience of Jonah in the great fish, there is a lesson for him, and in Jonah's prayer, pardon and successful preaching, an encouragement. A synoptic view of these Jonah pericopes yields a coherent story It presents symbols, imagery and a prophetic message that is a counterpart to that of the biblical Book of Jonah, notwithstanding this relationship is one of motifs and thematic structures, not of literary dependence.

One of the distinctive features of the Qur'anic presentation is the intense concentration of its language. One might say that Jonah's prayer within the great fish which occupies Chapter Two of the Book of Jonah, is in essence concentrated into one verse in *Sūrat al-Anbiyā'*

> *There is no God but You! Glorious beyond compare are You* (Q 21:82).

In both presentations of the story however there is implicit a shared theodicy: that divine mercy is a more powerful attribute than justice, and that God's preference is to grant life rather than death. This is the message of the Qur'an, clearly stated in *Sūrat Yūnus—To every people have We sent a Messenger* (v 47). Just as does the Book of Jonah, it carries the assurance that God's message is preached to those outside Israel.[33] This theodicy is encapsulated in the prayer of the people of Nineveh that Rāzī attributes to Ibn 'Abbās), 'O God, our sins are great and innumerable, yet you are greater and more sublime than them. Deal with us then as proper for You, do not deal with us as is proper for us.[34]

Ibn 'Arabī in the *Fuṣūṣ al-Ḥikam*[35] devotes a *faṣṣ* to Jonah. In it, he sees God's love and care for human life, and His readiness to forgive exemplified in the final belief of the people to whom Jonah was sent and the fact that belief availed them. He expresses it sublimely in this *faṣṣ*,

'Be sure you understand that care for God's servants is more to be nurtured than excessive zeal on behalf of God. David wished to build the Temple, and attempted to do so a number of times. But

33. *The Oxford Companion to the Bible*, Bruce M Metzger, Michael D Coogan, editors (New York/Oxford: Oxford University Press 1993), s.v. The Book of Jonah, 381.
34. Rāzī, *TK*, 17:165.
35. *Muḥyi'l-Dīn ibn 'Arabī*, *Fuṣūṣ al-Ḥikam*, Abū'l- 'Alā 'Affifī (ed.), al-Ḥalabī, Cairo, 1946. '*Faṣṣ ḥikmat nafsiyyat fī kalimat Yūnusiyya*', 167 *et seq.*

each time he completed it, it collapsed in ruins. So he complained to God and God revealed to him "This house of mine will not be raised by the hands of one who has spilt blood". David replied to him, "Was not that blood spilt in pursuit of your cause?" God said to him, "Yes, indeed! But were not those slain My servants?""[36]

For Ibn 'Arabī, God's acceptance of the belief of the people of Jonah is proof of God's preference for life over death, and the preservation of human life is better than its destruction, for He created Man in His image.

This exploration of the account the Qur'an gives of Jonah, a so-called minor prophet, is but one way to experience its power and vitality. It contributes to a perception of the shape of the mission of the Prophet Muḥammad, and the challenges he faced; it highlights aspects of his response to these challenges, God's dealings with him, and the wonder of God's works; it leads to the discovery and experience of new dimensions and emphases in the Qur'an. Ibn 'Arabī's encounter with Jonah expressed in the *faṣṣ* devoted to him, communicates something both of the passion of the Qur'anic message, and its humanistic dimension. It shows the Qur'an as a world open to infinity. One might apply to such a vision the words of Martin Buber, who said to those who regarded the Torah as a closed world, 'To you, God is one who created once and not again; but to us God is he who "renews the work of creation every day". To you, God is One who revealed himself once, and no more; but to us He speaks out of the burning thornbush of the present'.[37] The Qur'an puts this concept incomparably in *Sūrat al-Raḥmān, Every day He is in a new activity—kulla yawmin huwa fī sha'nin* (Q 55:29).

> *Which then of your Lord's blessings can you both deny*! (Q 55:30).

---

36. Ibn 'Arabī, *Fuṣūṣ*, 167.
37. *The Oxford Companion to the Bible*, 527.

Solomon and the Queen of Sheba Fakhr al-Dīn al-Rāzī's Treatment of the Qur'anic Telling of the Story

Solomon is one of the great figures in Islamic Salvation history. References to him, and pericopes presenting episodes in his life are distributed over a number of suras of the Qur'an as are those of other prophets, such as Adam, Abraham and Moses, revealing perspectives of his prophetic role and personality. In *sūrat al-Anbiyā*' (21:78–82) are a number of references to him and his father David: of the judgement he gave with David when sheep wandered into a cornfield, of the knowledge and skill in judgement given them (vv 78–79), and of the subjection of the wind to Solomon (v 81). In *sūrat Ṣād* (38:30–33) is an account of his admiration for horses, and in *sūrat Saba'* (34:14) of a staff that held him erect after his death for a year, until a worm devoured it from within, and it collapsed. In addition, his name has a place in lists of prophets in the company of Isaac and Jacob, Job, Joseph,Moses and Aaron in *sūrat al-An*'ām (6:84) and *sura al-Nisā* (4:163) The most extended pericope however is in *sūrat al-Naml* (27:15–44) that tells of his meeting with Bilqīs, the Queen of Sheba, an event which has a counterpart in the Book of Kings (1 Kgs 10 vv 1–13). It is a striking presentation of Solomon as prophet and ruler. and invites comparison with pericopes that present episodes from the lives of Moses, David and Joseph. It is significant that a number of these narratives of prophet as ruler appear in passages of the Qur'an revealed in the so-called third Meccan period, the years immediately preceding the migration to Medina, and may perhaps be seen as foreshadowing the path Muḥammad's future career was to follow.

This essay is devoted to Rāzī's treatment of the story in his *Mafātīḥ al-Ghayb*,[1] noting the relation of this treatment to that of Zamakhsharī, his predecessor by forty-five years, in *al-Kashshāf*.[2] Rāzī has arguably the richest mind of all the classical commentators on the Qur'an. Although an Ash'arite, almost in spite of himself, he admired Zamakhsharī's work, and quoted from it frequently in the *Mafātīḥ*.

A suggested English rendering of the pericope is set out below. It is divided into scenes to highlight a characteristic feature of Qur'anic story-telling: the deft construction of scenes which move swiftly from one to another without link passages, often without any indication of change of place or identification of speaker, the necessary connections implied both by the outline of the story and the resonances of rhetoric which hold together the sequence of events in the minds of the hearers.

Scene I

15. *We bestowed on David and Solomon knowledge, and together they said, 'Praise and thanks be to God who has favoured us above so many of his believing servants.'*
16. *Solomon was heir to David. He said, 'People of God, we have been taught the language of the birds, and been given abundance of everything. It is a most evident favour'.*

Scene II

17. *Solomon's army of jinn, mankind and birds were assembled before him, and arrayed in ranks,*
18. *then marched until when they reached the Valley of Ants, an ant said, 'Ants, return to your homes, lest Solomon and his forces, without realising it, trample you down.'*

---

1. Also widely known as *Al-Tafsīr al-Kabīr*. Bibliographical information and referencing as in, 'Joseph in the Qur'an', p. 24 fn 6. References are to *TK*, volume and page.
2. The work is *al-Kashshāf 'an ḥaqā'iq ghawāmiḍ al-tanzīl wa 'uyūn al-'aqāwīl fī wujūh al-ta'wīl*. Beirut: Dār al-Kitāb al-'Arabī 1947, 4 Volumes. References are to *Kashshāf* volume and page. Zamakhsharī's dates are 1075–1144 CE. He completed the *Kashshāf* in 1134. Rāzī lived 1149 –1209 CE, and worked on the *Mafātīḥ* from around 1200 CE until his death.

19. *Solomon smiled, laughing at her words and said, 'My Lord, keep me constantly thankful for the favours you have bestowed on me and on my parents, that I may do good deeds pleasing to you. Out of your mercy, set me among your righteous servants.'*

Scene III

20. *He surveyed the birds, and said, 'Why do I not see not see the hoopoe? Can it be that it has flown off? Is it among the absent?'*
21. *'I will punish it severely, or I will even slay it, unless it gives me a convincing reason [for its absence].*
22. *The bird did not stay far off for long. It returned, and said, 'I have been where you have not been, and I come to you from Saba' with indisputable news.*
23. *'There, I found a woman ruling over them, a woman who has been given an abundance of all that is, and she has a mighty throne.*
24. *'I found her and her people worshipping the sun instead of God. The devil had made their acts pleasing to them, turning them aside from the Path, so they are not rightly guided*
25. *'and worship God who brings forth what is hidden in the heavens and the earth, and knows what you hide and what you do openly.*
26. *'God! There is no god but He, Lord of the Mighty Throne'.*
27. *He said! 'We will discover whether you speak the truth, or whether you are of the liars.*
28. *'Go with this letter of mine, and give it to them; then draw aside from them, and watch how they respond.'*

Scene IV

The Queen of Sheba

29. *She said, 'Ministers! a noble letter has been delivered to me,*
30. *it is from Solomon, it is in the Name of God, the Merciful, the Compassionate,*
31. *Do not be arrogant towards me, but come to me in submission.'*
32. *She said, 'Give me an opinion on the matter. I am not to decide on an issue until you have given me a view'*
33. *They replied, 'We have great power and awesome might. The matter is yours to decide, so consider the order you decide to give.*
34. *She said, 'Kings when they enter a town lay it waste, and make the most powerful of its citizens the lowliest. It is thus they do.*
35. *I will send them a gift and see with what response the messengers return.*

Scene V

Solomon's reaction to her gifts

36. *When the envoy came to Solomon, he said, 'Are you offering me wealth? What God has bestowed on me is better than what He has bestowed on you, yet you rejoice in the gifts you offer.*
37. *Return to them! for we will come upon them with armies that they cannot withstand, and we will expel them, the lowliest, from Saba' abased and servile.*

Scene VI

Solomon has her throne brought to him

38. *Solomon said, 'Ministers! Which of you will come to me with her throne before they come to me in submission?'*
39. *A daemon from among the jinn said, 'I will bring it to you before you rise from your tribunal. I have the strength to do this. You can rely on me.'*
40. *One who had knowledge of the Book said, 'I will bring it to you in the twinkling of an eye'. Then, when he saw it standing before him he said, 'This is a favour from my Lord, putting me to the test to see whether I am grateful or ungrateful. One who is grateful, is for his own sake; one who is ungrateful—my Lord has no need of him and yet still is gracious.'*
41. *He said, 'Disguise for her her throne. Let us see whether she is guided, or whether she is of those not guided.'*

Scene VII

Arrival of the Queen of Sheba

42. *When she arrived she was asked, 'Is your throne like this one?' she replied, 'Well, it could be.' We had been given knowledge of God before her and made our submission to him*
43. *What she worshipped in place of God impeded her. She had come from an unbelieving people.*
44. *She was ordered, 'Enter the palace!' But when she looked at the forecourt, she thought it was a deep pool of water, she revealed her legs (by raising her garment). He said, 'The forecourt is paved with smooth blocks of glass'. She said, 'My Lord, I have sinned against myself. Now, with Solomon I make my submission to God, Lord of the worlds.'*

It is difficult to recapture in English the devices by which Qur'anic presentation of the story makes its impact, with its taut, intense dialogues, strong rhythms and tantalising ellipses. There is no doubt however as to the concentration of energy within it, and its potential for a haggadic type of expansion. It makes use of various of the techniques I have drawn attention to elsewhere:[3] the action broken up into scenes; the repetition of key words, the differentiation of character by style of utterance. It can be studied from a number of aspects—its audience appeal, its role in the development of Muḥammad's understanding of himself and his vocation, and its Talmudic antecedents.

At the simplest level however it is a reward story.[4] telling how a prophet king converts a pagan queen to belief in the true God. As such, it communicates basic truths of the economy of salvation, and offers proof texts on the basis of which theological formulations can be defined. Yet for Muslims it is more than this. The pericope presents not only salvation history, but history. The *dramatis personae* are historical figures and real people. The situations in which they play their roles are real situations, and the words they speak express their motivations, concerns and experience. Rāzī is aware of this, and is as much concerned with the human personalities of Solomon and Bilqīs as in the conversion of Bilqīs to Islam. He is deeply concerned with the spiritual values it enshrines, but equally with what he regards as proof texts to justify Ash'arite theology and refute the doctrines of the Mu'tazilites.

3. AH Johns, 'Joseph in the Qur'an', in *Islamochristiana*, 7 (Rome 1981): 29–55.
4. Hence the obverse of the punishment stories analysed by Wansbrough in his seminal Wansbrough, J, *Quranic Studies. Sources and Methods of Scriptural Interpretation* (London: Oriental Series. Volume 31, Oxford University Press, 1977). Wansbrough gives an example of a literary analysis of a 'punishment story', 21–25. The elements that he distinguishes in the example he gives, the story of Shu'ayb, may be found in this story. I) The formula of commission—Solomon is given knowledge. II) Corroboration—Solomon and the army obedient to him march to the valley of the ants. III) The diatribe—Solomon's letter to Bilqīs. IV) The threat of disaster—Solomon's response to the gifts sent by Bilqīs. V) Contestation—Bilqīs before Solomon and the test he gives her (repeated twice) followed by VI) her responses to each test and VII) her acceptance of Islam. VIII) and IX). Reversion from dialogue to narrative and epilogue do not occur in this case, but are elaborated by the *quṣṣaṣ* (story-tellers).

These issues are at the core of Rāzī's exegesis of the story although they far from exhaust it. In expounding them, he brings together all his learning and skills as a teacher; occasionally, however it must be admitted, taking up matters with only a tangential relationship with the Qur'an.

It is not always easy to engage with an author's personality on the basis of what he has written, whether on *tafsīr,* a field of study in which there may be a complex confluence of traditions, or any other discipline. This is true of Rāzī, whose work summates so much of the concerns of his predecessors.

He works through the Qur'anic text seriatim, raising points and issues, providing explanations and offering excursuses as he proceeds. To present a clear idea of his concerns and individuality from this pericope of twenty-nine verses, it is helpful to bring together thematically the issues he treats, even though this may detach some items from their place in the sequence of the Qur'anic narrative.

First there is his response to the characters in the story. For him, they are real persons and his writing on them suggests the insights of a proto-novelist. He examines their motives for action, and their responses to events as real people, building up details of their personalities, as he clarifies and explores further layers of meaning not made explicit in the text.

Of Solomon, for example, Rāzī emphasises that he had been given knowledge of a special kind, and with it the ability to understand the speech of animals.[5] His power is shown when his army of jinn, men and birds is assembled, and he leads them. The Qur'an itself presents a human reaction on his part. He laughs when, as he approaches the valley of the ants, he hears an ant saying, *Ants, return to your homes, lest Solomon and his forces, without noticing it, trample you down* (v 18). Rāzī stresses that Solomon's reaction to the ant's words went beyond a smile and became a laugh.[6] Indeed, in many places in the *Mafātīḥ* he highlights the expression by the prophets of primal emotions. He finds psychological reasons to explain this laughter.[7] One is Solomon's delight at hearing the words of the ant *without noticing it* (v 18). They were proof of how well-known was his

5. al-Rāzī introduces the story TK 24: 184, and begins his exposition on 185.
6. TK 24: 188.
7. Rāzī gives no less than nine suggested reasons for Sarah' s laughter at the visit of the angels to Abraham *ad sūrat Hūd* (11:71), TK 18: 25–26.

compassion and that of his army, a compassion that would not allow them to trample down without noticing, even an ant. His pleasure was such that he laughed. It is a shrewd psychological perception. But there is a second reason for his laughter: his joy that God had given him a gift given to no-one else, the ability to understand the speech of animals. His pleasure and joy, which result in the emotional release of laughter, then prompt him to utter a prayer of thanksgiving which Rāzī is to analyse in detail later, *My Lord, keep me constantly thankful for the favours you have bestowed on me and on my parents* (v 19), words expressing a sense of thankfulness that is repeated later in the story. Many of the prophets offer thanks for the favours their vocation has brought them. A striking example is Moses when he has escaped from Pharaoh after killing the Egyptian.[8]

Solomon also gives vent to another primal emotion: anger. He surveys the birds, and discovers that the hoopoe is missing. He is furious, and declares that he will torment it or slaughter it, the vehemence of his rage being conveyed by the energetic forms of the two verbs *la uʿadhdhibannahu* and *la adhbabannahu* (v 21). Rāzī gives an account of the stages by which Solomon realised the bird was missing to emphasize that his anger was real. Thus he visualises the situation: Solomon surveys the birds and does not see the hoopoe. He offers several reasons as to how Solomon had missed the bird, and why he had needed it. He then traces Solomon's growing uncertainty about where the bird is, and it then dawns on him that it has gone off somewhere, and so exclaims 'Has it gone off'?, as though querying the truth of what had become apparent to him: that the hoopoe was summoned, but did not come; that it was needed to find water, that it had been providing him shade from the sun, but the shade suddenly ceased. The reasons themselves are not intrinsically interesting. More intriguing, however, is his treatment of Solomon's words, 'How is it that I do not see the hoopoe' (v 20). He suggests that Solomon looked where he expected the hoopoe to be, and was slightly puzzled when he did not see it. Then it dawned on him that it was not there. As Rāzī puts it—he didn't see it. Then it dawned on him that it was missing and he said, 'It is missing', as though enquiring about the truth of what had dawned on him, just as one might say, 'That's a camel—or is it a sheep?'

8. Qur'an 28 (*al-Qaṣaṣ*): 24 My Lord, how in need have I been of the good You have bestowed upon me.

His initial bewilderment then becomes anger, *I will punish it severely or even slay it, unless it gives me a convincing explanation for it absence.* (v 21). Rāzī then gives some of the punishments suggested that Solomon had in mind for the bird, all of them severe: that it be tarred, that it be thrown down to be eaten by ants; that it be plucked and thrown down into the open sun. To demonstrate Solomon's prophetic impeccability however, it is necessary to show that Solomon's anger was justified. To do this, Rāzī argues that the bird had reached the use of reason, or a stage close to it, that is. one legally equivalent to that of a *murāhiq*, an adolescent, and so might be considered guilty of disobedience, and deserve the punishments Solomon threatened.[9]

The hoopoe's report that it has seen a queen who worships the sun instead of God stirs him to concern for the honour of God. He sends the bird back to Saba' with a letter demanding the queen come to him in submission. Rāzī adds details from the haggadic tradition, a source he uses sparingly, to fill in how the bird delivers his message to the queen and observes her reactions to it.[10]

When Bilqīs does not obey at once, but plays for time by sending him gifts, Solomon is again enraged and sends another message, threatening to destroy her kingdom. Rāzī elaborates the reason for this anger: that Bilqīs' gifts are worth so much less than the gifts God has given him, yet she still takes pride in them.[11]

She therefore agrees to come in submission. But Rāzī makes clear that Solomon is not satisfied simply with her physical submission. He is concerned to find a way to bring her to recognise both his prophethood, and the reality of *God who brings forth what is hidden in the heavens and the earth, and knows what you hide and what you do openly. God, there is no god but He, Lord of the Mighty Throne* (v 25–26).

He has her throne brought to Syria from Saba', and to test her intelligence, disguises it and puts to her the trick question: 'Is your throne like this one?' Rāzī finds the incident of special interest, for it represents a sharp change of mood on Solomon's part from the scene in which he angrily dismisses her gifts, and threatens total war

9. TK 24: 189.
10. TK 24:193–194.
11. TK 24:196.

unless she comes in submission to him. His interpretation hinges on Solomon's command: disguise for her throne (*nakkirū lahā ʿarshahā*). Rāzī explains *nakkirū* as meaning change or alter, as a man disguises himself so that he will not be recognized.[12] He explains Solomon's motives. Had he left it as was, she would certainly have recognized it. However, by his wording of the question, Solomon has presented her with a situation in which a judgement involving the use of intelligence has to be made. Rāzī analyses the formation of the question closely. Note, he says, that *hākadhā* consists of three words: *hā*, calling for attention; *ka* the particle of comparison, and *dhā* a demonstrative. He stresses the significance: Solomon did not ask 'Is this your throne?' but 'Is your throne like this one?'. She replied 'Well, it could be'. She did not say 'It is it', nor did she say 'It is not it'. This answer demonstrated the excellence of her mind, because she hesitated to give a categorical answer in a situation in which hesitation was appropriate.[13]

It is clear that the scene fascinated Rāzī, for he discusses it further. He notes the view that Solomon set this intelligence test because he planned to marry her, and wished to disprove the allegation of those who opposed the match that she was deficient in intelligence. However he rejects this, and argues that Solomon tested her to discover *whether she is guided, or whether she is of those not guided* (v 41).

In these words *a tahtadī am takūnu mina' l-ladhīna lā yahtadūn,* Rāzī sees concealed a double question: whether she would recognise the throne or not, and whether she would recognize Solomon as a prophet. As to the first, she gave an appropriate answer, and Rāzī presents Solomon and his ministers as so impressed that they exclaim: she is correct in her answer; she is intelligent and discriminating; she has been provided with the means to embrace Islam (*ruziqati'l Islām*):[14] the means, let it be stressed, for imbeciles and minors lack

12. TK 24: 199.
13. TK 24: 199. I am indebted to my colleague Dr Street for pointing out the close parallel between this answer and the 'aporetic' approach of Rāzī, who indeed is sometimes referred to as *Imām al-mushakkikīn.*
14. TK 24: 200. Rāzī's use of the word *ruziqat* in this context is intriguing. It cannot mean 'she has been granted Islam' for at this stage she has not accepted the religion. In the light of Rāzī's general ideas, and his earlier distinction between means and the efficacy of means (as in his treatment of v 19) the interpretation suggested seems appropriate.

the means and so cannot accept Islam. Bilqīs has the means, but has not yet made her submission. Solomon therefore sets her another test. He constructs a wonderful palace, the forecourt of which is made of blocks of clear glass. When commanded to walk across it she becomes confused. She thinks that the glass is a deep pool of water, and draws up her skirt to walk through it, revealing her legs. Solomon this time has outwitted her, and in recognising her error she declares: *My Lord, I have sinned against myself. Now, together with Solomon, I make my submission to God, Lord of the worlds* (v 44). Both events, not to put too fine a point upon it tricks, show the lengths to which Solomon goes to convert her, to fulfill his role as a prophet by bringing to Islam the great ruler of the south.

Rāzī's analysis of her conversion is significant. First he sees Solomon as concerned to prove that she has intelligence, that is to say she is qualified to accept Islam. Her intelligence however, is only an enabling condition. It does not of itself bring her to Islam. It is not until after the second test, in which Solomon outwits her, that she makes her spiritual submission. Intelligence alone is not adequate to acquire belief. There is a gap between means and the means having their effect. In this case, an experience in which sense perception and judgement are proved wrong is the occasion that opens the way for *tawfīq*, the actual grace necessary for the commitment of faith. This analysis is consistent with Rāzī's Ashʿarite position, which is that the efficacy of the means to acquire faith (in this case intelligence) and the act of faith do not exist in a causal relationship, any more than possession of the means to gain salvation automatically results in salvation.

Rāzī finds much of interest in Solomon, but it is the figure of Bilqīs that awakens his sympathetic imagination. In the Qur'an itself, the features of her personality revealed by the situations in which she appears, the words she utters, and what is said of her, show the potential for her conversion already exists. She is introduced into the Qur'anic narrative by the hoopoe bird, who describes to Solomon both the extent of her authority and the fact that she and her people worship the sun. Rāzī's interest in her quickens after she has received Solomon's letter summoning her to come to him in submission. The scene offers broad scope to the imagination. The Qur'anic account of her words to her ministers is succinct. She says simply, *Ministers! a noble letter has been delivered to me* (*innī ulqiya ilayya kitāb karīm*) (v 29). Rāzī here again adopts information from the haggadic tradition that he presents by means of a flashback to realise a context for the situation: that she was asleep on her bed, having locked the doors and put the key under her pillow; that the hoopoe entered through the window and cast the letter on her breast as she was lying there, adding the detail. 'Some say that it pecked her, and she awoke with a start.'[15]

After her announcement, Rāzī makes explicit the ministers' questions in response to her words that he finds implicit in the Qur'anic text: From whom is it? What is it? To which she replies in the Qur'anic words: *It is from Solomon. It is in the name of God, the Merciful, the Compassionate-it says Do not be arrogant towards me, but come to me in submission* (v 30-31).

The dialogue that follows between herself and her ministers—a policy discussion between a female ruler and her ministers—is unique in the Qur'an. She says to them, *Give me an opinion in the matter. I am not one to decide on an issue until you have given me a view* (v 32).

They reply, *We have power and awesome might* (v.33). She however rejects the option of war, and reminds them, *Kings when they enter a city lay it waste, and make the greatest among its inhabitants the lowliest. It is thus they do* (v 34).

Rāzī remarks that she has described to them the consequences of war, but he is equally interested in her motives in consulting them. He suggests it is out of concern for their feelings. She wishes to assure their satisfaction (and loyalty) by giving attention to them. Asking their counsel was her way of doing this.[16]

In their response, Rāzī sees an exquisite tact: they have the resources to make war and are ready to do so if such is her will. At the same time they assure her: '*The matter is yours to decide, so consider the order you decide to give* (v 3), to show their readiness to obey, even if she decides for peace. Rāzī, having thus extracted the meaning coiled within the condensed language of the Qur'an, and having reflected on it, cannot refrain from the spontaneous comment, 'No answer could have been better than this'—as though he himself had views relating to the proper attitudes of ministers to their ruler.[17]

15. TK 24: 194.
16. TK 24: 195.
17. TK 24: 195.

Rāzī then turns to her words, *I will send them a gift and see with what response the messengers return* (v 35). Here too it is what goes on in her mind that concerns him. He sees in her decision not simply a device to play for time, but believes that she had no confidence that the gifts would be accepted, and was prepared for their rejection. What she wanted was to find out what Solomon had in mind before deciding how she would respond to his letter. The scene in which Bilqīs creates her greatest effect however, and in which she makes the greatest impression on Rāzī is that in which she gives her reply to Solomon's carefully prepared question: *a hākadhā 'arshuki—is your throne like this one*, a reply which not only has the simplicity and immediacy of colloquial speech, but which in its pert tone is characteristically feminine *ka annahu huwa—Well, it could be*. Rāzī's opinion that it establishes her intelligence deserves universal assent.

It is the second test that Solomon set her, that of the forecourt of the palace made of blocks of clear glass that appeared to be water, that brings her to accept Islam. Rāzī notes the opinion of some that Solomon, since he intended to marry her, wished to disprove allegations that her legs were hairy, and that instead of feet, she had hooves like a donkey. These claims were made by jinn who feared that since she was part jinn, were she to marry Solomon, she might bear a child who combined the intelligence of jinn and human creatures.

Rāzī rejects these allegations, just as he had rejected the view that the first test, to assess her intelligence, was also set because he wished to marry her. The central issue for Solomon is that she accept Islam - this is why he went so far as to construct the palace on the route she was to follow on her way to him, with its forecourt of blocks of clear glass, beneath which were placed fish to heighten the illusion that she had been ordered to step into water. He has little to say of the incident itself—and the Qur'an itself is brief—noting simply that she was astonished (*'ujibat*), and from this (it is not clear whether the referent is her experience of mistaking glass for water and revealing her legs, or the sight of the palace itself), she turned to God. His comment on her words *I have sinned against myself* (v 44) is likewise brief. He gives two explanations. One, following the literal sense of the words, is that she had sinned by her previous worship of the sun. A second has a psychological touch: that when she mistook the glass for water, she thought that Solomon had intended to drown her, and so her sin would have been to think ill of a prophet.

Rāzī concedes that some take the view that she married Solomon. He however, disagrees, for, he says, no authority gives a reliable opinion on the matter. He concludes his discussion of her with a report from Ibn 'Abbās that when she had accepted Islam he said to her, 'Choose someone from among your people to whom I can marry you'. She replied, 'The likes of me, with my authority, do not marry ordinary people'.

He replied, 'Marriage must be to a Muslim'. She said, 'In that case, marry me to Dhū Tubba', King of Hamadan so he married her to him, and sent them both back to the Yemen, and he continued with her as King—*wa'llāhu a'lam*.[18]

Rāzī's positive response to her personality is all the more striking because he was a mysogynist, and held no high view of women's intelligence. In *sūrat Yūsuf* (12:94) to explain the word *tufanniduni* in Jacob's words, 'I sense the fragrance of Joseph, 'Did you not regard me as senile (*tufanniduni*), you would believe me', he quotes Zamakhsharī's explanation of the word, 'One speaks of *shaykh mufnid* (a senile old man) but, not of *'ajūz mufnida* (a senile old woman) since a woman does not have the wits in youth that she could lose in her old age.'[19] When however he comes face to face with a woman such as Bilqīs in the pages of the Qur'an, he responds to her as a person of genuine intelligence.

Rāzī's discussion of the letter that Solomon sends to Bilqīs gives him an opportunity to confront its use as an argument in favour of *taqlid*—the acceptance of a prophet and his message without an adequate *mu'jiza* (testatory miracle). Thus he raises the question: does Bilqīs' response to Solomon's letter serve as an indication that *taqlīd* is adequate as a basis for faith, for it could appear that she accepted the status both of himself and his letter without such proof.[20]

Rāzī's answer to the question is characteristic. He finds the necessary *mu'jiza*, not in the manner of its delivery by the hoopoe but in the letter itself. He says, Solomon's messenger to Bilqīs was the hoopoe, and the miraculous proof (*mu'jiza*) is in the letter the hoopoe carries. Since this letter furnishes a complete proof, the

18. TK 24: 201.
19. TK 18: 208.
20. TK 24: 195.

Qur'an mentions no other. She says, *It is from Solomon, and it is in the name of God, the Merciful the Compassionate it is Do not be arrogant towards me. Come to me in submission* (vv 30–31). Rāzī points out that it is brief, consisting of only nine Arabic words, *Bi'smillāhi'l-raḥmāni'l-raḥīm; allā ta'lū 'alayya; wa'tūnī muslimīn.* It is this brevity, he argues, that is proof of its authenticity. Such brevity is characteristic of a prophet's utterance, for prophets do not express themselves at length, but limit themselves to what is essential.

He explains: The obligations of the creature are knowledge and action. Knowledge must precede an act, thus the Almighty's words *Bi'smillāhi'l-raḥmāni'l-raḥīm* (*In the name of God, the Merciful the Compassionate*) are an expression which attests both the existence of the Creator—may He be praised and exalted—and declare that He is Knowing, all Powerful, Living, Willing, Judging and Merciful. The words *allā ta'lu'layya* (*Do not be arrogant towards me*), forbid yielding to the passions and self pride. And the words *wa'tūnī muslimīn* mean either *Come to me in submission*, or *Come to me as believers*. This proves that the letter, despite its brevity, includes everything necessary for religious belief, and for proper conduct in this world. This is the miracle (*mu'jiza*) that Biliqīs recognised.

Rāzī's spiritual response to the pericope adds a special dimension to the *Mafātīḥ*. It is prompted in various ways. Sometimes it arises from his perception of the silences in the Qur'an, silences deriving from the elliptical use of language which leaves words understood, words that an exegete needs to understand from the context. He is determined to uncover every layer of meaning, to identify the significance of every particle, and to make clear what is meant, but not expressed. Yet, and this should be stressed, he does this not do this by claiming the privilege of *kashf* (a divine disclosure) but by the use of reason informed by the content of a positive theology that he adds to the traditional techniques of Qur'anic exegesis. His analysis of the first verse of the pericope is a good example.

wa laqad ātaynā *Dāwūda wa Sulaymāna 'ilman wa qālā 'l-ḥamdu li'llāhi—We bestowed on David and Solomon knowledge, and they both said: thanks be to God* (v 15).

He raises the question, 'Is this not a place where one would expect the conjunction *fa* rather than *wa*?'. To explain the point he wishes to make, he gives an example from everyday usage, *ataytuhu fa shakara*—I gave it to him so he was thankful.[21]

He then explains what is required if *shukr* (thankfulness) is to be valid, giving an explanation possibly taken from a work on ascetical theology: the expression of *shukr* by the tongue is valid only if it is proceeded by an act of the heart and an act of the body. The heart must resolve to embrace obedience and abandon disobedience; the limbs must occupy themselves with deeds that derive from obedience. It follows then that implied in the Almighty's words, after '*We bestowed on David and Solomon knowledge*,' is the clause 'so they both put it into practice with heart and soul', and they said (*wa qālā*) (with the tongue) *al-ḥamdu li'llāh*.[22] His grammatical sense has alerted him to the significance of use of the connective particle *wa* in a context in which *fa* at first sight appears more appropriate. He understands as a signal that there is something in the text understood (*muqaddar*). He 'decodes' the signal, supplies the missing words that complete the meaning of the verse, and shows how the insertion into the text of what is *muqaddar* indicates that the use of *wa* in the Qur'anic verse is in accordance with grammatical norms.

He treats the word *'ilm* (knowledge) in similar manner. In the text, it is indefinite. Rāzī sees it as indicating a great and resplendent knowledge, the possession of which distinguished David and Solomon from most of mankind. As such it must be higher than any other knowledge and beyond the capacity of ordinary people, a knowledge of God and His attributes. It is, in fact, an immediate intuitive knowledge of such a kind that once the creature is profoundly aware of it, no trace of doubt enters his mind, and his heart is never for an instant forgetful of it. For Rāzī this knowledge has virtually a mystical dimension, and his account of it suggests the depths of his own spiritual yearning. But at this point he stops and takes the matter no further, just as he alludes to the mystical dimension of meeting of Moses with al-Khidr, then turns aside from it.[23]

The spirituality that he expounds in the *Mafātīḥ* has mostly a practical bent. In the course of his comment on the words of the ant *Ants, enter your homes lest Solomon and his forces without realising*

21. *wa* is a simple connective, whereas *fa* suggests a consequential relationship with what precedes it.
22. TK 24: 185
23. TK 21: 150.

it trample you down (v 18) he quotes with approval a commentator of the allusive (*ishārī*) school who, understanding *trample you down* (*yaḥṭimannakum*) as 'cause you to fall into the sin of ingratitude', interprets the ant's words as meaning they should return to their homes because it feared that if they saw Solomon in his glory, they might fall into ingratitude for God's gifts to them—at the sight of Solomon so much more highly favoured than themselves. This leads Rāzī to formulate the general admonition that social intercourse with the great should be treated with caution.[24]

In his treatment of the scene in which Bilqīs' throne is brought to Solomon's court *in the twinkling of an eye* (v 40) Rāzī shows skill in his mastery of the rhetoric of persuasion and argument. The Qur'an says that this miracle was performed by *one who had knowledge of the Book* (v 40), but does not identify who this person was. Rāzī believes it was Solomon himself, and he argues the point, using every rhetorical device at his disposal.

He perceives in the antiphonal contrast between the words *I will bring it to you before you rise from your tribunal* (v 39) and *I will bring it to you in the twinkling of an eye* (v 40), a dramatic structure to the scene. It is as though the events are acted out before his eyes: Solomon addressing his ministers, putting to them the challenge, who can bring me her throne? A daemon from among the jinn claims to be able to bring it before Solomon rises from judgement. Solomon himself responds to this claim directing his words to the daemon jinn and echoing his words—always an effective device—*I will bring it to you in the twinkling of an eye*. The point is clearly made: a daemon can work wonders, but the power given to a prophet is many times greater, a power no one else can match.[25]

Rāzī then goes through the exercise of reviewing current opinions as to who it was who brought the throne: either that it was an angel, some identifying it as Gabriel, others as an angel charged by God to assist Solomon; or that it was a human being: either al-Khidr, or Solomon's minister Āṣif b Barkhiyā who was *ṣiddīq* (had spiritual insight) and knew the Mightiest Name of God (*al-ism al-aʿẓam*), a name so powerful that whatever he prayed for, when he called on God by it, was granted; or some other person who also knew the Mightiest

24. TK 24: 187–188.
25. TK 24: 196–197.

Name or even simply a just man living on an island in the sea who had come to the court that day to look on Solomon. Only after exhausting the possibilities from among angels and men does Rāzī come to the climax of his own opinion, that it was Solomon himself.

Then he sets out his arguments. One of them is linguistic: that the relative pronoun *al-ladhī* in the phrase *al-ladhī 'indahu 'ilm min al-kitāb* (v 40) would only be used correctly if it referred to Solomon. He then considers possible alternatives. Only one of these deserves serious consideration: Āṣif b Barkhiyā, Solomon's minister. There are however three considerations that rule him out: One is that Solomon, as a prophet must know far more of the Book than his minister; another is that for anyone to perform so great a miracle in the presence of a prophet would be harmful to the status of the prophet; the third and ultimate argument lies in the word of the Qur'an itself, for on the appearance of the throne, Solomon exclaims, *This is a favour from my Lord, putting me to the test, to find out whether I am grateful or ungrateful* (v 40).

Rāzī's argument for this interpretation of the verse is that Solomon could only have regarded the miracle as a test to discover whether he was grateful or ungrateful if it had been an answer to his prayer, a result of the existence of his *mu'jiza*.

By comparison he says little of what is meant by the Book. He quotes several views: that it was the *lawḥ al-maḥfūẓ*, the inscribed tablet, known by Gabriel, that it was the book delivered to Solomon himself, or that of another of the prophets, or that it was the Mightiest Name of God.[26] The essential point is that it was knowledge of the Book that brought about the transportation of the throne, and that it is invocation by the Mightiest Name that brings the swiftest answer to prayer.

Rāzī includes a variety of other points not directly relevant to an understanding of the words of the Qur'an. For example he deduces from the warning of the ant to her followers, *return to your homes* (v 18) a traffic law: that it is not the responsibility of the person travelling along the road to exercise caution, it is the responsibility of the person on the road to watch out—a counsel that still has its value.[27]

26. TK 24: 197–198.
27. TK 24: 187.

He also includes some of the attacks made against the Qur'an by the *mulāḥida* (unbelievers). One of them throws doubt on the Qur'an's internal consistency, by asking how Solomon could have been ignorant of the existence of Bilqīs if she was queen of a great empire, and was distant from him only three days flying time for the hoopoe bird. To such attacks he gives no answer other than to say that belief in the dependence of the world upon *al-Qādir* (the powerful one) *al-Mukhtār* (one who acts as he wills) puts an end to such doubts.[28] In addition he draws attention to formal aspects of the linguistic beauty of the Qur'an. He shows, for example, how the word *naba'* in the phrase *min Saba' bi naba'* (v 22), because of the rhyme, is aesthetically more pleasing than would be *min Saba' bi khabar*. He explains this exemplifies a proper use of embellishment of language by enhancing both form and meaning.[29]

Behind all such points of detail, however, lie certain philosophical convictions that condition and inform a number of his interpretations and emphases. One has to do with the inviolability of natural law, the *'āda*, which may be suspended only on rare occasions. He shows for example how the speed with which Bilqīs' throne is transported from the Yemen to Syria (that is *in the twinkling of an eye*) does not exceed what is possible in nature itself. His argument is as follows: Geometricians say that the sun is one hundred and sixty-four times greater than the earth, yet it rises in a brief time. So if we divide the time of the complete rising of the disk of the sun by the distance between the Yemen and Jerusalem it can be shown that the twinkling of an eye is sufficient for it to cover this distance.[30]

His Ash'arite credentials are shown on several occasions. For example, when discussing Solomon's ability to understand the speech of animals, he accepts without question that in Solomon's day animals could speak, even though in his own time they were no longer able to do so, albeit retaining some of the skills for the service of man that God had taught them.[31] Thus, so far from finding the ability of animals to speak at one time, and not at another an intellectual problem, Rāzī it as consistent with Ash'arite occasionalism which readily accepts the possibility of discontinuity in the abilities of particular species of living beings.

28. TK 24: 191.
29. TK 24: 190.
30. TK 24: 198.
31. TK 24: 187.

It is his Ashʿarism that leads him to attack the Muʿtazilites at three points in his treatment of the pericope. The first is at Solomon's prayer on hearing the words of an ant: *Return to your homes* (v 18): *My Lord, keep me (awziʿnī) constantly thankful for the favours you have bestowed me and my parents that I will do good deeds pleasing to you. Out of your mercy, set me among your righteous servants* (v. 19). These words, he says, prove the correctness of our (the Ashʿarite) position. Paradoxically, to support his view he quotes Zamakhsharī's (Muʿtazilite) treatment of the same verse in *al-Kashshāf*, 'The meaning of *awziʿnī* is keep me constantly thankful for your favour to me, and keep this thanks from ever departing from me'.[32]

He then attacks the Muʿtazilite position, analysing the verse in a way that reflects the occasionalism of Ashʿarite doctrine. He sees Solomon praying first for the means to achieve salvation, and once they are provided, for the efficacity of those means. (In Ashʿarite theology, it will be recalled, the efficacity of means resides not in themselves, but in discrete creative acts of God). He contrasts this position with what he puts forward as the Muʿtazilite view that every human act and thought is the result of a *luṭf*. Every *luṭf* is fully realised. Thus once one has the *luṭf* of the means of salvation, one has no longer the need to pray for salvation. The cause (the means) will necessarily produce its effect. *Luṭf*, it should be remarked is a concept of considerable subtlety in the Muʿtazilite system, and Rāzī in this case is guilty of an oversimplification, not to say caricature of the Muʿtazilite position.[33]

A second instance occurs in his discussion of the words of the hoopoe bird, *I found her and her followers worshipping the sun instead of God. The devil has made their acts pleasing to them, turning them aside from the path, so they are not rightly guided* (v 24) and *worship God who brings forth what is hidden from the heavens and the earth* (v 25).

Rāzī states that the Muʿtazilites use the phrase *worshipping the sun* as a proof text for their view that the creature is the author of his acts,

32. TK 24: 188
33. See GC Anawati, R. Caspar and M El-Johdeiri, 'Une somme inédite de théologie muʿtazalite: le moghni du qadi 'Abd al-Jabbār', Mideo (Cairo: Dar el-Maaref, 1957), 281–318. It lists 25 chapters on lutf in volume 13 of al-Mughnī, 1–226.

but gives no source for this claim. In any case Zamakhsharī does not discuss this phrase in the *Kashshāf*.

Rāzī summarizes the Muʿtazilite arguments: God attributed their act of worshipping the sun to themselves, the devil had made what they were doing attractive to them; they were condemned for choosing to do this; they were following a wrong path.

Rāzī presents three arguments against these views. One is that the words are uttered by the hoopoe, an animal and so provide no basis for an argument; the other is based on an alleged inconsistency in Muʿtazilite doctrine. In their view, the devil does not impede people from following the right path, for were he able to do so, an unbeliever could no longer to be under legal obligation, for he would not then be able to exercise his free will; this however contradicts the obvious sense of the words of the Qur'an, that *The devil had made their acts pleasing to them, turning them aside from the Path* (v 24).[34] The third is based on the words, *What she worshipped in place of God had impeded her. Indeed she came from an unbelieving people* (v 43).

Rāzī here puts forward, again without identifying a source, an attempt by the Muʿtazilites to use this verse as an argument against the Ashʿarites by a *reductio ad absurdum* of the Ashʿarite position: Had God created unbelief in Bilqīs, it could not have been a prior unbelief that impeded her from the right path, nor yet the fact that *she had come from an unbelieving people*: it would have been God's continuous creation of unbelief in her [which is absurd].

Rāzī does not face this issue, but merely remarks that her being from an unbelieving people was a situation necessarily requiring unbelief (*al-dāʿiya al-mustalzima li 'l-kufr*).[35]

Attention has already been drawn to the apparent paradox in alRāzī's quotation from *al-Kashshāf* to support the Ashʿarite position. In fact Rāzī took more from Zamakhsharī's work than this one quotation. Even a cursory comparison of the two works reveals a sufficient number of passages either identical with, or slightly abbreviated from Zamakhsharī's work, even taking into account the use of common sources—to establish that Rāzī had a detailed knowledge of the *Kashshāf*, and made frequent use of it, but omitting, modifying and adding to passages from the work according his own

34. TK 24: 191
35. TK 24: 200.

intellectual and theological preference.[36] It is not possible to generalize from this instance for the *Mafātīḥ* as a whole, but the issue it raises is significant. It has to do with the whole question of the extent of Rāzī's relationship with the *Kashshāf*, and this in turn has to do with the background of Rāzī's work, and ultimately with the range and variety of the sources he had at his disposal during the years the *Mafātīḥ* was being compiled, and the shifts in emphasis of his concerns during this period.

It is possible however, even on the limited data base afforded by such a comparison to suggest some of the critical differences between the two authors. Although both are concerned with exact definitions of words and *qirā'āt* (this is an area in which the *Mafātīḥ* may be dependent on *the Kashshāf)*. Rāzī is more sparing than Zamakhsharī in the quotations of poetry he adduces to justify the meanings he gives for words. In the pericope discussed he gives only one quotation as opposed to four given by Zamakhsharī, and this one quotation used to illustrate a particular reading of the beginning of v 25 was also cited by Zamakhsharī *apropos* the same verse and for the same purpose.[37] A more striking contrast between the two men however is in the space they give to haggadic material. Zamakhsharī is fond of adding to the Qur'anic narrative embellishments of distances, numbers and names, and a wealth of stories introduced by words such as *yuḥkā* (it is narrated) or *yurwiya* (it is told), some of them corresponding closely with episodes related in Tha'labī's *Qiṣaṣ al-Anbiyā'*.[38] Although it does not follow that these passages were taken directly from Tha'labī's work, since the same sources could have been available to both, it is likely this was the case.[39] Rāzī however, disregards this

36. Here, a few examples must suffice. *Ad* verses 15–19, approximately 32 lines of al-Rāzī (TK 24: 185–188) are taken verbatim from *the Kashshāf*: *Ad* verses:20-24, approximately 32 lines (TK 24: 188–191) are taken verbatim from *the Kashshāf*. *Ad* verses 29–33 approximately 26 lines (TK 24: 193–194) are verbatim from *the Kashshāf*. A more detailed examination of these striking correspondences will be given in a separate study

37. Rāzī, in fact, lists four *qirā'āt* with wording virtually identical with that of Zamakhsarī using this line of verse to justify one of them. Each results in a different relationship between this and the preceding verse, and a range of sometimes contradictory meanings. TK 24:191–192.

38. Abū Isḥāq Aḥmad b Mḥd b Ibrāhīm al-Tha' labī. *Qiṣaṣ al-Anbiyā' al-musammā al-Arā'is*, Cairo: al-Ḥalabī Cairo AH 1347

39. Tha'labī died in 1036 CE, thus Zamakhskarī could easily have had access to his work. Moreover Zamakhsharī follows closely Tha'labī's distribution of sources. See following note.

material completely, even in cases where he repeats Zamakhsharī's exegetical information *ipissimis verbis*. For example he follows exactly Zamakhsharī's treatment of the sentence, *We have been taught the language of the birds* (verse 16), but omits the account of thirteen types of bird, and the pious phrases each utters, that follows it. Similarly, after introducing the words *Solomon's army of jinn, mankind and birds were assembled before him* (v 17), Zamakhsharī gives an account of the numbers of each species, the distances they covered, and the magnificence of the thrones and palaces their leaders, and the prophets and *'ulama'* occupied. This too Rāzī omits. After Solomon's words, *Why do I not see the hoopoe? Can it be that it has flown off?'* (v 20) Zamakhsharī adds an account of its adventures in the Yemen before it returns to Solomon (having been told by the king of the birds how angry with it Solomon is) and making its report to him, again not in Rāzī. Finally, after introducing v 36, telling of Solomon's angry response to the gifts Bilqīs has sent him, Zamakhsharī gives a long account of what these gifts were and of the questions Solomon puts to her.[40] This too, Rāzī disregards. At the end of the story, Zamakhsharī clearly favours the 'happy ending' that Solomon married Bilqīs.[41] This conclusion Rāzī rejects. He acknowledges that some take this view, but insists that no reliable authority gives any support for it. It is this principle, that events narrated must have the support of a reliable authority, and his rationalistic bent, lead him to leave aside fanciful embellishments of this kind. They also influence his interpretation of the text. Verse 18 tells of the arrival of Solomon and his forces at the valley of the ants, *they reached the Valley of the Ants* (*ataw 'alā wadī' l-naml*), Zamakhsharī takes the preposition *'alā* (upon, over) literally, and synthesising the Qur'anic text with the data given in his haggadic sources, visualizes the whole army travelling on a flying carpet, with consequently no danger to the ants below unless the wind dropped. Rāzī tacitly rejects this view, and although repeating Zamakhsharī's list of the possible meanings of the combination

40. Examples in the *Kashshāf* (Edition Beirut, No date). with corresponding places the *Qiṣaṣ* are as follows: *ad* verse 16 'We have been taught the language of the birds, *Kashshāf* 3: 352–353, *Qiṣaṣ* 204–205; *ad* verse 17 'Solomon's army of jinn, mankind and birds' *Kashshāf* 354–355, *Qiṣaṣ* 204; *ad* verse 20 'How is it I do not see the hoopoe ?', *Kashshāf* 3: 358–359, *Qiṣaṣ s* 216–217. *ad* verse 36 'When the envoy came to Solomon', *Kashshāf*, 2: 365–366, *Qiṣaṣ* 220.

41. *Kashshāf*, 3: 370.

ataw 'alā, does not include the sentence by which the latter indicates that the journey is being made by air 'because as long as the wind continued to carry them in the air, there was no reason to fear their destruction.' (*li annahum, mā dāmati'l-rīḥ taḥmiluhum fī 'l-hawa', lā yukhāfu ḥatmūhum*).[42] This is an extension of his rationalism on the one hand—a rationalism within the framework of a positive theology, none-the-less—and on the other his reluctance to add to information given by the Qur'an. It is this that leads him to show how the speed of the transfer of Bilqīs' throne from the Yemen to Syria does not exceed what exists in nature—in the *'ājda;* in fact, an issue Zamakhahsarī does not touch on.

In some places Zamakhsharī has details not in Rāzī. For example after the words *ataytuhu fa shakara* (*ad* v 15) Zamakhsharī has *wa mana'tuhu fa ṣabara* (I detained him and/so he was forebearing).[43] In discussing the rhetorical beauty of the phrase *min saba' bi khabar*, he adds the technical term for rhetoric *badī'*,[44] not in Rāzī.

Their arguments are from different premises or concerns. One of the criticisms levelled against the Qur'an by the *mulāḥid*, is how could Solomon could have been ignorant of the existence of Bilqīs. Rāzī's answer is that the Almighty Creator could act freely as he chose. He was *Qādir* and *Mukhtār*. Zamakhsharī's answer is, 'Perhaps God concealed it from him as this being in his best interest, just as He concealed from Jacob the fact that Joseph was in Egypt',[45] an explanation consonant with his Mu'tazilism. Rāzī is concerned to emphasize the unlimited power of God (*qādir, mukhtār*) even in the absence of an overtly 'rational' solution to the problem. Zamakhsharī however looks to the system of *luṭf* or *islāḥ* that 'governs' God's treatment of his creatures. He expands the text of Solomon's letter to Bilqīs by recourse to variant recitations (*qirā'āt*) of the text. He does not see the *mu'jiza* of Solomon's letter in in the manner of its delivery by the hoopoe bird,[46] not in its brevity, Finally he offers several suggestions as to what the *ism al-a'zam* (the Mightiest name of God) might be.[47] Rāzī does not attempt to identify it, being content to explain it is terms of its effect: to secure the swiftest

---

42. *Kashshāf*, 3: 355.
43. *Kashshāf*, 3: 352.
44. *Kashshāf*, 3: 360.
45. *Kashshāf*, 3: 361.
46. *Kashshāf*, 3: 364.
47. For example *yā ḥayy, yā qayyūm* and, *yā dhā 'l-jalāl wa 'l-ikrām, Kashshāf*, 3: 367.

possible answer to prayer. Even in such relatively minor variations, basic differences in their theology may be discerned.

There are further differences of emphasis or perspective deriving as much from personality as from philosophical preferences. In commenting on the punishment that Solomon threatens to mete out the hoopoe bird (v 21), Zamakhshaī is concerned to show that such punishment is allowable, since the bird is subject to him.[48] Rāzī, on the other hand, is concerned to demonstrate that it was legally responsible, or at least was sufficiently close to legal responsibility for it to be proper to administer punishment. Zamakhsharī, it appears, is concerned more with the rights of Solomon, Rāzī with the bird's capacity for moral responsibility. Another point of difference is that although Zamakhsharī has included Solomon as one of those who by virtue of knowledge of the book might have transported Bilqīs' throne from the Yemen to Syria, he rejects this possibility in favour of Solomon's minister Āṣif who according to him performed the task because Solomon was irritated by the length of time (two hours?) the daemon from among the jinn required to transport it.[49] The unequivocal support for Solomon himself appears to be Rāzī's own contribution to discussion of the issue.

There still remain two major, over-reaching concerns in the *Mafātīḥ* that distinguish Rāzī from Zamakhsharī. One is the consistency of his interest in character for its own sake, and his probing of the dynamics of human motivation. This is shown in his treatment of Solomon, and even more in his response to the personality of Bilqīs. The other is in his spiritual response to the text—as shown in his perception of the spiritual dimension of the knowledge of God and His attributes, which he sees as the distinguishing character of the knowledge given to David and Solomon. The same sensitivity is shown in his response to the feeling of thankfulness that overwhelms Solomon when he perceived two signs of God's goodness to him: One that enabled him to understand the words of the ant, and the other when he saw the throne of Bilqīs in front of him. This spirituality infuses Rāzī's *Ash'arism*.

In his consistent restraint in the use of haggadic stories and his determination not to go beyond what can be supported by reliable

48. *Kashshāf*3:359.
49. *Kashshāf*, 3: 368

sources, he shows a more rigorous approach to the Qur'an text than Zamakhsharī. He has no interest in Solomon's flying carpet! In a real sense he is dedicated to the use of reason, albeit within the framework of a theological system. Yet paradoxically, once again, the spirituality and awareness of God that informs his Ash'arism, so far from restricting his use of reason, allows him greater room to manoeuvre in matters requiring faith than is available to the Mu'tazilites. He has an intuitive awareness of God as transcending utterly the reaches of human reason, yet shows himself more rigorous in the use of reason to understand the Qur'an than the Mu'tazilite and so 'rationalist' Zamakhsharī in areas where this is called for. He sees reason as essential to the profession of Islam but recognises the mystery in the fact that it is not in itself a cause for the profession of Islam.

His treatment of this story, once the sense and flow of his argument is released from the confines of the formal analytical apparatus of his excursuses *baḥth, su'āl, wajh* and the rest, is remarkably rich. The repertoire of intellectual concerns which extend his Qur'anic commentary on this pericope are specific: the impeccability of the prophets, the need to repudiate *taqlīd* (as he understands it), the *i'jāz* of the Qur'an and the defence of Ash'arism. Yet the acuteness of his mind, and the largeness of his human concerns are at the heart of his greatness. He has his dull patches, where he applies mechanically the procedures of scholastic reasoning, although even these may have their insights. But on so many occasions he turns away from routine. An idea crosses his mind. There is an awakening of human interest as he becomes totally immersed in a scene, or identifies with a predicament. He takes up an issue related to the spiritual life. The pulse quickens, and the reader is spell-bound.

Sufism in Southeast Asia: Reflections and Reconsiderations[1]

In 1961 I published in this Journal a paper on the Islamisation of peninsular and insular Southeast Asia.[2] It was a paper I had presented to the first meeting of the conference of historians of Southeast Asia organized in January of that year at the University of Malaya in Singapore by the then Raffles Professor of History, KG Tregonning. It was a paper subsequently referred to in discussions concerning the coming of Islam to the Malay world, and attracted its share of approbation and criticism.

The starting point of these reconsiderations after a thirty-year odyssey in the field is the thought that the critics were more correct than I was then prepared to concede, although perhaps the misgivings they raised at that time were no closer to the whole truth of the matter than the ideas that I had put forward.

In 1961, it had seemed that there was a simple explanation to this vast, further expansion of the domain of Islam: it could be understood largely in religious terms reducible to a single factor, the

1. Earlier versions of this paper were prepared during my tenure of a Special Foreign Professorship at Chiba University, Japan, 1 October. to 31 December 1991, sponsored by the Japanese Ministry of Education, Science and Culture, and presented in the seminars held at the Institute of Asian Culture, Sophia University, Tokyo; Institute of Middle Eastern Studies, International University of Japan, Urasa, Niigata Prefecture, and Centre of Southeast Asian Studies, Kyoto University, I would like to express my sincere appreciation to my colleagues at these institutions for their fruitful discussions,
2. 'Sufism as a Category in Indonesian Literature and History', in *Journal of Southeast Asian History*, 2/2 (1961): 10–23.

appeal of 'Sufism'[3] to the peoples of those areas of Southeast Asia that now include the modern nation states of Malaysia, Singapore, Brunei, Indonesia, Thailand and the Philippines.

It could never have been as simple as that. Nothing ever is. There were political and economic factors involved. The facts of social life in the port cities of the island archipelago before Islam certainly included political structures of considerable sophistication. Urban activities inevitably had to be seen in reference to the position of the ruler and his entourage, a religious elite and religious institutions. The bureaucracy must certainly have included a harbour master and tax collectors. The security of the state would have required armed forces, however organised, on land and sea. Trades people would have included carpenters, ship-builders, weapon-makers, smiths and a range of service industries. There was a need for regular supplies of food—rice, vegetables, fish, and meat, which would have led to a merging of urban life with that of the rural hinterland. All these activities inevitably were among the challenges confronting the appeal and adaptiveness of the new religion.

Thus my idea of the primacy of the mystical dimension of Islam in the Islamisation of Southeast Asia with was woefully inadequate, and along with it, tacit assumptions as to the nature of 'Sufism' that lay behind it, that the word Sufism could be used as an abstract noun in such a context, even if it might suggest that Sufism could be considered as an optional extra to Islam, or, perhaps worse, that Islam be regarded as an optional extra to Sufism.

In the discussion of religious change there is need for a profound respect for the people whose lives and deepest personal values are under discussion. We are not dealing with abstractions but with individuals following a particular way of life, choosing to live their lives one way rather than another, and embracing as their highest goal, a complex of values deriving from an authority beyond time.

Such considerations have led me to reflect on Islamisation from a perspective different from that which came to me so naturally in the 1960s. They have led me to avoid using the words 'Sufism', and even 'Islam' itself as abstractions and yielding to the temptation to

3. Although Sufism is a convenient portmanteau word, difficult to avoid, it is a European coinage, often used by orientalists to approriate something in Islam they like. The Arabic word it purports to translate is *taṣawwuf*, a verbal noun which indicates living according to a particular spiritual discipline.

assess what happens in Muslim communities in Southeast Asia against the norms of that abstraction, as though Sufism and Islam were limited self-defining identities, and that the term Southeast Asia was little more than a convenient piece of shorthand. Instead there was a need to attempt a more dynamic approach, seeing Muslims in Southeast Asia as members of communities participating in the global commonwealth of Islam in their own right.

Islamisation in this context need not necessarily be understood as synonymous with conversion, at least in the first instance. At this stage the word conversion is best avoided, for it has connotations of an individual choice of one religion rather than another on largely theological considerations, such as one finds motivating religious change in the modern world, at least in the individualistic West. But were such unmixed considerations always the determinant factor? Is it not likely that religious change was gradual, and came about after a long process of association between local peoples and Muslims, beginning with curiosity, followed by a perception of self-interest leading eventually to attachment to and finally entry into that religious community, rather than a response on an individual basis to the preaching of a message? In the light of such considerations, my idea of the primacy of the mystical dimension of Islam in the Islamization of Southeast Asia rested on an inadequate foundation.

The end of the thirteenth century, which saw the earliest physical evidence of an Islamic port city in north Sumatra, marked the beginning of a strong forward movement of Islam in the region. By this time *tarīqa* (Sufi brotherhoods) sometimes described as international 'corporations', however various in the forms they assumed, were already playing a major role in maintaining the unity of the Islamic world after the fall of Baghdad to the Mongols in 1258 and the destruction of the Abbasid Caliphate. In fact a process was in train which by the eighteenth century led Gibb to remark 'membership of such brotherhoods was practically synonymous with the profession of Islam'.[4] When Ibn 'Arabī died in 1240, a monistic theosophy of the Sufi tradition was well articulated and widely diffused. This, together with the fact that the earliest extant manuscripts from North Sumatra,

4. HAR Gibb and Harold Bowen, *Islamic Society and the West* Volume I Islamic Society in the Eighteenth Century Part II (London: Oxford University Press, 1957), 76.

showed evidence a serious interest in such a theosophy, had seemed to suggest a possible causal relationship between the development of a theosophical tradition of Sufism and lslamisation in our region.

This was after all a view to which my early (alas skimpy) research on Sufi texts from Sumatra during the seventeenth century disposed me.[5] I was at that time, intoxicated by the writings of Nicholson and Massignon, and fascinated by the theosophy of Ibn 'Arabī.

Ibn 'Arabī's visionary Sufism is indeed intoxicating. His philosophical monism expressed in the term *waḥda al-wujūd* (the Unity of Being) transforms the emanational ideas of an Islamic Neo-Platonism into an extraordinary system of aspects and relationships, generated by the lines of force inherent in the Ninety-Nine most Beautiful Names of God, vehicles of His power and being, names such as al-Raḥmān (The Merciful), al-Ḥayy (The Living), al-Qayyūm (The Self-Subsistent or The Eternal) and al Muḥaymin (The Guardian). Even so, such elaborations were for a spiritual elite, not for every Muslim, and even with this qualification, they were not universally accepted.

Islamisation is a word with a variety of meanings, depending on the mix of trends and tendencies within the world of Islam at any one time. Such trends and tendencies are responses to the internal and external challenges that Muslim communities have faced since the religion was first preached in Arabia, and still continue. The division between Sunni and Shi'a, as a response to different views concerning leadership of the community, and the nature of that leadership after the death of the Prophet Muḥammad, is one example. There are however others, which sometimes led to schisms, at others resulted in no more than a shifting distribution of varying emphases in the formulation of doctrines which all Muslims shared. Examples of such issues can be seen in debates as to whether the Qur'an should be interpreted in a literal or allegorical sense, whether the foundation of the religion should be primarily rationalistic or gnostic, whether Law or spiritual insight should have the primary role in determining its norms and ideals.

Spiritual insight is at the heart of the Sufi quest. It is a dimension of Islam that springs from longing for an experiential awareness of

---

5. Published as 'Malay Sufism as Illustrated in a Collection of Anonymous Malay Tracts', in *Journal of the Malayan Branch of the Royal Asiatic Society* 30/2 (1957).

God: in Qur'anic language, a yearning to see His face. This yearning is expressed in different ways, and associated with varying styles of spirituality and spiritual taste. They range from the severely ascetic and sober, based on techniques of self-scrutiny, to the ecstatic, induced by recitation of the Qur'an, and even by music and dance leading to exuberances of theosophical expression. But these differences are not always mutually exclusive, and there is a difference of emphases within them and between them.

Such modes of spirituality are spread across the broad range of the Islamic peoples, Southeast Asia not excepted. Islamised Southeast Asia, however, presents special problems to Islamicists. One of the reasons is that the region, by and large, does not have a continuing stable urban tradition. In it the oral tradition is stronger than the literary. It is therefore difficult to bring to it the philological and historical methodologies developed in the study of Islam in the Middle East or the Indian sub-continent. Thus scholars concerned with the traditional Islamic disciplines have found little there of interest compared to the intellectual excitement to be derived from the literary traditions of South and West Asia. And many of the scholars who devoted themselves to the study of the history and societies of Southeast Asia lacked both a training in the foundational knowledge of Islamic disciplines, and an awareness of the wider world of Islam. The result was in many writings a prominence given to issues such as 'syncretism,' and the 'conflict' between *adat* and Islamic law, suggesting that such tensions were distinctive features of Islam in the region and not encountered elsewhere in the Muslim world.

In fact, the presence and role of Islam in Southeast Asia, until recent years has been consistently underestimated. This is in part because in a number of critical regions, Central Java being a case in point, many cultural forms of the pre-Islamic past still have a vigorous life, notably the shadow theatre and the gamelan orchestra. Moreover, in the search for a classical tradition (every country has to have one!) the pre-Islamic archaeological and literary culture represented by monuments like the Borobudur and the retelling in old Javanese poetry or prose of episodes of the Hindu Buddhist epics from the pre-Muslim past have exercised a stronger appeal for philologists and scholars of religion than the living tradition of Islam, which for many lay unobserved. In addition, thanks to the tendency to regard Central Java as representing the core of insular Southeast Asian culture, Islam appeared to lack legitimacy and cultural status, and was seen not as a new element in the mix but as the cultural blight that put an end to the splendour of Hindu Java. The presence of Islam was noted, and needed cursory reference, but often scholars were uncertain as to how to deal with it, and either dismissed it, or looked the other way.

This attitude was compounded by the currency of such terms as the heartland and the periphery of the Islamic world to refer to the Middle East and the Indonesian islands respectively, as though the further one got from Mecca the more diluted and weaker Islamic faith and practice became. Such are the ways in which we are made captive to metaphors of our own creation!

A corollary of this has been that what passes for conventional wisdom concerning Islam in the area ranges from the bizarre to the patronising. There is the view, for example, that Javanese Muslims are tolerant, and do not exhibit the aggressive characteristics of Middle Eastern Muslims because pre-Islamic beliefs are still strong, the implication being that the Javanese in revealing this dimension of tolerance are not behaving as Muslims at all, or that a tropical climate with its heavy rainfall, has dampened religious enthusiasm.

It is difficult to exaggerate how widespread such generalizations are, or how superficial. Tolerance and intolerance are not distributed geographically. There are in Egypt and Pakistan, for example, Muslims with a far broader range of religious sympathies than many Indonesians. There are Indonesians with a far more narrowly scripturalist understanding of the religion they profess than some Saudi Arabians. The reverse of course is also true.

If such were the views simply of European non-Muslims, it would be problematic enough, but in fact one finds similar attitudes among Muslims in the Middle East who speak patronisingly of their co-religionists in Indonesia or Malaysia, as though to say, due to their distance from the Holy Land, they are not really Muslims, or at best, that their way of being so is so diluted that there can be no strength of identification with them as fellow-members of the Muslim community.

A different perspective, one that takes as its starting point the active engagement, of Southeast Asian Muslims in the commonwealth of Islam, yields a different picture. It has its own exigencies.

It is necessary, by way of example, to take account of their observance of the daily ritual prayer, the passage rites of passage such as circumcision, marriage and burial, and alongside these, those areas of life in which Islamic Law of the Shafi'ite school is applied, and the great annual events such as the Fast and the Pilgrimage. One should consider, likewise, their participation in revival movements such as that of the Wahhabis, or the reformist movement initiated by al-Afghani and Muhammad Abduh, or in the radicalisation of Islam in modern times by Mawdudi, Sayyid Qutb and Khomeini. One has to appreciate the part Southeast Asian Muslims played in the transmission, development and vernacularisation of the Islamic disciplines in their part of the world: their knowledge of Arabic, the manuscript copies they made of foundational Arabic texts before the advent of printing, and the acceptance of its use for religious works and their competence in the Islamic disciplines. One might remark that at the turn of the century, Singapore had an important role in this process. In addition, one can look to their association with outstanding teachers in other areas of the Muslim world, the part they played in the Islamic commonwealth of religious scholars, and their preparation of text books for local conditions, making their own contribution to such disciplines as Qur'anic exegesis, dogmatics, jurisprudence and eschatology. Not least one should be aware of the implications of their adoption of the Arabic script to write Malay and other local languages. Finally one should take account of the establishment of Islamised forms of the state, and the role of sultanates in the region in the days before sultans were forced to give way, at least in some areas, to Colonels, Presidents and Prime Ministers.

It is only in such a wider context that the more specific question may be asked: how did Southeast Asian Muslims participate in the various Sufi traditions known in other parts of the Muslim world? How did they share in and make their own contribution to the mystical dimension of Islam? It is in this context that one may ask whether there were any aspects of Sufism that facilitated the spread of the religion, or may have predisposed Muslims in the various areas of what is now 'Indonesia' as the name of a modern nation state is an obstacle to a clear understanding of the processes of Islamisation in the region. It is easily overlooked that the word had no political content before the early twenties of this century. The fact that it is an over-arching term does not imply any homogeneity in the regions it subsumes, and certainly does not wipe out a millenium or more of the histories of a variety of languages and cultures, all important in their own right. People in different areas of what is now Indonesia naturally participate in the Islamic world in different ways.

It is from such a perspective that one should attempt to highlight the various aspects and emphases in the lslamisation of the region from the time that it began. Self-evidently, it cannot be separated from the trading system of the Indian Ocean. As soon as Muslims took part in that system, and eventually they were to dominate it, a discreet, silent process of Islamization began, as Muslim trading communities became established at focal points along the northeast coast of Sumatra and on the Malay Peninsula, the north coast of Java, Borneo and the Celebes. Such points were convenient stopping places to exchange goods, to take on water and firewood and to wait for a change of the monsoon—either to journey on to China for silks and porcelain, or to take on board spices and locally produced goods.

How long these communities had remained silent and discreet before appearing on the pages of history with a political profile there is little way of knowing, any more than whether they formed settlements in areas largely uninhabited, to which they attracted other traders, or whether they formed autonomous quarters in already existing centres of population and trade. At any rate, as Muslims, they had their networks of international contacts within which business confidence was guaranteed due to the writing of contracts according to Muslim Law. Business confidence is infectious, and the association of non-Muslim peoples in the trading enterprises of Muslims with contracts written according to Islamic Law, followed by the growth, stability and prosperity of Muslim communities is a widely recognized mode of Islamisation.

Now if Muslim communities are to function effectively as communities, they require the presence of *'ulamā'*, those individuals trained in Islamic jurisprudence who understand the principles of contracts—whether for trade or marriages—who can work out legal solutions to the conflicts that arise in any community, and who can lead prayers, officiate at funerals, perform the necessary astronomical calculations to determine the times for prayers, the approach of the fasting month, and the pilgrimage season. Such an elite, a class of scholars, have their own networks, both among themselves, the teachers from whom they had studied and acquired their legal expertise or by whom they had been inducted into one or another of the great *tarīqa (Brotherhoods).*

Once these things have occurred, there is already effective participation in the world of Islam, even if, in the thirteenth century, as far as Southeast Asia is concerned, documentation is sparse. But there is another development to take into account. By the thirteenth century, the new institution of the sultanate had become well-established. The first ruler whose coins bear the title *Sulṭān* was apparently Tughril Beg who stablished the Seljuk dynasty in 1055.[6] From his time on, sultanates sprang, up like mushrooms in the Middle East, the Indian sub-continent and Southeast Asia. Once the precedent had been established, any leader of a community who had established an adequate power base could when he deemed the time ripe, consolidate that power base by declaring himself sultan and claiming an area of territorial jurisdiction. A sultanate, barring coups and/or assassinations is a hereditary institution and given a measure of stability, and a succession of able rulers, is able to expand its area of authority. At some stage, this happened in Sumatra, and the culmination of the process of silent lslamisation is marked by the first evidence of a sultan on the island, the gravestone of Sultan Malik al-Saleh at Pasai with an inscription giving as the date of his death a year corresponding to 1297 or 1307, depending on how the inscription is interpreted.[7]

Pasai was a harbour principality, and it is the establishment of such harbour principalities under a sultan with their religious and mercantile orientation across the Indian Ocean, that provides the political and economic mechanism for the further expansion of Islam. It is likewise this institution that provides the means of a closer relationship with other Muslims, and creates opportunities in the structure of the state for the establishment of religious schools, the participation in teaching of foreign with local *'ulamā'*, and the creation of libraries.

If one asks whether during this period there is any direct evidence of Sufi involvement in the Islamisation that had reached the level at which the leader of a Muslim community might declare himself sultan, the answer is no. But if the question is put differently: What is the likelihood of individual traders and *'ulamā'* law brokers essential for business confidence being members of *ṭarīqas*? then by the thirteenth century, the answer must be that it is high, particularly if

6. Philip K Hitti, *History of the Arabs* (London: Macmillan [Papermac], 1979), 474.
7. DGE Hall, *A History of Southeast Asia* (London: Macmillan, 1955), 177.

the trader, as so many of them were, was from Indian sub-continent. There is indirect evidence in the traditional stories that elaborated in the court chronicles which attribute the coming of Islam to the preaching of itinerant holy men from abroad, one of them commissioned by Muḥammad himself.[8] But such stories are largely *ex post facto* fabrications.

There is evidence that the Pasai court was aware of personalities and events in other, older established centres of authority in the Muslim world. Fatimi,[9] using information provided by Hitti, has drawn attention to the possible significance of the name of the Pasai sultan, Malik al-Saleh (as it is usually spelt in histories of Indonesia) mentioned above. This name, Fatimi points out, is eponymous with that of the Ayyubid ruler al-Malik al-Ṣāliḥ (r 1240–1249), who restored Jerusalem to Islamic rule in 1244. Might this not have been a reason for him on becoming or declaring himself sultan, to adopt this name? It is possible to see a similar motivation in his naming of two of his sons Malik al-Ẓāhir [*sic*] and Malik al-Manṣūr [*sic*], both eponymous with two near contemporary figures in the Middle East. al-Malik al-ḥāhir Baybars was the fourth Mamluk sultan (r 1260–1277). He aspired to be a second Ṣalāḥ al-Dīn, and played a major role in blocking the Mongols' advance towards Cairo.[10]

al-Malik al-Manṣūr (r 1279–1290), was likewise a great anti-crusader, and the most outstanding Mamluk figure after Baybars. He achieved such renown that even the ruler of Ceylon sent an embassy to his court with a letter no one could read![11] The correspondence of names may be coincidental, but it is not inherently unlikely that the Malik al-Ṣāliḥ of Pasai was sufficiently in touch with events across the Indian Ocean, mediated perhaps also through trading contacts, perhaps through Pasai pilgrims or a Pasai community in Mecca, to be aware of these three famous names from the Middle East and to be heartened by reports of Muslim victories against the Crusaders. After all, such events there would have had economic implications

8. See Russell Jones, 'Ten Indonesian Conversion Myths', in *Conversion to Islam*, edited by N Levtzion (London: Holmes and Meier, 1979), 129–158.
9. SQ Fatimi, *Islam Comes to Malaysia* (Singapore: Malaysian Sociological Research Institute Ltd [MSR], 1963), 11.
10. Hitti, *History*, 656.
11. Hitti, *History*, 678. Fatimi's summary and interpretation of these events should be read against the information given in Hitti, 655–656 & 677–678.

for Pasai. At the very least, Fatimi's implied point that to be a Sultan was to become a member of an exclusive club of Muslim rulers is important.

It is not until the late sixteenth century that local manuscript sources from Sumatra become available. All are written in the Arabic script, adapted to indicate those sounds in Malay that have no counterpart in Arabic, and all show a significant stratum of Arabic loan words and a number of features of syntax that could reflect Arabic influence. Although relatively young, it is clear that they belong to a tradition that is much older and are evidence of a long and close participation of local peoples in Islamic life and culture. The earliest example is the poems of the Acehnese Hamzah Fansuri (d 1599?). He is an author belonging to the theosophical tradition of Ibn 'Arabī mediated by the Iraqi al-Jīlī (d *circa* 1408). His rendering of numbers of Qur'anic verses into Malay and interpretation of them as they are understood in this mystical tradition, no less than his vernacularisation of Arabic words and concepts, is extraordinary. His writings show an ecstatic passion for union with God, and include a brilliant tangential allusion to al-Hallaj's identification of himself with the burning bush in the vision of Moses, by an identification of himself with the tree burnt to yield camphor.[12]

By the seventeenth century, it is possible demonstrate a close relationship between religion and political authority in the Aceh sultanate (1496–1874). This relationship is evidenced in a number of ways: through the investiture of the ruler Sultan Iskandar Muda (1607–1636) into Sufi *tarīqa* by his *Shaykh al-Islām* (perhaps a conscious use of an Indo-Ottoman title), Shams al Dīn. It is also seen in his Shaikh al-Islam acting in a political role both as foreign minister and as vicegerent when Iskandar was incapacitated by bouts of insanity. This combination in a single individual of the roles of Sufi adept, *murshid* to the ruler, and holder of two senior positions of state, is noteworthy.[13]

The position of Islam in the state is likewise illustrated in the nonchalant and unstudied manner in which, to two well-known mystical verses of Ibn 'Arabī in a Malay work published under the title

12. See GWJ Drewes and LF Brakel, *The Poems of Hamzah Fansuri*, Bibliotheca Indonesica 26 (Dordrecht: Floris Publications, 1986). The specific verse reference is to page 143 v 13.
13. CAO Van Nieuwenhuilze, *Shamsu'l-Din van Pasai* (Leiden: EJ Brill), 6–21.

Hikajat Atjeh, a lengthy fragment of panegyric to Iskandar Muda.[14] When a remote ancestor of Iskandar finds his future bride in a clump of bamboo, to quieten her alarm at this unexpected discovery, he says to her, God has made manifest today our former hidden union (within His knowledge), before individual existents were differentiated one from the other). In this allusion there is both reference to the predestined greatness of Iskandar, and a sophisticated sexual conceit, the product of close, even playful familiarity with the formulations of the doctrine of the Unity of Being.[15]

Chance allusions of this kind are more revealing of the currency of religious ideas than the fact that Shams al-Dīn wrote a number of treatises in Arabic, still extant, among them, *Jawhar al-Ḥaqā'iq*, a masterpiece in its own right.[16]

In this Arabic work Shams al-Din sets out a structure of five levels or manifestations of Being, the same as that presented by Hamzah Fansuri. In the Malay (and presumably) later works attributed to him, he presents a structure of seven levels of of Being deriving from a work by a North Indian scholar Muḥammad b Faḍl Allāh al-Burhānpūrī (d 1590), *al-Tuḥfa al-mursala ilā'l-rūh al-nabī* (The Gift addressed to the Spirit of the Prophet). This was rapidly to establish itself as a basic text in many regions of the Muslim World, and it appears that in his Malay works, Shams al-Din too was quick to adopt it[17]

It should be remembered that the lbn 'Arabī tradition represents only one way of participation in the mystical life of Islam, and that

14. Teuku Iskandar, *De Hikajat Atjeh,* Verhandelingen van het Konial-Land-en Volkenkunde, volume 26, The Hague (1958): 67.
15. An English rendering of the lines in question is:

    We were lofty sounds unuttered held in the highest peaks of the hills
    I am you in Him, and we are you and you are He
    All is He in Him -ask those who have attained.

    For a Malay commentary on these lines by. the Achehnese 'Abd al-Ra'uf see AH Johns, '-73, 'Dakā'ik al-Ḥurūf by 'Abd al-Ra'ūf of Singkel', in *Journal of the Royal Asiatic Society of Great Britain* (1955): 55–73, 139–158.
16. For an account of his life and work see A.H. Johns, 'Shams al-Dīn al-Samaṭrā'ī (1560 - 1630)' in *Essays in Arabic Literary Bibliography 1350-1850*, Joseph E. Lowry and Devin J Stewart, editors, Mizan Band 17 (Wiesbaden: Harrassowitz Verlag, 2009), 357–371.
17. An edition of the Arabic text along with an English rendering is in AH Johns, *The Gift Addressed to the Spirit of the Prophet*, Oriental Monograph Series No 1 (Canberra: Australian National University, 1965).

other models are represented in fragments of works in Javanese from the late sixteenth century, dealing with dogmatics and spirituality, from one or another of the north coastal towns of Java.[18] These works have little to do with the monistic theosophy of the Ibn 'Arabī tradition but are based largely on the ethical mysticism of al-Ghazali. These examples are sufficient to demonstrate the independent networking of groups of religious teachers with varying spiritual taste at centres of trade and authority in the archipelago, and the discrete character of local traditions all over the archipelago.

By the mid-seventeenth century, a fuller documentation of this participation becomes possible, with evidence in Arabic sources of the presence of Sumatrans in Mecca and Medina and their attachment to a particular teacher. This is sufficiently important to present in some detail. We are able to put together a Kurdish scholar, Ibrāhīm al-Kūrānī (1615–1690) who was affiliated to a number of *tarīqa*, and a *khalīfa* of the Shaṭṭāriyya order, who settled in Medina; 'Abd al-Ra'ūf, an Acehnese who studied with Ibrāhīm in Arabia (1640–1661), and Yūsuf[19] a Makassarese who was in Medina with 'Abd al-Ra'ūf for some years; and Ibrāhīm's pupil al-Ḥamawī, who wrote *Fawā'iḍal-Irtiḥāl wa Natā'ij al-Safar* (The Benefits of Travel and the Results of Journeying) a biographical dictionary of the '*ulamā*' of Mecca and Medina in the eleventh Islamic century (seventeenth century AD) which includes an entry on his teacher Ibrāhīm and the Sumatrans who studied from him, reporting what they said to Ibrāhīm and what Ibrāhīm said to him about them.[20]

In this entry Ḥamawī says:

> Our Shaikh (Ibrāhīm) told me that one of our Jawi associates—and he was reading with him the [work entitled] *al-Tuḥfa al-mursala ilā rūh al-nabī* while we were present—told him that this treatise and the matters it treats of was popular and

18. GWJ Drewes, *The Admonitions of Seh Bari*, Bibliotheca Indonesia 4 (The Hague, 1969) and Een Javanese Primbon uit de Zestiende Eeuw (Leiden: H Brill, 1954).
19. Yūsuf al-Maqāsirī (1626–1699), a major religious-political figure in Java in the middle years of the 17th century. See Nicholas L Heer, The Precious Pearl (Albany:SUNY Press 1979), 15.
20. For a general survey of tafsīr in the region see AH Johns, 'Qur'anic Exegesis in the Malay World: In Search of a Profile', in Towards a History of the Interpretation of the Qur'an, edited by A Rippin (Oxford: The Clarendon Press, 1987), 257–287.

> well-known in the lands of the Jawi, and that it is read in their religious schools.

Ibrāhīm had a special relationship with Jawi students, foremost among them 'Abd al-Ra'ūf whom he designated as his *khalīfa* to spread this *tarīqa* in Sumatra when he returned to his homeland. They asked him questions about the correct understanding of the work referred to by Ḥamawī, and the system of seven manifestations of Being that it set out. It was in response to their questions that Ibrāhīm wrote a major work on the topic; entitled *lthāf al-Dhakī* In his introduction to his work he refers to the Sumatrans and the questions that they put to him:

> We have reliable information from a group of Jawi that there have become wide-spread among the inhabitants of the lands of 'Java': some books on Realities and esoteric teachings by men attributed with knowledge because of their study and the teaching of others, but who lack any understanding of the Law of (Muḥammad) the Chosen, the Elect.

He continues:

> They told me that among the best known of books among them was the compendium entitled *al-Tuhfa al-mursala ilā ruh al-nabī* (the work by Muḥammad ibn Faḍl Allāh mentioned by Hamawi in the biographical entry referred to above), and more than one of them has asked my humble self to prepare a commentary on it to make clear the conformity of the questions (it discusses) to the basis of the principles of religion, confirmed by the noble Book, and the *Sunna* of the Lord of the Messengers.[21]

This was not the only work that he wrote at the request of the Jawi. Another treatise on the correct understanding of the lbn 'Arabī tradition, *al-Maslak al-jalī fi ḥukm shatḥ al-walī*, also stating that it was written at the request of a Jawi, is in the Leiden library [Cod Or. 5660 (2)].

21. The work has been critically edited, the text established and translated into Indonesian by the Indonesian scholar Dr Oman Fathurahman, *Itḥāf al-Dhakī Tafsīr Waḥdatul Wujūd bagi Muslim Nusantara* (Jakarta: Mizan, 2012).

What kind of a man was Ibrāhīm? What did his teaching communicate to 'Abd al-Ra'ūf, and how did it contribute to the participation of his countrymen in Islamic life and devotion? In other words, what was the range of learning and the kind of spirituality to which he attracted them? In the introduction to his work *Itḥāf al-Dhakī*, he plays on the most beautiful names of God as though they were a musical instrument with the compass and resonances of a great organ, 'God is the First and the Last, the Outward and the Inward: the First before who in nothing was, the Inward beneath whom nothing is more hidden'. He justifies the seeking of inward meanings in the Qur'anic verses and *ḥadīth*, but condemns any abandonment of their literal meaning, quoting from al-Ghazālī's *Mishkāt al-Anwār* his use of the tradition, 'Angels do not· enter a house in which there is a dog' to condemn the *bāṭiniyya*. To discover an inward sense to the *ḥadith*, that is that the word 'house' may signify heart and 'dog' the spirit of anger, and thus that it may mean 'angels do not enter a heart in which is the spirit of anger' does no violence to the words of the Messenger. It would only do so were one to claim that the only meaning of this *ḥadīth* is this inward one. Knowledge of such an inward meaning however, does not exempt the believer from the duty of obeying the literal sense of the word. But, Ibrāhim says, the Sufis do not do this, rather they affirm the outward sense of the words, and refrain from keeping a dog; and, in addition, understand them in whatever inward way that Allāh reveals to them, for there is nothing impossible in God giving to any one of His servants He chooses an understanding of meanings in His Book and the sayings of His Prophet that are not explicitly expressed.[22]

What was he like as a teacher? There is an anecdote told in a biographical dictionary,

> Ibrāhīm used to say: The *Fātiḥa* should be recited at the end of every meeting. There was once an old *faqīh* who said, 'I married a young woman when I was advanced in years. Her family loved me and trusted me, but secretly, she disliked me because of my old age, and only pretended affection for me for the sake of her family'.

22. These passages are summarised from a draft English translation of the *Ithāf al-dhakī* based on the Leiden Ms Cod Or 7050. made before the edition of Dr Oman Fathurahman was published.

> Now one day a woman friend visited her, and I listened to them talking without their knowing it. Every word she spoke complaining about me I wrote down on a piece of paper I had by me. Then the woman visitor made to leave, but my wife said to her: 'Not until we have recited the *Fātiḥa* together, as do the *faqīh* and his friends when they part.' So the pair of them recited the *Fātiḥa* and I wrote that down too, as they recited it.
>
> Then I told her brothers all that she had said about me, and said to them, Do not make her stay with me, for I wish to divorce her. They were displeased with her and reproached her, but she denied everything I had accused her of having said against me. So I said, Here is the paper on which I wrote everything down as you were saying it'. And lo! there was nothing on the page except the *Fātiḥa*, and so I realised that the *Fātiḥa* had blotted out every evil thing she had said.[23]

A number of maxims are attributed to him. They include, 'It is better to reconcile two conflicting points of view rather than to choose one of them or the other'; 'Truth lies at the mid-point between excess and inadequacy,' and 'The philosophers got close to ultimate truth, but did not quite succeed in attaining it'.

And what of 'Abd al-Ra'ūf? He lived for thirty years in Acheh on his return from twenty years in Arabia. He exchanged letters with Ibrāhīm across the Indian Ocean. He was supported by the court, by the Sulṭāna Ṣāfiyatu'l-Dīn (r 1641–1675). He wrote prolifically, and his contribution to the vernacularisation of Islam in Malay is remarkable. He wrote a treatise, on the orders of the sultana, on the branch of *fiqh* known as *al-mu 'āmalāt* called *Mir'āt al-ṭullāb*—a work of 600 pages in manuscript; he prepared a Malay rendering of much of the *tafsīr* of *al-Jalālayn* that is still in use today and is regularly reprinted. (This work, entitled *Tarjumān al-Mustafīḍ* was accepted by Snouck Hurgronje as a translation of Bayḍawī's *Anwār al-Tanzil* taking at face value a codicil to the work added by three nineteenth-century Malay scholars in Mecca.)[24] He wrote a lengthy treatise on the

23. al-Afrānī al-Marakīshī *Ṭabaqāt al-ṣulāhā'* (Lithograph, no place, no date), 210–211.

24. For a general survey of *tafsīr* in the region see AH Johns, 'Quranic Exegesis in the Malay World: In Search of a Profile', in Towards a History of the Interpretation of the Qur'an, edited by A Rippin (Oxford: The Clarendon Press, 1987), 257–287.

spiritual exercise of *dhikr* (Reflection and Recitation) called *'Umdat al-muḥtajīn*, and a theoretical work on the concept of the Unity of Being, which may be summarised: The world is from God. Everything is The Reality, al-Ḥaqq, but not as it is here and now. Being is one, but only at the level of non-manifestation in the knowledge of God.[25]

'Abd al-Ra'ūf's concerns were broad. He brings together the exterior and interior disciplines (as did his teacher Ibrāhīm). Yet he knew how to discriminate between the levels of spiritual attainment of the students he was addressing. He writes on *tafsīr* without reference to the mystical dimension of exegesis, as well as on *ḥadīth* and *fiqh*. Yet he also writes on the spiritual exercise of *dhikr*, and on the Unity of Being. As a teacher, he inducted many individuals into the Shaṭṭāriyya order, and contributed to its popularity in Java.

This is the first occasion in the history of Islam in the region in which it is possible to bring together such a constellation of facts, individuals and sources of information: a Sumatra scholar, 'Abd al-Ra'ūf; the ruler of Acheh, Ṣafiyatu'l-Din, who was his patron; the Kurd, Ibrāhīm al-Kūrānī, who was 'Abd al-Ra'ūf's teacher in Medina, and the biographer of Ibrāhīm, Hamawi, who is our source of information for the presence of Sumatrans in the circle of Ibrāhīm's students. In addition, we have works that they produced. We can put our hands on their writings and in some cases manuscripts of the letters they wrote to each other across the Indian Ocean.

A later instance of a comparable constellation of elements occurs in the mid-eighteenth century under the aegis of the Sultanate of Palembang in south Sumatra. It is possible to document the relationship between 'Abd al-Ṣamad (1703–1788) of Palembang, and Arab scholars in the Holy Land, including the Egyptian Azharite professor Aḥmad b 'Abd al-Mun'im al-Damanhūrī who visited Mecca in 1763, and Muhammad b 'Abd al-Karīm al-Sammān (1719–1775) who founded the Sammāniyya *tarīqa*. 'Abd al-Ṣamad was inducted into this *tārīqa*, and through his students in Mecca returning home to Sumatra, it was established in Palembang where it flourished within the founder's life-time.[26]

25. See P Voorhoeve, 'Bayān Tadjallī', in *Tijdschrift Bataviaasch Gennootschap voor Indisch Taal-, Land-en Volkenkunde*, 1 (1952): 109–115.

26. GWJ Drewes, *Directions for Travellers on the Mystic Path*, Verhandelingen van het Koninklijk Instituut voor Taal-, Land-, en Volkenkunde (VKI) 81 (The Hague, 1977), 219–220.

Palembang was a centre of Muslim learning that deserves detailed study. Within a period of fifty years or less, Malay versions of such works on dogmatics as Ibrāhīm al-Laqanī's (d 1631) commentary on the rhymed credal statement *Jawaharāt al-Tawḥīd*, works of ethical mysticism as the *Ḥikam* of Ibn 'Atā Allāh, and the *Risālat fi'l-Tawhīd* by Raslan al-Dimishqī enlarged by the Cairo author Zakariyya al-Ansārī (d 1520) and later 'Abd al-Ghanī al-Nablusī (d 1731), a Sufi text that lays greater emphasis on inner worship, purity of motivation, and the spiritual stages of *shukr, riḍa* and *ṣabr*, than spiritual union with the Divinity. And then perhaps most important, 'Abd al-Ṣamad's rendering into Malay around 1788 of *Lubāb iḥyā' 'ulūm al-dīn*, an abridgement of al-Ghazali's *Iḥyā' 'ulūm al-dīn*, by al-Ghazali's brother Aḥmad. Here again is documentation of a Sumatran scholar who spent years in Mecca, his association with Arab and Egyptian scholars, his induction into a *ṭarīqa*, his spreading of this *ṭarīqa* in Palembang in person, and through the students who came from Sumatra to study with him in Mecca, the major contribution he makes to the vernacularisation of Islam with a work that is still reprinted, and the role of the Palembang court in supporting religious learning.[27]

A nineteenth century example is furnished by the career of al-Nawawī al-Bantanī. He was born in 1814 went to Mecca in 1829 and lived there for most of the remainder of his long life. He wrote on the various disciplines of *ḥadīth*, jurisprudence, Qur'an exegesis, mysticism grammar and rhetoric. He was teacher and guide to many generations of Jawi in Mecca over forty years. Snouck Hurgronje met him in 1885 and in his book *Mekka in the Latter Part of the 19th Century*[28] notes that he was acknowledged as head of the Jawi community; and had just published, on the newly established Mecca Press, a two-volume commentary on the Qur'an.

Nawawī was the author of over 100 works in Arabic, a number of them still in current use in religious teaching institutions and regularly reprinted in Mecca, Cairo, and a number of major cities in Indonesia. His two volume *tafsīr, Marāḥ Labīd*[29] deserves special mention. In the introduction he lists the authors and the works on whom he depends. They include Fakhr al-Dīn al-Rāzī (d 1209), Shirbini (d 1570), and

27. Drewes, *Directions for Travellers on the Mystic Path*, 36–37.
28. Snouck Hurgronje, *Mekka in the Latter Part of the 19th Century* (Leiden: EJ Brill, 1931), 268–272.
29. *Marāḥ Labīd -Tafsīr al-Nawawī* (Cairo: Ḥalabi, 1965).

Abu'l-Su'ūd (d 1574). In fact about seventy per cent of his *tafsīr* is selected from Rāzī's great work *Mafātīh al-Ghayb* (also known as *al-Tafsīr al-Kabīr*), giving his own compilation, following in Rāzī's footsteps, a markedly rationalist character. Moreover, following Rāzī, he omits many illustrative stories to the qur'anic text which modern Muslims tend to dismiss as *Isrā'īliyyāt*. Thus Rāzī's influence on him is significant, an influence that he passed on to thousands of his students from the Indies over a period of forty years. A case can be made that he not only anticipated and facilitated the spread of Muḥammad 'Abduh's reformist ideas in the then East Indies, but also, thanks to his staunch loyalty to the Shafi'ite *madhhab*, the school of Islamic Law widely followed in Southeast Asia, also helped prepare the ground for the rise of the *Naḥḍat al-'Ulamā'*, distinguished from the *Muḥammadiyya* and other reformist groups by its insistence on recognition of the authority of the traditional schools of law,[30] and its own adherence to the Shafi'ite *madhhab* in particular. As a digression, it may be remarked that I owe Nawawī a personal debt, for it was through him that I discovered Rāzī, and found a new field of research in Rāzī's great work of *tafsīr*.

These examples are far from exhaustive. They are, however, sufficient to show that references to Islam in Sumatra and Java as though these regions belonged to a remote periphery of the Muslim world are misleading. Rather the islands of Indonesia were linked to the Arabian Peninsula by the Indian Ocean, not separated from it. Modes of participation varied from place to place. During the silent years of Islamisation preparing the ground for the appearance of Islam with a political face in the region the Sufi dimension was present, both explicitly and implicitly at appropriate levels in Muslim communities.

In giving a primacy to the Sufi movement in the Islamisation of the region, the issue was wrongly put, but the putting of it was not wholly wrong. If the generalisation that the Indies became Islamised due largely to the spiritual appeal of Sufism was too broad, it is not necessarily wrong to say that many, if not a majority of the *'ulamā'* who played a role in the establishment of Muslim communities and institutions in Southeast Asia had Sufi affiliations. By the same token,

30. For a more detailed study of this work of Nawawī see my 'On Qur'anic exegetes and exegesis: A case study in the transmission of Islamic learning' in *Islam:Essays on Scripture Thought and Society*, Peter G Riddell and Tony Street, editors (Leiden: EJ Brill, 1997).

it is certainly overly simplistic to speak *tout court* of Islam being brought to the Indies by traders, without reference to the central role of the *'ulamā'* in any Muslim community enjoying stability over time.

During the early years of Islamisation, local evidence is so scarce that it is necessary to proceed by inference. Nevertheless it must be recognised that we have to do not simply with local peoples encountering Muslims, and eventually adopting a new religion in a particular geographical area, but with their involvement in a wide-ranging international community through a variety of networks and institutions comprising related ethnicities, merchant groups, religious teachers and *tarīqas*. All this was a continuing process that by zealous networking at an individual level *pari passu* with the expansion and contraction of political authority at the level of the ruler, extended the domain and depth of Islam in the region, particularly when the Muslim ruler allied himself with (or fought against) another local Muslim ruler.

During this period (eleventh-eighteenth centuries) Sufism should not be thought of as distinct or separate from the vast body of jurisprudence it complemented and alongside which it grew out of the primary sources of the Qur'an and the *sunna*, notwithstanding that the house of Islam has long been divided in its attitude to the Ibn 'Arabī tradition of theosophical Sufism. The Sufi Shaikhs were not necessarily to be thought of as individuals or a class separate from the *'ulamā'*. It is in part the anti-*tarīqa* stance of the reformists of Muhammad Abduh's generation that has at times exaggerated the extent of this tension, an exaggeration that has been projected back anachronistically, and tacitly accepted by a number of Western scholars.

The Sufi movement is but one dimension of Islam, and in so far as it has a separate identity, represents only one aspect of Islamisation in the region. There are many others which complement and support each other. Among them is story-telling, especially as represented by local re-tellings, adaptations and enlargements of Qur'anic presentations of scenes from lives of the prophets, *qisās al-anbiyā'* (Stories of the Prophets) which long before the Germans invented the term *heilsgeschicht*, established a widely socialised perception of a universalistic salvation history, from Adam to Muḥammad. The Malay corpus of manuscripts representing this genre of Islamic literature has been woefully neglected.

My examples have been limited to Acheh, Palembang and Banten, and they are far from exhaustive. One could refer to other centres and periods with similar kinds of documentation. But this brings us to a paradox: of how intensely local such communities and centres of trade and culture are, and how the religious elites were embodied in these communities in a way that produced a fusion of universal forms of Islam with local beliefs and life-styles.[31] This is indeed true of Indonesia today, with its distinctive styles of fusion of local elements with the universalistic doctrines of Islam in say Aceh, Minangkabau, Central Java and the Celebes, but it is certainly not peculiar to Indonesia and its neighbours. Lapidus' great work makes this abundantly clear.

The processes of Islamisation in Southeast Asia and the outcome of those processes are more like than unlike what happened elsewhere in the Islamic world; in the so-called polarisation between what is called *sharīa* and *'adat* law, we are only seeing the same processes that were to yield the so-called classic formulations of Islamic Law—the uniting and infusing with an Islamic spirit and norms of a whole range of practices in familial, commercial and criminal law, administrative regulations, adding Persian, Byzantine and Hellenistic maxims, elements of the canon law of the orthodox church, Talmudic and old Babylonian law bringing all into conformity with God's will.[32] Equally, 'syncretism', no matter how this troublesome word is understood, is a phenomenon well attested in all parts of the Muslim world, not least in its so-called heartlands.

Sufism then had and has its role in a variety of styles of Islamisation in different regions and periods in combination with many other things besides in Southeast Asia. It is a dimension which offered a variety of modalities of participation in the universe of Islam according to the spiritual taste, cultural traditions and Zeitgeist of those parts of Southeast Asia that were to become part of the domain of Islam.

So let me conclude: the role of Sufism in our region is not all that different from that of Sufism in other parts of the Muslim world. There is little reason to regard the Muslims of Southeast Asia overall

---

31. Ira M Lapidus, *A History of Islamic Societies* (Cambridge: Cambridge University Press, 1990), 259.
32. Lapidus, *A History of Islamic Societies,* 102–103.

as being necessarily more legalistic, more mystical or more prone to 'syncretism' than other peoples of the Muslim world. From Morocco to the Moros, the Domain of lslam comprises a mix of shared emphases, and a varying distribution of them within that mix. Indeed, a major challenge to Southeast Asianists is to learn to recognise that the presence of Islam as a living, dynamic element permeating the diverse traditions of the region is far greater than much of conventional wisdom on the subject has up to the present allowed. To echo the striking metaphor of the Qur'anic words: 'The dye of God! And who better than God can tincture with a dye? (Qur'an 2:138)', this 'dye of God' is more widely and deeply infused than many have realised.

Perspectives of Islamic Spirituality in Southeast Asia: Reflections and Encounters[1]

Points of Departure

This essay attempts to subsume a universe of discourse. The terms it comprises question our understanding and experience of realities of different kinds. Southeast Asia is a geographical expression. Spirituality has to do with human experience of things unseen. It is a vital element in every religious tradition and, in Islamised Southeast Asia, is generated by the cumulative interactions of this great monotheistic religion with the diverse communities and cultures that have their home there, interactions symptomatic of an ongoing creative energy.

After forty years of concern with some of the realities implicit in these terms, they still present me with questions so searching and so personal that responses at any level are difficult. This essay nevertheless attempts to offer answers to such questions in the form of reflections on a number of the issues they involve, reflections which, even if they present little that is radically new, may serve to broaden the parameters of discussion, and suggest paths of further exploration.

As terms, 'Islam' and 'Southeast Asia' have been used so often that their meaning and implications may be taken for granted; and habitual ways of associating, thinking and writing about them have produced ideas that set our minds moving in fixed directions or possibly mis-directions. Islam in Southeast Asia', for example is a popular title for seminars and books alike. Two approaches arc well-established.

1. Based on a paper originally presented at an international workshop on 'Islam in Southeast Asia' organized by the Center for Muslim-Christian Understanding of Georgetown University, Washington DC, and the University of Malaya, Kuala Lumpur, in 1996.

One is via a focus on a limited area deemed to represent one of far wider compass. Geertz's study of a central Javanese town code-named Modjokuto appears as a book with the mildly presumptuous title *The Religion of Java*,[2] and in the literature, its scope is expanded even further for it to be offered as a guide to Indonesian society.[3] The other may be epitomized in that inspired and deathless phrase from the film *Casablanca*. 'Round up the usual suspects.' Both approaches have their limitations. Rarely if ever can a part of something stand for the whole, no matter what its intrinsic interest and importance. And interrogation of the usual suspects tends to become a routine exercise. True, we have ways of making them talk, but there still remain questions that have not yet been asked, and the need remains to ask ourselves whether we have put into the suspects' mouths what we wanted them to say.

Reference to the film *Casablanca* may sound light-hearted, if not frivolous. But spirituality needs to subsist in humanity as soul in body, and humor is as essential a part of being human as rationality. There is then a need to discover ways and means of moving beyond what has become habitual, of finding new questions to ask, and more suspects to round up.

In a book that now in its way is a classic, Southeast Asia has been described as a cross-roads of religion.[4] The expression is a metaphor and it serves as a convenient piece of short-hand to fix the region and one aspect of it in our minds. Yet, like all metaphors, vivid and apt when first coined, after the passing of years it may he misleading.

Historians tell us that Southeast Asia, due to its geographical position as a great archipelago between the two land masses of South and East Asia, was accessible to religious traditions from East and West, and then give accounts of how Buddhism began to spread, Islam began to spread, Christianity began to spread and so on. This too is a convenient piece of short-hand to account for the fact that in Southeast Asia today there are a number of different religions, but at best it is only half the truth. The situation existing there is a result not just of Buddhism, Islam and Christianity 'coming' to

2. C Geertz, *The Religion of Java* (Glencoe IL, 1960) (numerous reprints).
3. As in Ira M Lapidus, *A History of Islamic Studies* (Cambridge: Cambridge University Press, 1988), 969.
4. Kenneth Perry Landon, *Southeast Asia: Cross-roads of Religion* (Chicago IL: University of Chicago, 1949).

South East Asia—from Burma to the Philippines—at particular points in their history commencing a vigorous response to the stimuli of these non-autochthonous religious traditions, and while maintaining the authenticity of their allegiances to them, expressing their identities as Buddhists, Muslims or Christians in ways that are culturally rich and distinctive. In the case of Islamisation, one can document a reaching out for, an ingesting of and a vernacularisation of the foundation texts of the religion, together with the disciplines of religious learning deriving from them. This was accompanied by a quickening participation in its spiritual and cultural traditions, a complex process that has left a mark on virtually every area of social and intellectual life.

One of the striking cultural features of Southeast Asia is the way in which these religious traditions have developed there. Rather than 'a cross-roads' of religion, perhaps a metaphor more apt to express this aspect of Southeast Asia might be 'a seed-bed' of religion, the diverse peoples of Southeast Asia having in common a genius and extraordinary resource for realising and giving expression to the inner genius of these religious traditions, resulting in cultural achievements on a par with those in the lands of their birth. The outcome is marked by paradoxes. Buddhism is virtually absent from India, but artistically, socially and spiritually still flourishes in Southeast Asia. The region has the largest complex of Muslim communities in the world; the Philippines is the only Asian nation with a Christian majority. And there are significant minorities of Muslims, Buddhists and Christians in the regions in which they are not the majority religion. Is it then, or is it not, paradoxical that there are Vietnamese Catholic priests serving Australian congregations, or Indonesian *imams* in Australia serving Muslims from all over the Muslim world, and caring for Muslim communities in Australia?

Islam In Southeast Asia

Despite this immense fruitfulness, one of the consequences of the historians' short-hand expression 'Islam comes to Southeast Asia', is a perception that this is all that happened: Islam came and a certain homogeneous stasis ensued. Perhaps this is one of the reasons that many Muslims from the so-called heartlands of the Islamic world sometimes give a patronising smile when they hear Islam in

Southeast Asia mentioned. Even leading Southeast Asian Muslims have been known to be apologetic about their contribution to the Muslim world, and remark that their region is a consumer rather than a producer of Islamic culture. Thus it frequently happens that in surveys of the Islamic world, Southeast Asia is overlooked, or else described from secondary sources that are factually and conceptually out of date, by authors with little knowledge of the local languages, and less of Arabic.

A well-established approach in university courses devoted to the study of Islam in the modem world is to view its historical development as mediated through three core politico-cultural dynastic zones: the Ottomans (1281–1924), the Iranian Safavids (1501–1722) and the Moghuls (1526–1857).[5] In teaching survey courses of this kind, 1 invariably include Southeast Asia as a zone in its own right, worthy of a parity of esteem with the others, and stress that this region too participates in and contributes to the cultural variety of the Islamic world alongside a so-called 'big three'. This too, however, is incomplete, for it takes no adequate account of the presence of Muslim communities in Africa, Central Asia and China. And to avoid any danger of complacency, it is important to remember that time does not stand still, and there are yet new transformations of Islamic culture and civilisation emerging in Europe and North America.

A study of the ways in which Muslims in Southeast Asia participate in the world of Islam not only tells us something about these Southeast Asian Muslim communities, but also shows them an integral part of the Islamic world as a whole. But in many ways such a study has hardly begun. The study of Islam in this region is uneven, fragmented by discipline, cultural sub-region and period. In university courses on Southeast Asia, interest in the social sciences far outweighs that in the development of the traditional Islamic disciplines and the religious life and values of Muslim communities. Very few foreign anthropologists or political scientists know what *fiqh* is, or study the Qur'an in such a way as to realise what it means to experience it as a revealed book, even to the limited extent that this is possible from an English rendering. There are numerous studies on the history

5. JO Voll, *Islam: Continuity and Change in the Modem World* (London/Colorado: Longman/Westview, 1982).

of Muslim political organisations in Indonesia, such as the Nahdat al-'Ulama' and the Muhammadiyya, their role in social and political life, the rivalries between their leaders and the tactics by which they compete for power and influence, or the demographic distribution of the supporters of the radical PAS *(Partai Islam Se-Malaysia*—The All-Malaysia Islamic Party) in Malaysia, and the socio-economic reasons for its role in Kelantan and Trengganu. There are, however, few studies on the formation of personal values, the development of conscience and the commitment to ethical ideals that guide people's lives and that direct their commitment to *jihād* in the deepest, truest sense of the word, and the expression of this commitment and the way it is endued in people's lives as the 'the dye of God' *(ṣibghat Allāh)* (Q 2: 138).

Reflections on Spirituality

'Spirituality' is a word of protean significances that has changed its meanings over the centuries, and anyone using it can give it a different nuance according to circumstance and emphasis. The *Shorter Oxford English Dictionary* includes, among its meanings in modern usage, 'The quality or condition of being spiritual; regard for spiritual as opposed to material things; the study and practice of prayer as leading to union with God'. One could add further that it involves an awareness of a sacred dimension of experience and, beyond it, the encounter of mystery in religion. This is crucial. The absence of an apprehension of mystery may well mean that commitment to religion, or to any sense of values transcending the self, is reduced to little more than a game played with the recitation of formulae and external observances.

Spiritualty is activated by a challenge and requires a commitment. The challenge may be accepted, resisted struggled for; it may be so intense as to involve a struggle to abandon everything other than the imperatives it demands. It exists in different individuals at different levels. It goes beyond confessional allegiance. It involves a tension between one thing and another, the making of a commitment to one thing to the exclusion of another, a tension exquisitely expressed in the Muslim confession of faith, *lā ilāha illā'llāh.*

There are difficulties in giving an adequate account of any tradition of spirituality: whether it is one that is inherited, by stepping back to observe its contours, so as to achieve at least some measure of detachment. or that of another community, by opening one's self to all that empathy requires to gain an appreciation of it. This is in part because religious traditions develop a way of presenting their internal coherence in a special kind of language, one that includes not just the passing round of a currency of specific concepts but a tone and colouring that accompany and are distinctive of all internal communication within the community living by this tradition. Mastery of this language is not just an ability to state a given set of doctrines; tone and colouring are equally part of the reality a religion represents. The language, like any language can be studied, in the case of Islam ideally by a number of years in a *madrasa,* but the tone and colour can only be learned by living the language, by sharing in some way in the life of the community for whom they are native. Even so—to continue the metaphor of foreign language learning—no matter how hard the learner tries, mistakes will occur, one will get things wrong, one will misunderstand and in tum one may be misunderstood.

Spirituality is a many-sided thing. It is not limited to any single religious tradition and strikingly, similar spiritual types can often be recognised in every universalistic religion. Spirituality is expressed in a variety of ways and attitudes, a number of them, on the surface at least, mutually contradictory, some world affirming, others world denying—such general characterizations are points on a continuum—but each with the potential to be rich and fulfilling within individuals and communities.

In some cases a spirituality may be recognised through its effects as it prompts certain individuals to look beyond themselves, to relate in a special way to those near them, or awakes in them a concern with issues of the environment and social justice. The roots of this aspect of an Islamic spirituality are at times overlooked. The prophetic ḥadīth and others like it, 'Pay heed to the cry of the oppressed for there is no barrier between it and God' *(itqi da'wat al-malūm, fa innahā laysa baynahā wa bayna Allāh ḥijāb,*[6] are not widely known outside the lslamic community, but are at the heart of Islamic concerns for social justice. Spirituality may well prompt a constant state of dissatisfaction with what and where one is, and open one to an honest encounter with others. It can provide an impetus to reach across boundaries of differing religious allegiances.

6. H Hadiyah Salim, *Tarjamah Mukhtarul Ahadits* (Bandung, 1980), 17.

It is not easy to encounter spirituality at second hand. In the accounts and analyses we read of great religious writings, we may at times sense that something vital has been lost, or at best reduced to a private agenda. It is necessary to remember that the true value of a secondary work lies in the degree to which it equips one to experience not simply what the spiritual author wrote, but beyond that, the experience, the perceptions that made him or her write in the way they did, the reality to which the act of writing is a response.

If one searches for spirituality, it is often hard to know where and how to look. In one sense it is everywhere, in some ways explicit, in others hidden in an interplay of competing drives and desires. Spirituality may involve one in, impel one to searching and questioning. Yet it may pass unnoticed unless one seeking it can recognise the cues that point to its presence. Part of the difficulty is that there is no such thing as a chemically pure spirituality. All spirituality finds its expression within the context of an interplay of cultural and religious situations. It may be evident with an overwhelming, transparent clarity; it may be the hidden sub-text of writings that at a cursory glance appear secular.

Some spirituality leads on to mysticism. All mysticism is an expression of spirituality, but not all spirituality finds its expression in mysticism. There is a tendency to regard spirituality as a synonym for mysticism, yet the connotations of the word 'mysticism' may lead us astray. Mysticism as it has been studied in Southeast Asia often has as its particular focus giants of the spiritual life such as the Acehnese (north Sumatrans) Hamzah Fansuri (d 1593?) and Shams al-Din of Pasai (d 1630). The study of these authors at times has been side-tracked by the use of inappropriate concepts such as orthodoxy and heterodoxy, and the intellectual analysis of a theosophy of many-sided complexity which may distract the student from the spiritual path the mystic has followed and the spiritual rigours of the quest, of which his writings are the expression, but not the goal.

Spirituality in Islam

We are concerned here with Islamic spirituality, and in the same sense as there is no such thing as a chemically pure spirituality, so there is no such thing as a chemically pure Islam once one moves beyond the words of the Qur'an and attempts to explain them. Any universal transcendent principle has to be mediated through forms that are culturally specific, and this occurs even when a monotheistic: history-oriented faith such as that of Islam comes into contact with the co-Abrahamic faiths that preceded it Judaism and Christianity, with the world of the Indian religions, Hinduism and Buddhism or and not least, with the so-called 'primal' religions.

In coming to terms with an Islamic spirituality, it is necessary in the first instance to establish a profile of the constituents of the essence of Islam: an Arabic revelation, a specific salvation history together with modes of and an apprehension of praise, adoration and asking for help concentrated in and flowing from the Qur'anic formula 'In the name of God the Merciful the Compassionate' *(b'ismi'llāhi'l-raḥmāni' l-raḥīm),* and with it the totality of the meanings and resonances of the Qur'an.

It is not possible to think of an Islamic spirituality in any culture without these elements having become part of it. But it is necessary to be more specific about the implications and concomitants of acceptance of Islam: an eschatology, a view of the world and the universe having a beginning and an end; a law, enshrining values, with sanctions divine or human, here or in eternity, to ensure faithfulness to it; an intimacy with the Most Beautiful Names *(al-asmā' al-ḥusnā),* the names by which God describes Himself in the Qur'an, and the divine attributes, which tell of how something of His Knowledge, Power and Will are to be seen in creation, and prompt varying complexes of human responses to Him. These names, which present a way of experiencing God and recognising His acts, are embedded consciously or sub-consciously in the minds of every Muslim. Ibn 'Arabī (d 1240 CE) and his school, well-known in Southeast Asia, have used these names in their writings like the keys of a mighty organ. But from the beginning of Islam, long before the time of lbn 'Arabī, they have had an important spiritual role. They have called forth human responses of great diversity according to the spiritual taste and personality of the individual, and generated a vocabulary of devotion. The words of this vocabulary were to become systematized by certain of the Sufis, but long before their crystallisation within the technical vocabulary of Sufism, from the time of the Prophet, they were part of the spirituality of Islam, as indeed they had been of its Abrahamic predecessor religions. These responses arc expressed by words such as hope *(rajā'),* fear *(khawf),* yearning *(shawq),* love *(maḥabba)* and thankfulness *(shukr).* These words are not to be taken as abstractions, existing simply as components of a system; they arc realities that cannot exist outside a human subject. They identify facts of human experience, the experience of individuals who feel guilt, who repent of sin, who hope in God, who fear His punishments, who yearn for Him, who love Him, whose sense of gratitude to Him impels them to prayer. They may be understood as psychological states, expressing spiritual taste, personality and character. One person may become aware of the presence of God, and be impelled to prayer by thankfulness—*shukr*, another by hope—*rajā'*; another by *fear-khawf,* another by a sudden awareness of and sorrow for sin—*ṭawba;* yet another by uncertainty, bewilderment—*taḥayyur.*

It is as expressions of such a wide range of constituents and individual encounters with them that an Islamic spirituality in art and literature may be identified. They are the markers, one might say, or parameters of living and praying, faith and doubt, searching and exploring, within which individual Muslims respond as best they can. It is such responses that lie at the heart of the myriad spiritualities to be uncovered in art and literature.

Such generalisations are the relatively straightforward part of these reflections. It is when we look for, and try to identify and respond to, expressions of spirituality in specific traditions of art and literature that ambiguities and confusions arise. For art and literature are not always easy to define.

This leads to another point: spirituality is not the preserve of artistic and intellectual elites and not everything written about or referring to religion necessarily breathes a genuine spirituality. Many works written on religion can be monumentally dull, concerned with technical questions of *fiqh* (Islamic jurisprudence) in commentaries numerous stages removed from their basic text. Rules for virtuous living may be presented in a way that arouses no desire for compliance.

Value judgements of this kind, however, if made at all, need to be made with care. Over the centuries, tastes change, and it is not always easy to be sure of the expectations of and responses to artistic and literary works among peoples of other times and places. How can we know for sure that a genuine spirituality is to be found in one work, or have the presumption to say that it is not present in another? Sometimes qualified judgments are best, even while conceding that it is no more difficult to free-wheel in religious writing than in other genres of literature, and that there are the Barbara Cartlands of religious writing as well as of romance.

Spirituality in Diverse Forms

Yet it is possible to suggest points of departure for our journeys of exploration in Southeast Asia from the sixteenth century to the present day and beyond—spirituality in art and literature is not limited to the past. They are to be found in architecture, in institutions such as the *madrasa,* in calligraphy and the illumination of manuscripts,[7] in the use of the human voice—above all in qur'anic recitation, in dance and drama. *A fortiori* they are to be found in the various genres of religious writing, whether in regional languages, above all Malay, or Arabic. All such forms of cultural expression are part of a continuum which began when the first Islamic communities were established in the region, and is still being extended today as artists and scholars re-present the spirit and achievements of the past in new forms: experimentation in new styles of calligraphy; dramatic performances of the Barjanzi (a poem celebrating the life of the Prophet); and equally in what has been called 'dakwa rock'—performances of songs with religious lyrics by popular singing groups, making use of developing fashions and styles of music, for alongside the profusion of works in contemporary literary forms such as the novel, the essay, lyric poetry and drama.

In Architecture

Architecture deserves a special mention. It constitutes one of the most powerful. and sustained revelations of the ethos and vitality of a culture, and the Buddhist and Hindu architectural traditions of Southeast Asia have produced consummate expressions of these belief systems. The Islamic contribution, like so much else of the Islamic heritage of the region, has largely been neglected. Yet the mosque is one of the great expressions of Islamic spirituality. It is above all a construction of sacred space set apart for divine worship, designed to create an atmosphere of cool and quiet for the flowering of the spirit, and the Southeast Asian mosque represents a valid and noteworthy contribution to the expression of the architecture of Islam, rarely if ever included in world surveys of mosque design.

7. Ann Kumar & John McGlynn, editors, *Illuminations: Writing Traditions of Indonesia* (Weatherhill NY, Lontar Foundation, 1996).

As a readily accessible introduction to this field, Hugh O'Neill's essay 'Islamic architecture under the New Order' is in many ways inspirational.[8] He draws attention to the indigenous building traditions of the region and speaks of the superb timbers, fibres, stones and earths suitable for terracotta that have given rise to a distinctive local tradition of mosque building throughout Islamised Southeast Asia. He describes them as splendid timber structures with rising tiers of tapering hipped roofs, supported on multiple columns threading through their cool interiors. He stresses their distinctiveness noting that such mosques, in avoiding the typology of dome, cube, courtyard and arch exemplify a tradition that has few if any references to Middle Eastern and Ottoman styles. There are, he continues, fine examples still standing in West Sumatra and Palembang, and the venerable mosques of Banten, Cirebon and Demak and Surabaya have been the model for those built through Java since the sixteenth century.

He gives a detailed description of the great mosque in Yogyakarta built in 1758 by Hamengkubuwono I as a prime example of such mosques, and draws attention to the principal features of its design: square hipped roofs supported by four tall master columns. Huge trunks of teak support the upper roof and open up clerestory windows. The lower layers of the roof are supported by twelve shorter columns and are linked by horizontal beams.

It was not until the nineteenth century that the forms and symbols of the Indonesian Moorish legacy characterised by domes, minarets and arched masonry openings (as opposed to split gates), became increasingly popular, a development for which he offers explanations that need not detain us here.

In the modern period, both traditions, the Southeast Asian and the Moorish have been continued. On the one hand he refers to the grandeur and size—not to say arrogance—of the great Istiqial mosque in Jakarta, inspired by the Muhammad 'Ali mosque in Cairo; on the other he also draws attention to the Taman Sari in Yogyakarta, built in 1972, which echoes the great mosque of Hamangkubuwono referred to above. In it a single column supports the uppermost roof on four struts, with curving brackets carved to represent stem and

8. In Virginia Matheson Hooker, editor, *Culture and Society in New Order Indonesia, South-east Asian Social Science Monographs* (Kuala Lumpur: Oxford University Press, 1993), 151–164.

branches of the 'celestial tree' or stem of the lotus. It is not difficult to see the single column as a symbol for the letter *alif* standing for the name Allāh, the unity of God, or the Lote tree of the highest point in Paradise, at the *sidrat al-muntahā* mentioned in Q 53:14.

It is hardly possible to go further here than to say what a rich field of explorations this field of study offers, given the spiritual significance of the mosque, and its multiple roles: a place of preaching, teaching, prayer and study, in which to discover a unique experience in the religious use of space.

In Literary Traditions

The literatures of the region have been more studied than the architecture of the mosque, but by no means exhaustively. Fruitful points of departure are numerous and the field is so rich and diverse that it is difficult even to outline a framework adequate to include genres, periodizations and relationships in which every component has its place. A central issue is how the word 'literature' should be understood. In the Muslim world of Southeast Asia, the categories and approaches developed in the study of literary cultures in the West are not always helpful. In the Islamic tradition, the Qur'an is the supreme example both of religious teaching and of literary art, and the story of Yūsuf (Joseph), sura 12 of the Qur'an, is the epitome of both. In a world-view in which the religious and secular are perceived as aspects of a whole, literature cannot be divided up into the categories religious—non-religious, imbued or not imbued with an Islamic spirituality, be its presence implicit or explicit. The values the Qu'ran proclaims and presents, the symbols its draws on, the way issues are presented and the way it juxtaposes type and anti-type, directly or indirectly colour the world of the creative imagination of the literary artist.

On a journey of exploration, then, there is a need to identify writings which thrust the reader into a new world of experience, with the potential to bring about a personal transformation. Writings in which there is both tension and an awareness of mystery, and a knot pulled so tight that it hurts.

In the Islamic Disciplines

If overtly religious writing is taken as our starting point, the earliest example is the writing of the great Acehnese poet Hamzah Fansuri (d *c* 1593). He is first among the 'usual suspects' to be interrogated and still has much to tell us. Notwithstanding the work done on his *thought*, appreciation of him as a poet, of the internal dynamics of his verse and of the superb technique by which he expresses his experience of God in great poetry drawing on the theosophical concepts of Ibn 'Arabi tradition has hardly begun. He is possessed by an awareness that nothing truly exists· other than God. He is nevertheless equally conscious of his own individuality. His poems are a personal account of his quest to resolve the paradox. In his passion to resolve the contradiction he experiences the searing presence of God's spirit. It sets him ablaze and consumes him so that nothing of him is left other than the reality that is God, the precious essence of camphor when the camphor tree is burnt to ashes, losing its own identity. Hence the final verse of one of his *syair*:[9]

> *Hamzah Shahrnawi terlalu hapus*
> *Seperti kayu sekalian hangus*
> *Asalnya laut yang tiada berharus*
> *Menjadi kapur di dalam Barus*

which may roughly be rendered into English

> Hamzah of Shahrnawi is totally obliterated
> like wood reduced to ashes
> Though his origin is the [infinity of] the tideless sea,
> in Barus he becomes camphor.

The verse, for all of its apparent simplicity, reveals an elaborate chiasmus setting the infinity of the 'tideless sea' against the tiny particularity of the place Barus; and the destruction of one thing, the tree, producing something other, infinitely more precious, camphor. And to this should be added the allusion to the encounter of Moses with another burning tree, when God spoke to him out of the fire on Mount Sinai.[10]

9. A poem of indeterminate length, often on a single topic, consisting of rhyming endline quatrainswith generally four pulses to the line.
10. GWJ Drewes & LF Brake], *The Poems of Hamzah Fansuri*, Bibliotheca Indonesica 26 (Dordrecht, Netherlands/Cinnaminson, USA: Foris Publications, 1986), 142. (I have not included the authors' renderings.)

Hamzah's work is a high point in the tradition of the use of Malay as a language of Islamic spirituality. Unfortunately, little or nothing of the tradition prior to the time of Hamzah leading to this high point has survived, although it must extend back over two or three centuries. It is only from the beginning of the seventeenth century that the strength of this tradition is evident, and from then on grows apace both with the vernacularisation of works representing the Islamic disciplines, foremost among them *fiqh* (jurisprudenc), *tafsīir* (Qur'anic exegesis) and *taṣawwuf* (mysticism), are represented.

Fiqh, by its nature, does not immediately disclose the spirituality that motivates and inspires the dedicated, patient sifting through the authorities and searching for precedent essential for the delivery of jurisprudential opinions. *Tafsīr*, on the other hand, can sometimes move beyond the careful word by word exegesis of qur'anic verses to communicate the thrill and passion of the exegete as he responds to the divine words of the Qur'an. The following passage from the *tafsīr Marāh Labid*, by Nawawī of Banten (1814–1897), is an example of a model of the faith and religious commitment that can glow through the terminology of positive theology in a response to the Qur'an, when word for word exegesis is transformed into spiritual excitement, as Nawawi expands the concentrated language of the opening of *surat al-Furqān* (25:1):[11]

Blessed is He who revealed the Furqān[12] *to His servant*, that is, Exalted is God who revealed the Qur'an to Muhammad, exalted in His Essence, in His Attributes and in His Deeds. For His Essence is exalted above the, possibility of change and extinction, and transcends comparison with any contingent thing; His attributes are exalted above anything created, and His deeds are exalted above any possibility that they be without purpose. The revelation of the Qur'an, which comprises all religious and worldly good is among His Acts; and His bestowal of the title of servant [upon the Prophet] proclaims that our Lord Muhammad is the greatest of all His servants; *that he might*, that is that that servant might, or He who revealed the Criterion might be *to the worlds*, that is those of the jinn and humankind subject to the

11. The English renderings of the qur'anic words commented on are italicised.
12. Since *al-Furqān* is here one of the names of the Qur'an itself, and the connotations of the literal rendering of the wored 'Criterion' are inadequate, it is left untranslated. It should be noted that Nawawī's commentary is largely based on the work of Fakhr al-Dīn al-Rāzī referred to in note 21 below.

Law, *a warner*, that is one to inspire dread of the punishment of God by means of the [message of] the Qur'an.[13]

These two examples from different genres of religious writing, apart from their content, show, in the case of Hamzah, the effectiveness of Malay as a literary language of Islam and, in that of Nawawī, the skill of a Southeast Asian scholar in the use of Arabic.

Another category of writing, one that has been seriously neglected, is the *Qiṣaṣ al-anbiyā'*. Stories of the prophets are the bed-rock of the world-view of members of the world community of Islam. Such writings have their place alongside other works in verse and prose of a variety of genres in numerous languages, stories of the heroes of Islam, court chronicles and a wide range of Malay works loosely categorized under the heading *hikayat.* These *qiṣaṣ*—they have been called 'novels of holiness'—are no less deserving of serious treatment as literature than works such as the *Hikayat Seri Rama* (an early Malay rendering of the Ramayana) or the *Hikayat Hang Tuah* (a 'romance' of a hero of the Malacca sultanate) (*c* 1400–1511). In a sense, logically, even if not always temporally, were one using Western categories, they may be regarded as having an intermediate position between 'secular' and 'religious' literature. Whether as literature or spiritual reading, their value is often underestimated. The Dutch scholar Hooykaas once remarked that he deliberately excluded discussion of them from the repertory of Malay literature because they were 'more general Islamic than Malay'.[14] In fact, the *Qiṣaṣ al-anbiyā'* in a special way are a manifestation of an indigenous literary art as well as Islamic spirituality. They establish clearly the configuration of type and anti-type. They employ techniques of structure to depict an arc of tension leading to a resolution. Even more, they serve to establish a universalistic structure of time and place in which every human individual, no matter who or where, has a role and a destiny.

In Secular Literature

But as I have insisted, spirituality is not restricted to writings that profess themselves to be religious. Northrop Frye looked at the whole corpus of English literature, and saw it virtually as a commentary on

13. Nawawī al-Bantanī, *Marāh Labīd*, Cairo, 1965, II, 92. The *Marāḥ Labīd* is readily available in numerous reprints in Malaysia and Indonesia.
14. C Hooykaas, *Over Maleise Literatuure,* second edition (Leiden: Brill, 1947), i.

the great spiritual themes presented in the Bible: Fall and Redemption, Death and Resurrection.[15] In the same way, the values, the symbols, the types and the anti-types presented in the Qur'an are to be found in virtually all writing with an Islamic provenance. Such a presentation may not be explicit and at a superficial level it may even seem to be denied. Yet it is the themes of the Islamic revelation that set the basic moral perspectives of human perception of personal identity and establish an arena in which conflicting drives struggle for dominance or resolution implicit in the social ambience of the Muslim world in which any story is set. Even works which have no overt religious content or reference point may suggest the religious dimension even when set outside it, simply by the fact of appearing to disregard it.

In Drama

This point is crucial, and its centrality is illustrated in an essay of Barbara Hatley's, 'Construction of tradition in New Order Indonesian theatre'.[16] She presents examples of ways in which playwrights use images from regional cultural traditions in modern style theatre to express attitudes to aspects of contemporary society. She singles out a group of such playwrights as 'Islamic voices'.

These Islamic voices are theatre groups in Yogyakarta with an Islamic commitment, and one of the plays she mentions is *Dajjal*, sponsored by Aisyah, the Muhammadiyya Women's Wing. The eschatological figure of *Dajjal*, a type of anti-Christ, is used as a symbol for the forces of development expropriating people from their land and poisoning the minds of the young, itself an echo of the hadith referred to earlier in this essay, 'Pay heed to the cry of the oppressed, for there is no barrier between it and God'.

That there should be Islamic voices in the theatre is interesting in itself, particularly since the legitimacy of drama as an art form is questioned in some traditions of Islam. And it is indeed legitimate to single out *Dajjal* and other plays with an overt Islamic purpose using an explicit Islamic imagery as representing these Islamic voices. Yet this cannot be the whole story. There may well be Islamic values and spirituality implicit in other of the dramatic pieces she refers to—and

15. Northrop Frye, *The Great Code: The Bible and Literature* (London: Routledge & Kegan Paul, 1983).

16. In Hooker, *Culture and Society*, especially 61–62.

indeed in literary works generally—of greater spiritual power and broader resonance than in those written with a single-issue focus. The essence of spirituality is that it exists in a human situation, is not reducible to a program, to slogans or sermonizing. Spirituality cannot exist outside humanity, and not to recognize this is to give no credit to the great tradition of Islamic humanism. 'Grace is everywhere' and the touch, the light of Islamic spirituality is often present under many guises and not always identified. What may be too self-evident to the participant in the culture to require mention, may be overlooked by the outsider who misses subtly nuanced cues.

The Novel and Short Story

Some prose writings may serve as examples. When Achdiat's novel *Atheis* (*An Atheist*), set during the Japanese occupation, appeared in 1949, some readers felt that it was anti-religious because of the vividness and honesty with which it portrayed characters hostile to religion and presented their views: the suave Rusli, for example, who remarks that one day it may be possible for man to create life. And when the devout Hasan objects, saying that this is tantamount to man making himself equal to God, simply replies, 'Why be obscurantist? There is no God'. And the anarchist Anwar who smears a concoction of opium onto the tip of his cigarette, saying, 'This is God I'm putting onto my cigarette. Didn't Marx say God [*sic*] was the opium of the people'.[17] The tension between belief and unbelief is plain. Each has its protagonists who speak in full voice. The spiritual message of the novel is clear, and it has as its sub-text a journey from faith, to loss of faith, and a return to faith as Hasan, shot by the Kempeitai, the Japanese military police, whispers with his last breath, 'God is most Great'—*Allāhu akbar*!

A Malaysian novel such as *Salina*[18] (the title is a woman's name), which appeared in 1961, makes no overt reference to religious values. All the ideals and hopes of the 'good' characters are destroyed. The whole course of the novel seems to suggest that it is not God but fate, time, *dahr*, that is in charge. But human values and personal relationships, trust, loyalty and love remain, and through the

17. Achdiat Karta Mihardja, *Atheis*, third printing (Jakarta:s Balai Pustaka, 1957), 68 and 106 respectively.
18. Abdul Samad Said, *Dewan Bahasa dan Pustaka* (Kuala Lumpur, 1961).

emphasis laid on these values, the background presence of God is implied. Expressed in different terms, the same tension is present.

It is also present in a short story by AA Navis.[19] An elderly man who has devoted his last years to religion comes from afar to visit his son, daughter-in-law and their two children. He reaches their village. Before he has an opportunity to meet them, he discovers the couple are half-brother and sister, both his children by different wives. Because he abandoned his responsibilities to them and their mothers, the children grew up unaware of the relationship between them and married. He faces a dilemma. An illegal, indeed incestuous situation exists. The tension is between the revealed Law which has stated the prohibited degrees of kinship within which marriage can take place, and the already existing human values of family, love and the well-being of children born to the marriage contracted by a couple ignorant of their relationship. Should he remain, meet them, tell them the situation and the family be broken up, or not? The situation is one in which the knot is pulled so tight its hurts. The conflict is between two goods. Both have a justification in religion. In the plot resolution the human rather than the legal good is given preference. The secret is not divulged. The old man departs without meeting his children: and grandchildren. It may be noted incidentally that the Qur'an itself does not impose rules retrospectively, and tolerated situations that had arisen in the time of ignorance.[20]

In Poetry

To turn to modem poetry: Amir Hamzah (1911–1946) merits further interrogation for a number of reasons. He was Western-educated, and his mastery of Dutch opened to him the doors of a number of traditions of spirituality. He wrote not conventional religious poetry, but a poetry that was the fruit of deep personal tensions and ambiguities. It communicates a faith that experiences doubt, bewilderment, incomprehension, even anger at God and anguish at His silence, yet remains unshaken, and enables him to continue to address Him as *kekasihku*, 'my Beloved'.

19. The story is 'Datangnja dan perginja' in AA Navis, *Robohnja Surau Kami* (Jakarta: NV Nusantara Bukittingi, 1961 (first printing 1956), 71–88.

20. Qur'an 4:23–25.

From childhood he had a fully Islamic upbringing; he completed study of the Qur'an, and listened to the recitation of stories of the prophets. During his years of study in Java from the age of fourteen, at the Christian Junior High School in Batavia, the curriculum included Bible reading.[21] In Solo, at Senior High School, he studied 'Oriental' literature. This variety of cultural experience provided multiple reference points for the diction, imagery and mood of a number of his later poems in the collection *Nyanyi Sunyi* (*Songs in Solitude*). One can recognise in them transformations of cries of adoration and despair from the psalms, of pain and frustration from the Book of Job, and of love and yearning from the Song of Songs alongside echoes of verses from the Qur'an, and allusions to the *Qisas al-anbiyā'*.

In *Permainanmu* (*Your Plaything*), for example, he wonders how can it be that God Himself should harden Pharaoh's heart, yet punish Pharaoh for his disobedience:

> *Bertanya aku kekasihku*
> *Permainan engkau permainkan?*
>
> And I ask, My Beloved,
> is it a game you are playing?[22]

In *Padamu jua* (*To You Alone*) he exclaims

> *Aku manusia*
> *Rindu rasa,*
> *Rindu rupa*
> *Di mana engkau*
> *rupa tiada*
> *suara sayup*
> *hanya kata merangkai hati.*
>
> I am human
> Long for touch
> Long for form
> Where are you?

---

21. It is possible to identify with some degree of certanity the Dutch Bible translation that Amir used, a reprint of *De Eerste Staten Bijbel* (Leiden: Paulus Aertsz, 1637).
22. *Njanji Sunji* (Jakarta, Pustaka Rakyat, 1954), 8. Note that as a result of spelling reforms, in more recent reprints of the work the title now appears as *Nyanyi Sunyi*.

You have no form
Your voice is distant
Only your word binds the heart.[23]

He is in near despair at the absence of God, pleading that as a human being, for assurance of His presence, he depends on the senses, and so cries out in pain, 'Where are you?'—for God has no form, His voice is distant and only His words can hold the heart.

But the *Qiṣaṣ al-anbiyā'*, elaborating the qur'anic account given in Q 20:10–47, tell how Moses, on his way back from Midian to Egypt, on a dark night lost his way in the mountains and saw a fire. He approached the fire, and saw a tree aflame, and God spoke to him. Moses could not tell where the voice was coming from-above, below, beneath him or at his side-and bewildered cried out, 'Where are you?'![24]

Almost certainly, Amir Hamzah was relating his experience to that of Moses. The figure of Moses appears a number of times in his verse. In the last verse of *Hanya Satu* (*One Thing Alone*) Amir exclaims, 'One thing alone do I desire, to feel you close beside me, as did Moses on the peak of Sinai'.[25] In *Padamu Jua*, Amir is perplexed and grieved at the apparent absence of God. Yet Moses too, in the *Qiṣaṣ*, even when God was speaking to him out of the fire, was constrained to utter in bewilderment the same words, 'Where are you?' This echo adds to the depth and intensity of Amir's poem.

23. *Njanji Sunji*, 5.

24. A classical telling of the story puts it like this: 'Moses thought it was a fire that someone had lit, and he gathered twigs, to light a torch from its flames. Moses looked up at its branches, and, lo, there was a brilliant green in the sky, and then a light between heaven and earth, with rays that dazzled his sight, and when Moses looked at it, he put his hands over his eyes, and a voice called him, "Moses" . . . he responded, "At your service. I hear your voice, I do not see you, where are you?" He replied, "I am with you, in front of you, behind you, and totally encompass you. I am closer to you than your very self." Then Satan put a doubt into his mind, and said, "How do you know that it is the voice of God you hear?" He replied, "Because I hear it from in front of me and behind, from my right and my left, just as I hear it from in front of me, thus I know it is not the voice of any created thing" Rāzī, *TK* 22:17. See also Robert B Crotty, editor, *The Charles Strong Lectures 1972–1984* (Leiden: Brill, 1987), 129. The *Qiṣaṣ al-anbiyā'*, retold in the works of the classical exegetes, form part of a great continuing tradition of religious education, and are well-known in Malay and other regional languages.

25. *Njanji Sunji*, 7.

In the last poem of *Nyanyi Sunyi, Istana Rela* (*Palace of Content*), he reveals the constancy of his faith in the verse beginning:

Jangan percaya hembusan cedera
Berkata tiada hanya dunia.

Put no trust in the evil whisper
that says there is nothing but this world.

The sense of the line *Jangan percaya hembusan cedera* is a brilliant expression in Malay of the sense of verse 4 of the final sura (114) of the Qur'an, which begins, I take refuge with the Lord of men, the King of men, the God of men 'from the evil of the sideways slinking whisperer'—*min sharr al-waswās al-khannās.* Amir knew all too well the evil of the sideways slinking whisperer, and sought refuge with God from him.

These examples, though far from exhaustive, show something of the skill and power of his writing, with a strength that comes from the superbly controlled diction, the multiple reference points brought into alignment and a total spiritual honesty. He was an individual whose Islamic faith showed the capacity to integrate elements of diverse cultures to form a new whole in a way characteristic of the great tradition of Islam, exemplifying a culture that was a genuine expression of Islamic humanism, one genuinely Islamic and genuinely human.

The tradition continues. A final example is the Indonesian poet, Emha Ainun Nadjib, born in East Java in 1953. His work reveals the depths of a complex spirituality. A number of his poems, even without mentioning the name Allah, or the conventional terms of religious devotion, express aspects of the relation between God and humankind through a variety of symbols and images, highlighting the tension between what man is, and what his yearnings and destiny—his essential vocation—summon him to be. Among them is *Berperan di Bumi* (*A Role on Earth*)—a poem making use of the Iqbalian theme of God discovering Himself in Man, Nature and the Universe.

Two stanzas suffice:

Aku berperan di bumi
berendam di kolam-kolam dunia
Sambil menatap cakrawala

Siapakah aku?
Jangan cari di kolam
Lacaklah ke cakrawala
Aku ruh tunggal
Namaku beragam
Petakku tigapuluh enam

which could be expressed in English:

I have my role on earth
Deep in all its waters
While contemplating the firmament.

Who am I?
Seek me not in the waters
Search for me in the firmament.
I am the unique spirit,
My names are manifold
my divisions six and thirty.

Another, *Kau Pandang Aku* (*You Look on Me*), represents God as addressing Man, telling him how he willfully misunderstands God's nature, imagining that he sees him in one thing at the expense of others. Four stanzas suffice:

kau pandang aku batu
        kau gempur dengan peluru
    padahal aku angin
kau pandang aku badai
        kau tahankan baja dan mantra
    padahal aku gunung membisu
kau pandang aku raja
        kau tinggikan singgasana
    padahal aku pemabuk
kau pandang aku ngemis
        kau taburkan mutiara
    padahal aku bumi

which may be expressed in English:

You look on Me as stone
        You try to shatter me with bullets
    Yet I am wind.

You look on Me as tempest
        You try to protect yourself against me with steel and spells
    Yet I am a mountain, ever dumb.
You look at Me as a king
        You raise high the throne
    Yet I am the drunkard [at the gate]
You regard me as one begging
        You scatter me pearls
    Yet I am the earth [on which you scatter them].[26]

The climax of the poem is in its last line, 'Yet I am Love!' (*padahal aku cinta*).

Poems such as these breathe the religious spirit in the sense of mystery that inspires them, and present the reader with a challenge that must be faced. They show how wide is the field in which Islamic spirituality may be explored, how it is growing and how many suspects there are, still unknown and still to be interrogated.

In the Essay

Spirituality is not to be found exclusively in religious journalism, and may be seen at its best and most penetrating in the secular press, and express the spiritual insights and encounters of individuals outside the religious establishment. Examples are to be found in a number of the essays Goenawan Muhammad wrote for the weekly journal *Tempo*—suppressed under the Soeharto regime. In 1979, in his essay 'A cube', he wrote of a visit to Mecca, and without pretension shares with the readers a religious experience and wisdom that comes straight from the heart:

> The Ka'ba is something very simple. Once I went inside. It was dark. There was nothing awe inspiring, nothing appealing about it, nothing to suggest that the essence of the Unseen World was here. But then something startled me. Something happened. I heard a whisper in front of me telling me to pray two *rak'a*—and at that moment I realized, not only mentally, but physically too, that God was nowhere here, that God was

26. Iem Brown & Joan Davis, editors & translators, *On the Veranda: A Bilingual Anthology of Modern Indonesian Poetry* (Cambridge: Cambridge University Press, 1995), 136–139. (The English renderings in the book should be taken only as a guide to the sense of the poems.)

> not here at all. He was still remote. He could not be embraced from where I was standing. That God is not within human reach. But the very moment we realize this, we can surrender ourselves to Him. As a poet might put it, 'We humble ourselves before the shadow of His greatness, for that is the moment when He is very near'.[27]

There is a likewise a deep spirituality in his essay 'Mosques'. He recalls the mosque of his home village, one without a minaret, without a dome and without a loudspeaker, blending harmoniously into its surroundings. If it differed from its neighbouring buildings at all, it would be only that the prayer chamber was cooler, the floor cleaner, the well deeper and the water cistern for the ritual ablutions before prayer never dry. It was not like the huge Istiqlal mosque, where the great officials in the religious establishment meet with their state counterparts, which can draw in copious funding and attract abundant alms giving:

> Our village mosques feel no need to put on airs, because they do not claim to be anything other than places of prayer. They reflect a community that feels no need to put itself on display because it is so much a part of its surroundings.[28]

He refers to Seyyed Hossein Nasr's expression of sadness at the loss of humility and sense of proportion that used to exist in the traditional architecture of Islamic communities, and comments:

In other words, he is speaking of a spiritual crisis. But is secularization really the root cause? Or has the narrowing of the field of religion gone so far as to reduce its scope to matters of law and social conduct at the expense of compassion and sensitivity to the human condition?[29]

In writing this, he is expressing the concern of O'Neill referred to earlier about the physical grandeur of the Istiqlal mosque in Jakarta.

---

27. In *Tempo*, No. 24, Yr XVII (15 August 1987): 18
28. See Goenawan Mohamad, *Sidelines: Writings from Tempo*, translated by Jennifer Lindsay (Melbourne, Hyland House in association with Monash Asia Institute/ Monash University, 1994). The two essays referred to are 'A cube', 133–134, and 'Mosques', 135–136.
29. In *Tempo*, No 39, Yr IX, 24 (November 1979): 7.

Conclusion

The use of the word 'spirituality' as a concept to assist a response to works of art and literature flourishing in an Islamic environment provides a kind of liberation from traditional approaches, even though it may not so easily fit into more rigorous categories of academic analysis.[30]

In using it, there are dangers. The spiritual life of an individual is something special and precious. It is necessary to guard against any temptation to reduce it to a topic for publication in an academic journal, something to add to a cv, the ultimate temptation, 'the evil of the sideways slinking whisperer who whispers into the hearts of men—we seek refuge with God from him!'—*sharr al-waswās al-khannās al-ladhī yuwaswisu fī ṣudūr al-nās*[31]—*na'udhu bi'llāhi minhu* the question of motive. What is the justification for anyone to pry into something so personal in a community to which one does not belong? Perhaps only that despite differences of emphasis and varying points of departure, the attempt to understand, appreciate and share such a dimension of experience in another tradition may yield new and positive perspectives of common human concerns.

There are indeed times when it may not appear so difficult, or the distance to be bridged so great. When we read in a great spiritual writer:

We offer God a spiritual adoration, consisting in the internal devotion of the mind, and bodily adoration, which consists in an exterior humbling of the body. In all acts of worship, that which is without is referred to that which is within as being of greater import; it follows that exterior adoration is offered on account of interior adoration, in other words we exhibit signs of humility in our bodies in order to incite our affection to submit to God—proceeding from the sensible to the intelligible,[32] does it really matter whether it was written by a Muslim or a Christian?

30. I am grateful to Professor Osman Bakar of the University of Malaya for suggesting the use of this word.
31. Q 114:4
32. Quoted in Margaret Smith, *An Early Mystic of Baghdad: A Study of the Life and Teaching of Ḥārith b. Asad al-Muḥāsibi AD: 781–857* (London: Sheldon Press, 1977 (first printed 1935), 287–288.

Can spirituality across religious traditions then be actively shared, in a way that goes beyond tolerance and even beyond acceptance? At present, perhaps, only between consenting adults in private. But this kind of exploration may help. Perhaps, to paraphrase a remark by Rabbi Lionel Blue writing in The Tablet, to get beyond the Me Tarzan, You Jane level in encounters of religious dialogue, touch a live wire and experience the electric shock of the realization of a shared human experience and destiny.

'. . . Abraham, our father in faith . . .'? A Reflection on Christian-Muslim Consociation.

This St Mark's Vigil address is a reflection, but more than that, a quest, a searching. The phrase on which it is based belongs to the liturgy of the Eucharist, in which it is an attestation of the faith of the Christian community in its most solemn of rituals, that Abraham is 'our father in faith'.

In the title, I give 'our' an extended meaning, raising the possibility of it being inclusive of Muslims, as well as Jews. Hence the question-mark. The unfamiliar word 'consociation', of course means 'companionship', 'fellowship'. In using it, I wanted to cause a hesitation, a moment of bewilderment. The connotations of the synonyms might seem pat, banal even, and lead the listener to imagine that the question was rhetorical. While not exactly clinical, 'consociation' does not carry this baggage. Rather there might lie within it a dynamic, positive nuance that could go beyond simply 'companionship' or 'fellowship' with its implication of the possibility of a shared association on equal terms. Yet the question is not rhetorical. It does not expect a 'yes' or 'no' answer. Rather it is implicit with qualifications and nuances that go beyond a plain 'yes' or 'no' or even 'yes but . . .', or 'no but . . .', and recognises that attempts to answer it may uncover a fusion of irreconcilable conflicts and tensions.

Abraham is a role model in all three religious communities. He has in their scriptures and daily religious life, an inspiring presence. He has also, in each, a pivotal, defining role in the revelatory unfolding of economies of salvation, that might in some respects appear exclusive.

In Christian ritual, he is indeed celebrated in the Eucharist as 'our father in faith'. In the Christian Scriptures he has a tangible presence. In the Magnificat (Lk 1:47–55) Mary proclaims that in the child she is carrying, God has

> *Come to the help of Israel his servant, mindful of His mercy,*
> *According to the promise He made to our ancestors*
> *of His mercy to Abraham and to his descendants for ever.*[1]

And when Zachariah, took his son John, cousin of Jesus, to the Temple to be circumcised, first he praised God,

> *Blessed be the Lord, the God of Israel.*
> *He has visited his people and redeemed them*

And then declares that the role his son is destined to play, is a fulfilment of God's promise, for

> *He swore to Abraham our father to grant us*
> *That free from fear, and saved from the hands of our foes*
> *We might serve him in holiness and justice*
> *All the days of our life in his presence* (Luke 1:68-79.

In the book of Genesis, the story of Abraham leads the patriarchal narratives, narratives that close with the death of Joseph, and establish the identity and vocation of the Jewish people.

The name Abraham (then Abram) first appears in Genesis 11:26, towards the end of the listing of a genealogy. He is the son of Terah, of the line of Shem. He was born in the land of Ur of the Chaldees and his wife Sarah (then Sarai) was barren. His father Terah took them and other members of the family from Ur towards Canaan, and they settled in Haran. There Terah died.

At the beginning of Genesis 12, however, there is a dramatic shift of focus. Abraham becomes central to the narrative, and his role as the first of the patriarchs of the Jewish people in the Judaeo-Christian reading of salvation history and all that this implies, is revealed.

'The Lord said to Abram, "Leave your country, your family and your father's house, for the land I will show you. I will make you a great nation; I will bless you and make your name so famous that it will be used as a blessing. I will bless those who bless you; I will slight those who slight you. All the tribes of the earth shall bless themselves by you." So Abram went as the Lord told him.' (Gen 12:1–4).

---

1. Bible translations are from *The New Jerusalem Bible*. Rendering of the Qur'an are my own.

When he arrived in Canaan, the Lord appeared to him again, and said to him, 'To your seed I will give this land' (Gen 12:7). After a journey to, and return from Egypt, the Lord addressed Abraham a third time, promising him land and progeny as numerous as the dust of the earth (Gen 13:14–16). And Abraham settled by the Terebinths of Mamre in Hebron. Sarah continued barren.

The Lord then appeared to Abram a fourth time, and again promised him a great reward. And since Sarah still had not conceived, Abraham as it were sulks, and said, 'Let a member of my household be my heir' (Gen 15:3). The Lord repeated his promise (for a fourth time) and assured him that his posterity would be as many as the stars of heaven. Abraham asked Him how could he be sure God would be true to his word. God then commanded him, as a sign of a covenantal agreement, 'Take me a three-year-old heifer and a three-year old she-goat, and a three-year old ram and a turtledove and a young pigeon'. And he took all of these and clove them through the middle, and set each half opposite the other (Gen 15:8–9).

Notwithstanding this covenant, Sarah still did not conceive, and so invited Abraham to take her slave girl Hagar to wife, to be a surrogate mother on her behalf. Hagar conceives, and proud of her own pregnancy, sneers at her barren mistress. Sarah harassed her, and she fled into the desert. The Lord's messenger found her, told her she was to bear a son to be called Ishmael, and ordered her to return to Abraham's household, there to give birth to her son (Gen 16:16)

Nine years later, God appeared to Abraham (Gen 17:1–3) and told him yet again that he and Sarah will have as issue many nations. Abraham threw himself on the ground laughing, but God continued speaking, and assured him that Sarah would have a son, Isaac, with whom God would establish an everlasting covenant, and that Ishmael too would beget a great nation, but that God's covenant would be with Isaac, who would be born within the year.

To confirm this promise, the Lord appeared again to Abraham in the Terebinths of Mamre (Gen 18:1). As he was sitting by the flap of his tent in the heat of the day, he saw three men standing before him. He welcomed them with generous hospitality. They said to him, 'This time next year, your wife Sarah will have a son'. Sarah, overhearing it, laughed. The men then took their leave. Abraham, learning that they were on their way to destroy Sodom, pleaded with God to spare the city, even if only as few as ten innocent men were to be found there.

Sarah gave birth to Isaac the following year. The promise had at last been fulfilled. When the child was weaned, Abraham held a feast. But when Sarah saw Hagar and her son laughing during the celebrations she ordered Abraham to send Hagar and her son from the house. Reluctantly, Abraham did so. But God reassured him, saying that although it was through Isaac that his seed should be acclaimed, of the slave girl's son too He would make a nation, because Abraham was his father.

Early the next morning, Abraham took provisions for Hagar, gave her the child, and sent her away. She wandered through the wilderness of Beersheba. When her water was exhausted, she flung the child under one of the bushes, and went off, not wishing to see him die. She sat and wept, but God's messenger called from the heavens telling her not to fear, assuring her that her son too would beget a great nation. Then she saw beside her a well. She took from it the water she needed, and gave her son to drink. He grew up strong and healthy, living in the land of Paran, and Hagar found an Egyptian wife for him.

The last episode relevant to this reflection is how God put Abraham to the ultimate test. He told him to sacrifice Isaac, the son on whom the fulfilment of God's promise to him depended, crucial both for the status of the Jews as a chosen people, and for Christians, for them to see the birth of Jesus, a Jew, as the promised Messiah. the ultimate fulfilment of the promise to Abraham. The faith of Abraham was equal to this test, and he took Isaac to Mount Moriah, ready to offer him in sacrifice. This son, Isaac is the child of promise, God's covenant is with him, and through him with the tribes of Israel, the Jewish people, and through the Jews to Jesus, the point of meeting and separation between Judaism and Christianity.

Abraham has a corresponding status and dignity in the Muslim reading of salvation history. He is honored as the friend of God—*khalīlu'llāh*, the Qur'an saying of him, *God took Abraham as his friend* (*Sūrat al-Nisā'*, 4:125) The perception of his status among the prophets is shown in the stories elaborated from the Qur'anic account of Muhammad's Night Journey and Ascension,

> *Glory be to Him who took His servant by night from the Sacred Mosque to the Furthest Mosque, round which We have spread our blessing, to show him Our signs.*
> *He, indeed He is the Hearing, the Seeing.*(*Sūrat al-Isrā,'* 17:1–2)

The exegetes tell how the prophet was first taken from the sacred mosque at Mecca, on the winged steed al-Burak, escorted by Gabriel to the site of the Dome of the Rock in Jerusalem. From there he was taken up to the 7th heaven, at each stage in the journey greeted by an earlier prophet. At the first (and lowest heaven) he is greeted by Adam, at the second by Jesus and his cousin John (the Baptist), at the third, by Joseph, at the fourth, by Elijah, at the fifth, by Aaron, at the sixth, by Moses, and at the seventh by Abraham, seated on a throne at the gate of *al-bayt al-maʿmūr* (the Celestial Mansion).

No less than in the Judaic and Christian traditions, Abraham has a continuing daily presence in the devotional life of Muslims. At the commencement of each of the five daily prayers, Muslims, following the example of Muhammad himself, recite the prayer of Abraham after he has been shown the transience of star moon and sun as objects of worship, *I turn my face to Him who created the heavens and the earth, pure in faith, and in submission to Him, I am not of the idolaters,* (*Sūrat al-Anʿām*, 6:79) professing membership of the community of Abraham.

Abraham is recalled again at the formulaic conclusion of each of these five daily prayers, where the one praying declares,

> *I testify that there is no god but God, and that Muhammad is his servant and his messenger.*
> *O God, pour out your mercy upon Muhammad*
> *And the family of Muhammad*
> *As You poured out your mercy upon Abraham*
> *and the family of Abraham*
> *Truly You are glorious and worthy of all praise.*

He is thus the only human being named besides Muhammad in this fundamental ritual obligation.

Finally, in the greatest of Muslim festivals, the *ḥajj*, the rite of pilgrimage to the House of God at Mecca, Abraham, Hagar and Ishmael are commemorated, and pilgrims stand and pray where Abraham stood and prayed.

There are 235 verses relating to Abraham in the Qur'an. Some are narrative, others are exhortatory or referential, and acoustically they re-echo like a drum roll from sura to sura as Muhammad is reminded of Abraham, and told to speak of him. The message Muhammad brings is one that has already been presented by his great predecessors Abraham and Moses. Abraham is the ultimate exemplar for Muhammad and his contemporaries. God says to him

> *There is a marvellous model for you*
> *In Abraham and his party* (*Sūrat al-Mumtaḥina* 60:4)

The religion revealed to Muhammad is that enjoined on Abraham, Moses and Jesus *Sūrat al-Shūrā* (42:13) *God has decreed for you the religion He decreed for Noah, and we have revealed to you, and which He decreed for Abraham, Moses and Jesus.* In other words he, Muhammad, bears to his people, and ultimately the world, the same primordial message of the Unity of God, the role of the Prophets and the Law they bring, and the warning of a Resurrection and Judgement, as the prophets preceding him had to other peoples.

But in addition to this underlying Abrahamic rhythm, there are narrative pericopes about him distributed over a number of suras, that clarify his role. They are, for the most part, discrete, and do not add up to a re-run of the Genesis story, let alone a birth to death account of Abraham's life story. For such a reconstruction, it is necessary to refer to the genre of religious knowledge called *Qiṣaṣ al-Anbiyā'* (Stories of the Prophets), biographical compilations based on the work of Qur'anic exegetes, and drawing on extra Qur'anic sources of various kinds including the Talmud. Episodes from the Qur'an are elaborated in the ensuing narratives. They set out a chronology of his life, they fill gaps, and provide a context for allusions. Qur'anic pericopes serve as anchors to the movement of the extended narrative, give it spiritual depth, and enhance its literary character.

The Qur'an introduces him not as a descendant of the line of Shem, but as a prophet appearing after Noah, in *Sūrat al-Ṣāffāt* (37:83), to bear the same prophetic message that Noah preached to his people and who were drowned in the flood because they rejected it

God gave Abraham an argument to prove His uniqueness and transcendence,

> *When night came over him, he saw a star, and said,*
> *'This is my Lord'. But when it set, he said,*
> *'I do not love what sets'.*
> *Then when he saw the moon rising, he said,*
> *'This is my Lord'. But when it set he said,*

> *'If my Lord did not guide me, I would certainly be of those astray'.*
> *Then when he saw the sun rise, he said,*
> *this is my Lord, this is greater by far. But when it set he said,*
> *My people, I have nothing to do with your idol worship*
> *I turn my face to Him who created the heavens and the earth,*
> *pure in faith, and in submission to Him, I am not of the idolaters* (*Sūrat al-An'ām* 6:75–79).

He asks God how the dead are to be raised

> *When Abraham said, Lord, show me how you raise the dead.*
> *God replied, Is it that you do not believe?*
> *He said Indeed I believe [but show me] so that my heart may be assured.*
> *God said Then take four birds, and divide them into pieces before you, then place a part of each of them on each mountain.*
> *Then call them. They will come swiftly to you.*
> *Understand that God is Mighty, Wise* (*al-Baqara* 2:260).

Confident in his understanding of his vocation, he challenged his father's worship of idols,

> *'What are these images to which you devote yourselves?'* (*Sūrat al-Anbiyā'* 21:52).

When left alone in the temple, he smashed all of them except the largest. When the devotees of the idols returned, they asked who had done this, and he replied, 'The one that stands unharmed'. They realised that he had done it, and threw him into a furnace, but God saved him, saying to the flames,

> *'O fire, be cool for Abraham'* (*Sūrat al-Anbiyā'*, 21: 69).

After rescuing him from the flames, God brought him and Lot from their homeland to

> *The land We have blessed for all the worlds* (*Sūrat al-Anbiyā'*, 21:71)

the land of Canaan.

The next episode is not referred to explicitly in the Qur'an. It is a counterpart to the Genesis story of Sarah's jealousy of Hagar and her son, and her ordering Abraham to take them out of her sight. In Genesis they go to Paran, a settlement on the way to Egypt. In the Muslim presentation of the story, Abraham takes them to Mecca, and leaves them there, trusting that God will care for them.

Why Mecca?

Because God says of this city

> *The first House [of worship] established on earth*
> *is indeed that at Bakka*[2]*,*
> *as a blessing and guide for all the worlds* (*Sūrat Al 'Imrān*, 3:96).

Abraham left them in a waterless place, near two hillocks about 200 metres apart, Safa and Marwa. The Qur'an says of these hillocks

> *The hillocks of Ṣafā and Marwā are indeed emblems of God* (*Sūrat al-Baqara* 2:158).

The exegetes (and *Stories of the Prophets*) explain that Hagar, fearing the death of her child, placed him under a shrub, and ran distractedly to and fro between these two hillocks praying to find water. Gabriel appeared to tell her that her prayer had been heard, and as the infant Ishmael scrapped at the earth with his finger, a well of copious water known as the well of Zamzam appeared. The abundance of water gushing from it attracted a passing caravan from the Yemen *en route* to Syria, and led it to Mecca, the sacred site of the Ka'ba then being repopulated. These two hillocks are emblems of this miracle, and one of the rituals of the *ḥajj*, the hurrying to and fro between these two hillocks commemorates the distress of Hagar, fearing the death of her child from thirst. The miraculous well is a counterpart to the Genesis account of how God saved the infant Ishmael from dying of thirst by the miraculous provision of a well after Sarah had driven Hagar from her house, and she was on her way with him back to Egypt.

The Qur'an alludes to Abraham's journey to Mecca with them in another pericope in which, as it were he 'reminds' God of his having brought them there:

2. That is, Mecca

Our Lord,
I have indeed made some of my descendants
To dwell in a barren valley
Next to your sacred House

Our Lord,
Let them pray there
That the hearts of humankind
May incline toward them
And Bestow on them the fruit [of the earth]
That they may be grateful to You (*Sūrat Ibrāhīm*, 14:37).

Abraham returns from Canaan to Mecca on a number of occasions, drawn by longing for his son. However, it is in Canaan that he received the visitors at his tent who told him that despite the advanced age of them both, Sarah would give birth to a son the following year, and that the people of Sodom would be destroyed.

This event is presented in the Qur'an in four accounts of differing emphases and character.

The most extensive of them is in *Sūrat Hūd*, may be rendered,

Our messengers came with good tidings to Abraham
They said,
  'Peace'
He replied
  'Peace',
Then forthwith had brought to them a roasted calf.
But when he saw that their hands did not reach towards it,
he was unsure of them, and filled with fear of them.
They said:
  Do not be afraid, for we,
  we indeed have been sent sent to the people of Lot'.
His wife was standing nearby, and she laughed.
Then We gave her good tidings of Isaac, and after Isaac, of Jacob.
She said,
  'What! Am I to bear a child,
  although an old woman, and this husband of mine is an old man.
  This is indeed an extraordinary thing.'
They replied,
  ' Are you surprised at what God has decreed?
  The mercy of God and His blessings are upon you, people of the House.
  He indeed is worthy of all praise, is glorious.

When the fear had passed from Abraham,
good tidings having come to him,
he began to plead with Us for the people of Lot.
Indeed, Abraham was forbearing, trusting in God.
'Abraham, desist from this!
The decree of your Lord has been uttered!
an inexorable punishment is coming upon them

(*Sūrat Hūd* 11:69–76.)

It is vivid and concise. The information it presents is carried by dramatic dialogue. After the exchange of greetings, it tells of Abraham's hospitality, his moment of fear, when his guests do not eat, the laughter of his wife, the announcement of Isaac the child she is to bear (and of his son Jacob), and her incredulity that at her age she should conceive. The visitors re-assure her—God's blessings are on the 'People of the House'. Finally, it tells of Abraham's pleading for the people of Lot (an event presented in detail in Genesis).

The questions exegetes put to the text are significant, and reveal an established hermeneutic. They note his hospitality, his kindness of heart. But they ask, why was he afraid - because they did not behave as guests should. Having been offered hospitality, they decline to eat. For when a stranger arrives and accepts the food offered to him, the inviolable relationship between host and guest is established. Why did they not eat - because they were angels; indeed angels do not eat. Why did Sarah laugh? She had not yet heard what the good tidings are. Is it a laugh of relief, of relaxation of tension, after the angels said - do not be afraid. Is it that she had just been saying to Abraham how wicked were the people of Sodom, and that God should do something about it, and just at that moment she is saying this, the angels come, and say that this is precisely what they have come to do. Is it a figure of speech, a hyperbaton, the placing of an effect, the laughter, before its cause?

When Abraham and his family are addressed as 'People of the House', what does it mean. By House here, some exegetes understand the house of God, the Ka'ba at Mecca, others, the family of Abraham, yet others the family and kin of the Prophet

The Qur'an gives a taut and moving account of God putting Abraham to the test by commanding him to sacrifice a son

Then, when the boy was able to walk with him,
Abraham said
My dear son,
I have seen in a dream that I am to sacrifice you,
Can you accept this?
He replied,
My dear father, do that with which you are commanded.
If God so will, you will find me one of the steadfast.
So when both had submitted to God's will
Abraham having thrown him face down . . .
We called on him saying,
Abraham, You have accepted as true what the vision told you.
Indeed in this way we reward those who do good
This was the test that would make clear [your faithfulness].
And we redeemed him with a worthy victim,
And we left on him for those yet to come [this blessing]
Peace be upon Abraham
Thus do we reward those who do good,
Indeed he was of our believing servants.
We gave him good tidings of Isaac,
A prophet among the righteous.
We blessed him and Isaac,
And of their descendants are some who do good, and some who do wrong to themselves (*Sūrat al-Ṣāffāt,* 37:102–113).

The Qur'an does not state which of his two sons Abraham was to sacrifice. The early exegetic tradition frequently identifies him as Isaac. The great Spanish mystic Ibn 'Arabī (d 1240) in the *Fuṣūṣ al-Ḥikam* devotes a chapter to Isaac as the sacrificial victim. But from the fourteenth century on, the tradition settles virtually unanimously on Ishmael.

The Qur'an tells how when Abraham was visiting his son in Mecca, God commanded them to restore this ancient place of worship, saying

'Cleanse My House for those who circle round it,
for those who are devout,
for those who bow [in prayer],
prostrate themselves [in adoration]

And they responded, as they re-laid the foundations of the house, saying,

> *'Our Lord, accept [this labour] from us,*
> *It is You, You who are all-hearing, all knowing.*
> *Our Lord, make us obedient to You,*
> *and our descendants a people obedient to You.*
> (*Sūrat al-Baqara*, 2:125).

And so they worked together to rebuild the Ka'ba, the House of God, from the fragments to which it had been reduced after the flood that destroyed the unbelievers in Noah's day, preparing it for the time of Muhammad, when its dignity should be fully restored, and people come in throngs, to make the pilgrimage. Among the reasons for this pilgrimage is that

> *In it are the clearest of testimonies.*
> *Among them the place where Abraham stood*
> *Whoever enters it is safe from harm* (*Sūrat Āl 'Imrān*, 3:97).

Therefore Muhammad is commanded

> *Proclaim to humankind the Pilgrimage!*
> *They will come to you on foot,*
> *they will come on every scrawny camel,*
> *they will come from every distant valley* (*Sūrat al-Ḥajj* 22:27).

And when they come, they are to stand and pray where Abraham prayed (2:125):

> *Take as your place of prayer the place where Abraham prayed.*

Abraham prays for this shrine and the people who live there, among them his descendants through his son Ishmael, and for the coming of Muhammad. He prays that God will send them,

> *A messenger from among themselves*
> *a messenger who will recount to them your signs,*
> *who will teach them the Book, and Wisdom,*
> *and purify them [from their sins]* (*Sūrat al-Baqara*, 2:129).

Despite common elements in the Judaic Christian and the Islamic Abrahamic narratives there are differences in their significance, even when the events related appear identical. One way of putting it is that although the cast of *dramatis personae* of Islamic salvation history is largely that of the Judaic and Christian traditions, the drama in which they are performing is subtly different.

For the Qur'an, the physical lineage of Abraham is not important. What is central, is that he has the faith that Noah had. When God calls him, it is not to promise him land and posterity (which God in Genesis does to Abraham on five occasions) but to show him why He, God alone, is worthy of adoration. The Qur'anic Abraham does not show the human weaknesses of Abraham in Genesis. He does not importune God to keep a promise. He does not sulk, he does not lie on his face laughing when the promise is made to him for the fifth time. His sacrifice of four birds (*Sūrat al-Baqara,* 2:260), is not to bind God to a covenant to ensure He keeps His promise, but to see for himself how God will raise the dead.

In this, at one level at least, there is no necessary contradiction between the two faith traditions, even though the Genesis emphasis on the progeny of Abraham does not have a place in it. The model Abraham presents is of a man of faith in the divine Unity, a man chosen as a messenger preaching this unity, a man given the title of friend of God, a man the model of hospitality, a man of compassion and justice.

It is with the journey of Abraham, Hagar and Ishmael to Mecca, and the status of the shrine at Mecca that crucial differences appear, and significant theological divisions between the communities of faith, and a profoundly different reading of the economy of salvation are revealed.

In general, the Qur'an and Genesis tell the same story of how Paradise was Lost. Adam and Eve eat the forbidden fruit, and are expelled from the Garden of Eden for the sin of disobedience. It is in the way that the consequences of the fall are to be repaired, and the way in which Paradise may be regained that the three religions, and their reading of the Abraham story differ.

In the Judaic and Christian traditions, human rehabilitation is through the coming of a Messiah, born to the Jews. Abraham is their patriarch. They are a people chosen and prepared for this responsibility through their history, spiritual and secular, as presented in the Tanakh. Their descent from him is from Isaac, the son long promised to Abraham and Sarah, along with the promise for his descendants of the land from the river of Egypt to the Euphrates (Gen 15:18). The story of God's visiting Abraham with/through the three angels, to announce that Sarah will give birth to this son within a year, and Abraham's willingness to sacrifice this son as the supreme test to which he is put, are a high point in the arc of tension of the narrative. There is indeed an honourable space for his descendants through Ishmael, but God's covenant is with Isaac. For the Jewish people then, the Messiah is yet to come.

In the Christian reading of the same scriptures, the Messiah has already come in the person of Jesus, expiating the sin of Adam, and redeeming humankind. The theology behind this is that as a result of Adam's sin, he and his descendants lost sanctifying grace and the gift of sharing in the divine life until the coming of a Messiah, a saviour, God himself incarnate, understood as the eternal word of God incarnate, the second person of the Trinity become man, to complete the sacrifice of redemption foreshadowed in Isaac. This inspires and informs the Eastern church apothegm, 'In the Eucharist we encounter the Trinity, just as Abraham encountered the three angels standing before his tent'. In Christ then, the primal debt of disobedience is paid, humankind is redeemed, the yoke of the ritual law central to Judaism is lifted, and participation in sanctifying grace restored.

In Islam there is a different paradigm of living in God's favour, while still enduring the consequences of the fall. Adam and Eve disobeyed God. They were expelled from the Garden. They repented. Their first home on earth was Mecca. There they built the first place of worship on earth, identified in the Qur'an as the Ka'ba, where it all began. Adam was the father of all humankind. He was the first prophet, the first teacher. In him is established the basic template of divine revelation, of an economy of salvation, that humankind must recognise that God is one (the Qur'an on a number of occasions denying that God is a 'threesome'), that He sends messengers telling of Himself and the Law humankind are to live by; (the Judaic *halaka* and Arabic *shari'a* both have the sense of road or pathway), and of a day of resurrection when they will be judged.

Original sin, understood as the loss of sanctifying grace as a result of the fall has no place in Islamic theology. Every individual in born with a natural disposition to the true religion, Islam. Muslims often speak not of conversion to, but reversion, return to Islam. Humankind can be corrupted by parents or their environment, and the deceit of Satan, 'Who lies in wait for them from before and behind, from right and from left' (*Sūrat al-A'rāf*, 7:17). They need teachers to guide and strengthen them. They do not need a redeemer, they do not need a Messiah, as the word is understood in Judaism or Christianity. Salvation does not depend on the coming of Muhammad; he is not a Messiah. Any people that has welcomed and obeyed its prophet will enter Paradise. God has sent many messengers, not all of them known, not all told of the in Qur'an, each from and to his own people. Noah was such a prophet. His people rejected his message, and they were drowned. Abraham was such a prophet. He had special qualities, and a special role. With Ishmael he rebuilt the first temple on earth where God had been worshipped after its destruction in the flood. In this, Ishmael, due to his close association with his father Abraham has a status above that of Isaac. Abraham was put to the test by the command to sacrifice his son. But this test, and the life of this son, was not to pave the way for a chosen people. Abraham indeed through Isaac, the ancestor of the Jews was one such prophet. The Jews were a specially favoured people, but not a uniquely chosen people. Jerusalem is a holy city, but not *the* holy city. The primal holy city is the shrine at Mecca, the first place of worship on earth, restored by Abraham after it had been destroyed by the flood, the shrine where the first humans Adam and Eve worshipped before their multitudinous descendants became divided into tribes and peoples of different colours and languages.

It is in the light of this understanding of Abraham that when Muhammad in Madina is confronted by Jews and Christians, each claiming to have exclusive rights as vehicles of salvation, and competed in trying to attract him and his followers to their religion, God tells him to respond to them

> *Abraham was not a Jew, nor A Christian,*
> *but one true in faith (ḥanīf),*
> *he was not an idolater* (*Sūrat Āl 'Imrān*, 3:67).

and

> *Reply, [to them] (on behalf of himself and his community)*
> *'Rather, we follow the faith of Abraham, one true in faith and*
> *Say, we believe in God, and what is revealed to us,*
> *and what is revealed to Abraham* (*2:135*).

thereby removing him from the exclusively Judaic and Christian paradigms. Muhammad was a messenger and a prophet in precisely the same sense as were Adam, Noah, Abraham and Moses. He was reminding those to whom he preached of a primal covenant behind and preceding all the prophets before time began.

> *Recall when your Lord drew from the loins of Adam their seed,*
> *and that of all their descendants,*
> *and had them testify to Him for themselves*
> *Am I not indeed your Lord?*
> *They replied, yes indeed, we so testify* (*Sūrat al-Aʿrāf*, 7:172).

Behind all covenants between God and various peoples and their prophets in time, lies this meta-historical covenant with all who are to be born, a covenant made before time began.

Are there two Abrahams? Are the two narratives, one leading through Isaac to Jesus, the other leading through Ishmael to Muhammad, irreconcilable? Or do they have enough in common for Muslims and Christians with Jews to share in a vision of him, jointly to refer to him as 'Our father in Faith', notwithstanding the different theologies, the different hermeneutic in which each situates its reverence for him. It must be emphasized that from a Christian perspective, the point at issue is not that Muhammad is a later prophet with a fresh revelation. It is not simply a case of a new prophet, but a different economy of salvation. It is a different reading of the consequences of Paradise Lost, and how Paradise is to be regained. The theology of Islam presents a different way of explaining and justifying the ways of God to humankind to that central to the Christian and Jewish traditions. Can common ground be found beneath the theological and cultural clothing with which the three traditions invest Abraham.

At the human level, there is the quality of his faith, his hospitality, his compassion and sense of justice, pleading for the people of Sodom - his vision of a vast world of his descendants, sharing in his covenant by the ritual of circumcision. At a higher level, there is his response when he is put to the test: he is prepared to forgo all that God promised him after at long last it appeared within reach, when God asked him to sacrifice a son. He said 'Yes' to God.

There are two beautiful verses in the Book of Judith which may be of help in answering the question. 'In spite of everything let us give thanks to the Lord our God who is putting us to the test. Remember that our fathers were put to the test to prove their love of God. Remember how our father Abraham was tested, and became the friend of God after many trials and tribulations . . .' (Book of Judith (8:25–26).

Perhaps the need to face the reality of these perceptions of Abraham, is one of the ways in which we are put to the test. How to recognise these divisions, and to find ways of making the best of the situation: not in a grudging manner, but with generosity and possibly even delight. To make the best of it by searching for shared values within or concealed by different theological narratives without falling into a post-modernist relativism, while recognizing the imperatives of and remaining faithful to one's own narrative; attempting to find what can be shared, while still respecting, preserving, being faithful to the definitive and distinguishing core formulations of each faith community.

For Christians, the doctrine of a triune God, the mystery of the Trinity, is a way of expressing something beyond all understanding, the inner life of God. In it, and in the Incarnation which is part of this life-giving mystery, Christians find an inexhaustible source of spiritual life and inspiration. Yet for Muslims, *Tawḥīd*, the declaration that God is One is, in an analogous way, full of mystery and also infinite in its implications. The common translation of *Tawḥīd* as 'monotheism' is overly cerebral, and gives little sense of the reality for which it stands. God is One, something of his nature can be learnt from the names and attributes revealed of Him in the Qur'an, but His life and being within that Unity is a life and mystery that draws humankind to Itself. As the Muslim mystic Taftazani (d 1390) put it, when, in awe, in this world, on what he calls this littoral of hope we try to understand this mystery, what we can do is no more than trying to empty the sea, by scooping out its water with a ladle. He continues, 'The mystic drawn by God, continues his journey onwards until he is plunged into the ocean of *Tawhid* . . . and sees nothing existing other than God . . . this is what the Sufis call annihilation (*fanā'*) in *Tawḥīd*. It is to this state that the Divine Tradition refers, 'When my servant approaches me through more than I have required of him . . . then I love him. And if I love him, I become the ear by which he hears, the the hand by which he grasps, and the leg by which he walks'.

In the Incarnation, Christians see in the humanity, love and compassion of Christ, the supreme model of what being human ought to be; they believe that these qualities regarded as supremely human, are revealed in the person of Jesus. For Muslims, the primal attributes of God are mercy and compassion, God is the Merciful, the compassionate, *al-Raḥmān al-Raḥīm*, and these qualities may be seen in the love and care that human beings show for each other in daily life, even in the most desperate of situations. Such a compassion exists within both faith communities, can reach across borders/frontiers and reveal itself to the other, sometimes in the most unpromising circumstances.

Anzac Day is a day that gave the name Gallipoli a continuing resonance in Australia and New Zealand, and had a key role in the development of an Australian national consciousness and identity. There is a hymn with plain words, and a simple but plangent melody that expresses the anguish of remembering those Australians who sailed away from Australia to war, to Gallipoli, and perished.

We would remember them today
Who from their homeland sailed away
So blithely and so willingly
To give their lives for you and me,
Father, guard their sleeping.

But the anguish they suffered was also the anguish of many thousands of Turkish mothers and wives whose loved ones perished.

It was not until over half a century later, in 1968 that Turkish migrants, descendants of those Turks who perished at Gallipoli came to Australia, and formed the first critical mass of Muslims in Australia. In coming to Australia, they were being put to the test, just as the Australians welcoming them were and are put to the test. Today, one of the largest Muslim communities in Australia is Turkish. In 1977, a community of Turkish new Australians established in Sydney a Turkish Islamic Centre to foster Turkish community life, a development that led to the building of a mosque at Auburn that accommodates over 2000 worshipers at the Friday congregational prayer. The leaders of their community, wished their mosque to be recognized as an integral part of the wider Australian community in which it was set. To express this ideal, they called it the Gallipoli mosque. The choice of name, and the cross-cultural resonances it evoked, grew out of shared memories, reaching back over three or perhaps even four generations, to the ANZAC landings in 1915.

The inauguration of the mosque in November 1999 celebrated this vision. The Turkish and Australian National Anthems were played; there was a recitation of verses from the Qur'an, followed by a rendering in English. Guests and speakers represented senior members of the Turkish local and diplomatic communities, and of the State of New South Wales and the Australian Commonwealth Government. And a climactic moment in the ceremony was the speech of the State President of the New South Wales branch of the Returned Services League, in which he gave a generous welcome to this non-Anglo Celtic community to Australia, and to the building of a centre for worship by members of the faith community of Islam declaring Australia its home

It brought vividly to mind some of the realities of the military encounter between Australians and Turks in 1915 commemorated on Anzac Day. This encounter took place in the geo-political context of World War I. But it was an encounter at various levels, and of multiple resonances. At one level it was in the context of World War I, between Britain, France with their antipodean allies, and Germany. At another it was inter-racial, between Anglo-Celts and the Turkic peoples of Central Asia. But at yet another, though not often construed in these terms, it was between Australian soldiers by and large Christians, and Turkish soldiers, defending their homeland, by and large Muslims.

Despite the bitterness of the fighting, there was mutual respect between Turks and Australians as fellow soldiers and human beings. This respect was shown by both sides during periods of cease fire despite the barriers of language; it was shown in the care both sides gave for each other's dead and wounded. They kept their compassion. It was commemorated in the immortal and inspired words of Ataturk speaking of the ANZAC war dead, 'Heroes, who shed their blood and lost their lives, you are now lying in the soil of a friendly country. Therefore, rest in peace. There is no difference between the Johnnies and the Mehmets to us where they lie side by side here in this country of ours . . . having lost their lives on this land, they have become our sons as well'[3]—words that perhaps exemplifying the ultimate in shared compassion.

3. Major General Peter R. Phillips, atioal President, Returned and Services League of Australia 1999, in *ATAM Australian-Turkish Assembly Magazine*, 1/1 (1999): 22.

Might the ceremony at the inauguration of this mosque, consecrating as it were such a fellowship—consociation dare one say—this shared compassion, this mutual respect born in the obscenity of war surviving, growing even, put to an end talk of a clash of civilisations, at least on one plot of earth. Alongside consecrating the fellowship between Turks and Australians born in the Dardenelles in 1915, perhaps be seen as symbolizing a burying of ancient hostilities between Muslims and Christians—both claiming to be children of Abraham. Is the figure of Abraham here then a sign of incompatibility or conciliation. Is the glass half-full or half-empty?

But there is yet another test. We live in a world—at least in Australia and Western Europe—in which those who believe are put to the test yet again as was Abraham. Matthew Arnold, in elegiac though stately Victorian verse expressed it,

The sea of faith
Was once, too at the full
And round earth's shore
Lay like the folds of a bright girdle furled
But now I only hear
Its melancholy, long, withdrawing roar.
Retreating to the breath
Of the night wind down the vast edges drear
And naked shingles of the world

Is this really so? Or are the folds of this bright girdle still gleaming, present in forms which we do not recognize or appreciate, hidden under different apprehensions of the faith of Abraham, which in this, as well as in other ways, put their respective communities to the test in their relations with each other. And with whom, as children of Abraham, it is still possible to celebrate a faith in One God, the forgiveness of sin, the resurrection of the body and life ever-lasting. AMEN

CPSIA information can be obtained
at www.ICGtesting.com
Printed in the USA
JSHW021515150723
44805JS00002B/106

9 781922 582850